Acclaim for Tudor Parfitt's

JOURNEY TO THE VANISHED CITY

"This is an exceptionally good book, lucidly written and exhibiting all the craftsmanship of a first-rate detective novel."
—*Weekend Telegraph*

"Parfitt's brilliant narration . . . has put the Lemba on the ethnic, cultural and historical map of Africa."
—*Journal of Oriental Studies*

"The book has an exciting feel of a race against time, of modernity—black and white—closing in over traditional ways. . . . Parfitt is careful to leaven his expertise with gently observed characters and incidents." —*The Independent*

"A haunting history-cum-travelogue, as Parfitt sleuths out the claims of the Lemba of South Africa . . . like Paul Theroux with a Ph.D: the best in adventure scholarship."
—*Kirkus Reviews*

"A unique blend of academic research and personal exploration has resulted in this fascinating story of the author's search for the Lemba and their original city of Sena."
—*Library Journal*

"Parfitt reveals a rare talent for combining rigorous academic standards with a sense of drama, an elegant style and most pleasing of all, the eye for fine detail of a first-class travel writer." —*Mail on Sunday*

"Parfitt's approach is a novelistic blend of setting, dialogue and lightly worn research. Unconstrained by the anthropologist's obsession with method, he manages to shed more light on this extraordinary people than any number of pedantic ethnographies." —*Spectator* (London)

Tudor Parfitt

JOURNEY TO THE VANISHED CITY

Dr. Tudor Parfitt is Reader in Modern Jewish Studies and Chairman of the Middle East Centre at the School of Oriental and African Studies, University of London. A broadcaster, journalist, and traveler, he is the author of numerous books.

Journey to the Vanished City

The Search for a Lost Tribe of Israel

TUDOR PARFITT

VINTAGE DEPARTURES

Vintage Books

A Division of Random House, Inc.

New York

Pour Sophie

 FIRST VINTAGE DEPARTURES EDITION, APRIL 2000

Copyright © 1992, 1997, 1999 by Tudor Parfitt

Library of Congress Cataloging-in-Publication Data
Journey to the vanished city : the search for a lost tribe of Israel /
by Tudor Parfitt.
p. cm. — (Vintage departures)
Originally published: New York: St. Martin's Press, 1993. With new epilogue. Includes bibliographical references and index.
ISBN 0-375-72454-0
1. Lemba (South African people) 2. Lost tribes of Israel. 3. Zimbabwe—Description and travel. 4. South Africa—Description and travel. I. Title.
DT1768.L45 P37 2000
968.91—dc21 99-089015

Author photograph © Sophie DeVergnette

www.vintagebooks.com

Printed in the United States of America
10 9 8 7 6 5 4 3 2 1

CONTENTS

JUN   2000

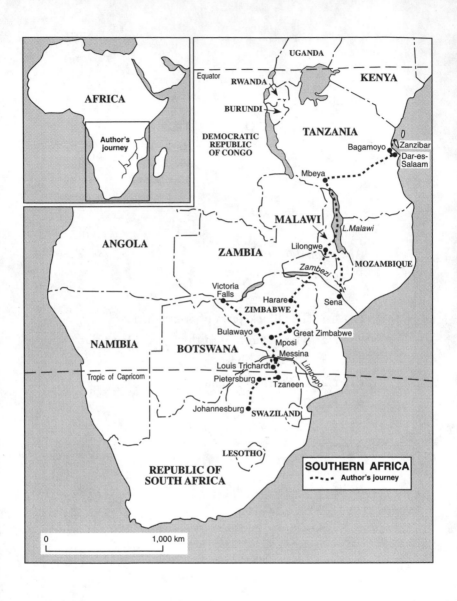

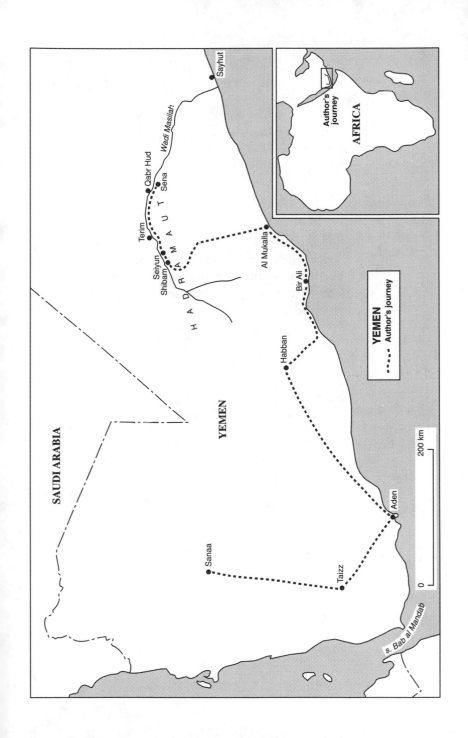

ACKNOWLEDGMENTS

I would like to thank the very many people who have helped me in the writing of this book. I owe particular thanks to the Lemba tribe of southern Africa, some of whose names have been changed.

PROLOGUE

One evening when I was about eight years old my mother came home with a cardboard box full of splendidly bound old books about Africa. There were stories of the Boer War, the Ashanti and Zulu Wars, and the exploration of the Dark Continent. These books became treasured possessions and I still have them. But two of them, *Prester John* by John Buchan and *King Solomon's Mines* by Rider Haggard, in their rich, purple bindings, I no longer have. I read them so often that the brittle, yellowing sellotape which held them together gave way and by the time I left home they had disintegrated.

Years later I had my first chance to visit black Africa. The Minority Rights Group had asked me to write a report on the Falashas, the so-called black Jews of Ethiopia. By a remarkable stroke of luck my visit coincided with the 1984–5 Israeli operation to rescue the Falashas from the refugee camps of the eastern Sudan and I went on to write a book about it – *Operation Moses*. Some time later I was invited to Johannesburg to give a paper on the Falashas at a conference at the University of the Witwatersrand. Most of the people who attended that conference were white, middle-class academics, but at the back of the hall where I gave my talk I noticed a small group of shabbily dressed black men wearing what looked like Jewish skullcaps. When I spoke to them, they announced with pride that they were members of the Lemba tribe, that they were Jews, a lost tribe of Israel, and that they were related to the Falashas of Ethiopia. Indeed, they were Falashas, they said, Falashas who had fled Ethiopia centuries before.

As a historical statement this seemed pretty implausible. The vast distances which separate Ethiopia from South Africa seemed to disqualify any link between these tribes. As far as Europe was concerned the very existence of the Falashas was unsuspected until relatively recent times. Had the Lemba maintained a memory of this heritage for many centuries, as they claimed? Or was their knowledge of the Falashas recently acquired? And if so, why had they wished to identify with them? Why did they wish to identify with Jews?

The Lemba urged me to accompany them to Venda in the north-eastern corner of South Africa. There, they said, I would be able to see traditional Lemba villages and study their beliefs at first hand. After a few days in Venda I realised that there were elements of the Lemba's traditions which seemed to be Semitic and which were unlikely to have derived from European influence. Their enthusiasm for sacred hills and animal sacrifice, their ritual slaughter of animals and food taboos, their circumcision rites, their tribal names, their refusal to marry outside the tribe – their endogamy – taken together clearly suggested a Semitic ancestry. In addition, certain parts of their saga of origin were of such a specific nature that they seemed to be rooted in historical experience. Some of what they said traversed territory not unfamiliar to me: stories of lost Jewish kingdoms, of Solomon and Sheba, of vanished civilisations – my boyhood realm of *Prester John* and *King Solomon's Mines*. But some was new: their traditions maintained that centuries before they had come from a mysterious city they called Sena; they had crossed 'Pusela' (although they did not know what Pusela was), and had come to Africa. There they had rebuilt Sena, perhaps in more than one place, and had helped to construct a great stone city which they identify as Great Zimbabwe – the ruins of which have intrigued archaeologists for the last hundred years.

They abandoned Great Zimbabwe because, within its walls, they had broken the law of their God, Mwali. There-after they were scattered among the other tribes: a black diaspora.

Was the Lemba's selection of a Jewish identity a mirror of some particular characteristic of their tribe in pre-colonial times? Or was it, in fact, the reflection of some historical Jewish influence, hitherto unsuspected, centuries before on the east coast of Africa?

There was a riddle here. I decided that I would return to Africa to try and solve it. But to do so I sensed that I would have to put aside my prejudices and whatever knowledge I happened to have. I would have to not know. I would have to approach these stories as I approached the stories of my boyhood. I was planning a journey, I thought, into a myth.

PART ONE

The Black Jews of South Africa

I

Gold was the first thing that struck me. You can smell it in Johannesburg because the city is surrounded by old gold workings and grassed-over slag heaps, yellow now in the parched winter, golden buttocks giving off a disturbing, aromatic, slightly sulphurous smell blown everywhere by the dry wind. And gold, I was sure, had some part to play in the story I was hoping to unravel. Who could even think of lost Jewish tribes in Africa without recalling the old belief that the gold-bearing regions of South-East Africa were none other than the biblical Ophir?

Many of today's gold miners live in Soweto. I made arrangements to visit the township in the company of Ephraim, a Lemba detective in the South African police force. Ephraim was waiting outside my hotel at least an hour before the time we had fixed. His old car was spotless. When he saw me approach, he opened the door and, with a shy smile, invited me to get in. An ironed towel with an embroidered Star of David had been placed on the passenger seat for me to sit on. He drove off slowly, glancing at me from time to time as if to assure himself that I was comfortable. It was not long before the neat lawns and sidewalks of white Johannesburg were replaced by beaten earth and piles of rusting mechanical detritus: here it only takes minutes to get from the first to the third world.

The sky was darkening and a cold wind was blowing off the high veldt, driving the smoke from hundreds of thousands of coal fires into a low, scudding cloud. We were passing through the Orlando section of Soweto. At a set of traffic lights a few black teenagers jeered at me. Ephraim put his hand-gun above the dashboard, where it could be seen.

'Don't worry,' he said, 'there is Lemba watchmen on the road to warn us of any trouble. There is three or four thousand Jews live in Soweto. They know you are coming. By the way, this is a Lemba shop,' he said, pointing at a corrugated iron shack outside which a crowd of dishevelled men were queuing for fish and chips. Ephraim stopped the car and led me in past the queue. The Lemba owner was protected from his customers by a thick metal grill.

They spoke to each other in an urgent whisper. I understood only the words Parfitt, London and book. Looking at me as if I were the reincarnation of a minor prophet, the shopkeeper put his hand through the grill and, holding the sleeve of my jacket, urged me to stay and eat with him. Ephraim shook his head: 'The Lemba is waiting. We have many places to visit. Tight schedule.'

We drove through Meadowlands and on into what Ephraim said was the heart of Soweto: 'This is Mofolo – and that is the hostel where I stayed when I first came from the north thirty years ago.' He pointed at a particularly bleak building, replicas of which are to be found in townships throughout South Africa. The men who live in these hostels come to the city in search of work, leaving their families far away in rural areas. A few of them were leaning against a scarred wall, drinking beer out of a bucket. Beyond the hostel I could see row upon row of identical box houses and corrugated iron shacks: there were no street names, only numbers. In between the houses there were wrecked cars and smoking rubbish dumps. Ephraim identified each location, carefully spelling out the unfamiliar names. 'Two million people live here. And so many Lemba.'

We crossed the railway line, blasted through brown granite, which takes hundreds of thousands of black workers from Soweto to Johannesburg every day. An armoured car was approaching us. Ephraim took a sharp left turn and said nothing. We were now in a slightly more affluent suburb of little bungalows with neat front gardens. Ephraim stopped the car and we went into a new house where two Lemba sisters were waiting for us. Tea cups and plates had been neatly laid out on a new plastic table in a tiny sitting-room. The sisters were wearing identical blue cotton dresses. 'Blue is the Lemba colour,' said Ephraim, 'it is the colour of heaven and the colour of our god, Mwali.' The sisters were eager to show me their three bedrooms and modern kitchen, but Ephraim hurried me out of the house even before the tea was ready.

A few streets further on we stopped again in front of a similar house. A strikingly beautiful woman wearing jeans and a T-shirt was waiting on her front step. Her name was Selinah Munuonde. Leading the way into her house she said, 'You're interested in the Lemba? I love to talk about the Lemba! Look! You can read this.' From a shelf in her sitting-room she reached down an article, badly typed on yellowing paper, called 'The ancient history of the Lemba' by a Professor Mathiva. With an ironical flourish she struck the pose of a tribal dancer and told me she would change into her traditional Lemba costume.

'I love my people,' she shouted out from her bedroom, 'we came from the Israelites, we came from Sena, we crossed the sea, we made iron and gold and pottery and, as we came down through Africa, we sold our handicrafts. To start with,' she was almost singing as she spoke, 'we had cattle. We had towns. We were free. But the cattle died and we turned poor. But we were so beautiful with beautiful, long, Jewish noses and so proud of our facial structure! We no way wanted to spoil our structure by carelessness, eating pig or marrying non-Lemba gentiles.' Among the Lemba, as I was soon to discover, these ideas are axiomatic: once, long ago, there had been a golden age when they had been white, free, rich and long-nosed. Now Selinah twirled into the room looking magnificent in the colourful, striped tribal cloak which, in the Lemba language, she told me, was called *chilemba*.

'First I can dance,' she announced, 'then I tell you about my nation,' and, clapping her hands, she started swaying from side to side to some imaginary Lemba music. Ephraim, who looked as if he disapproved of all this carry-on, stood at the window glaring at the passing cars and the panoramic view of Soweto. The telephone rang and he answered it.

'The meeting's waiting,' he said, turning to me.

'What meeting is that?' I asked.

'The elders of the tribe,' said Ephraim, taking my elbow and leading me out to the car. Selinah danced out into the street with us, a radiant butterfly in the drabness of Soweto.

The meeting-house was a poor, roughly built shack in the Diepkloof area of the township. Groups of youths stood around wood fires in the open spaces. A path had been swept through the rubble in the enclosed yard in front of the house. We went into a small room where ten Lemba men were sitting around a wooden table. The table was laid with a blue cloth embroidered in gold with a Star of David. A gold elephant occupied the centre of the star. The only other thing on the table was a large family Bible.

'*Mushavi, Mushavi,*' intoned the men, greeting each other

and me as well, it seemed, with this tribal praise-name, clapping in time with the words.

'*Mushavi, Mushavi,*' I replied, clapping my hands in turn. They looked at me with approval.

They introduced themselves. Many of them had Semitic-sounding names: Mr William Mhani, Mr Solomon Sadiki, Mr Samuel Hadji. Solomon Sadiki bowed and read out a little prepared speech: 'We all thank you for coming from far to visit a lost tribe of Israel. It is *really* a lost tribe and it is getting yet more and more lost. Most of my life I was crying for this lost nation of mine. It is dying away now. I have done all I can. Ask anyone. I have not spared myself.' The others nodded in agreement.

'Once,' he continued, 'I wrote an article for a newspaper to tell the whole world about us. Once I gave an interview to a journalist. And till now I am the vice-chairman of the Lemba Cultural Association and adviser to the Lemba Women's Club of Soweto. But it is not enough to save us. We need help! Some of the old men have said you will write a book about the Lemba like you wrote about the Falashas. If you do that, the Lemba cannot die, isn't it?'

Now it was William Mhani who spoke. He had the face of a Peninsula Arab or a Middle Eastern Jew. He was trembling with excitement. 'Like the lost tribes of Israel,' he said, 'we Lemba are made up of ten tribes: Sadiki, Hamisi, Mahdi, Tovakare, Hadji, Sharifu, Hasani, Bakari, Duma, Seremane. The tribes came from Sena. Each man here represents a tribe. And, like the Israelites of old, you will find out about us in this holy Bible.' Opening the Bible on the table, he read out the passage from *Nehemiah* which lists the names of those Jews who returned from the Babylonian captivity with Zerubbabel: '"the sons of Parosh . . . the sons of Shephatiah

... the sons of Pahath-Moab ... the sons of Azgad ... the men of Michmas ... the sons of Lod, Hadid, and Ono"'; then he paused, looking around at each of us in turn: ' "And then the sons of Sena, three thousand, nine hundred and thirty." And Sena', he continued, 'is a town in Israel north of Jericho.'

'Just a minute – I thought you did not know where your original Sena was?'

'We did not know until some little while back,' William replied, with some diffidence. 'Then, one day I was reading the Bible and the Lord made my eye turn upon this passage. This Sena near Jericho must be our original homeland.'

At the mention of Sena the other men smiled at each other, clapped their hands and in their own language repeated the words: 'The white men who came from Sena! The white men who came from Sena!'

Solomon spoke up: 'Not everyone agrees with Mr Mhani's discovery. The fact is, I think that you are right, we do not know where Sena is. It might be in Israel, but some believe it is in Egypt; others think it is in the Yemen or in Ethiopia. Really, we do not know. We *used* to know where it is. We do know it is in the north. If you go far enough, you can find it. This my father told me: we came from Sena; we went to Ethiopia where we were called Falasha. I once went to Ethiopia with my boss for the Company and I saw the Falashas and saw they were just like us. And they accepted me as a Falasha. I went to Gondar, prayed with them in their synagogues, broke bread and salt with them. After Ethiopia we travelled south. To start with we were called Jews, then Falasha, then Lemba. This name means that we refuse to eat pig and to marry gentiles. That is what Lemba means: the people who refuse. Best of all, we like to be known as Mwenye. What this word means we do not know.'

A bald, earnest man, Ebenezer, had been wanting to interrupt Solomon. Like the others he was dressed in a dark, shabby suit. Now, in the formal style of a debating chamber, he said, 'Point of interruption! What the Lemba used to be called is no matter. They still are the same holy nation whichever name they have. My grandfather,' he coughed into his hand and looked around to see if he was holding our attention, 'my grandfather noticed that the English people always call himself Welshman, Scottishman, Irishman, but he always the same Englishman – they still English people.'

William banged the table in agreement and the old man bared his yellowing teeth in appreciation.

Solomon seized this opportunity to carry on with his speech: 'Our forefathers reached the east coast of Africa. When they left the coast they went and built the great stone city of Zimbabwe. But the Lemba broke the law and the people thought Mwali was cross with them and they went and lived among the nations.'

Ebenezer interrupted again: 'The God of the Lemba is called Mwali. When it thundered when I was a boy, my mother used to say, "Mwali is moving from one part of heaven to another." Belief in God is one of the signs of the Mwenye.'

Solomon nodded: 'There is many signs of the Mwenye which can help you to find this holy people in the north. One sign', he said, 'is that everywhere, everywhere you will find our holy flag with the ancient sign of the Lemba – the Star of David and the Elephant of Judah. Another sign is that everywhere, everywhere the Lemba shave their heads at the time of the new moon.'

In fact, Solomon had a fine head of hair which showed no sign of having been shaved. And among the others, only Ebenezer looked as if he followed this tribal tradition. I glanced at his bald head and nodded.

13

'Don't be misled,' said Solomon. 'Not all bald heads are shaved at the new moon. Some bald heads are just bald heads.'

'Point of interruption – don't joke! It's a serious meeting. We always used to say that having your head balded made you brainier,' snapped Ebenezer.

'Does that mean that most Lemba do not, in fact, shave their heads?'

'Yes,' murmured Ebenezer. 'That used to be done in the past. In the olden days. Now that we live with the gentiles we do the things of the gentiles. But in the north they still do it in the Jewish way.'

This was all that the elders had to tell me. I asked a few questions but they shuffled their feet, muttered a few words and looked at each other with embarrassment. I presumed they knew nothing more. I was not really surprised. Soweto was not likely to be a rich repository of tribal tradition. And this had been well recognised by the Lemba themselves in the past. Half a century before, an ethnologist had noted that Lemba working in the mines were no longer regarded as Lemba by the people in the villages. When the miners came home, they were made to vomit publicly to rid themselves of the impurities they had picked up in the towns. To complete the purification an unblemished animal would be sacrificed. By the nature of things, the men in this room could hardly be reliable informants. They sat round the table, heads bowed, waiting.

A woman came in from a kitchen behind the shack carrying a tray with tea things: tea bags, powdered milk, scones. Her arrival was the sign for conversation. There was an immediate hubbub. The bald man wanted to know if I could get his thirty-five-year-old son a grant to study medicine at Oxford. Others wanted to know what I had discovered about the

Lemba, when I would be leaving for the north and which route I would take. They all urged me to speak to Professor Mathiva, a Lemba scholar at the University of the North near Pietersburg, and also to a learned Lemba called Wilfred Phophi, who lived in Vendaland. Some of them asked for news of Israel and particularly of the Falashas. As soon as the topic of the Falashas was mentioned, Solomon pulled *Operation Moses*, the book I had written about the Falashas, from a briefcase and asked me to sign it. While I was doing that, he clapped his hands together and the men started chanting, '*Mushavi, Mushavi,*' as a sign, it seemed, that the meeting was over.

Then William, his eyes closed and his hand raised, rose to his feet and started to pray. As he prayed, his other hand strayed over the open Bible, his index finger tracing a pattern over the page as if it were a map. And for him, and no doubt for others, it was a map, a map of possibilities for understanding the present and decoding the past. In *Journey without Maps* Graham Greene wrote that 'Africa has always seemed an important image'. In the mediaeval world the effort to understand that image had made icons out of maps and maps out of scripture; the Bible was always ransacked for clues to the mysteries of the continent. Here in this room the process continued. And part of that process was William's conviction that their Sena was mentioned in the Bible and was near Jericho. That the Lemba were descendants of a specific Jewish family which had returned to the Land of Israel from Babylon millennia before flew in the face of reason. It could hardly be historic. Nor, I was sure, was it part of the tribe's authentic mythology. In fact, as I was to find out later, the idea had only achieved currency because William's discovery had been published in a local newspaper and the article had been passed around within the tribe. But this was an interesting example of the uses to which the Bible might be put, and a good example of the way in which the tribe's identity might have been influenced in the past. The discovery that the name Sena was to be found in the Bible both sanctified and legitimised their own tradition in 'white' terms. What had happened here was obvious. But I could see that I would have to be careful to distinguish between what the Bible had suggested to the Lemba, or what specific clergymen had suggested (and what could be more exciting for any clergyman than that his prospective flock might be a lost tribe of Israel?), and what the original Lemba tradition had maintained.

But would I be justified *a priori* in rejecting any Jewish or biblical element in this tribe's tradition? Africanist friends in London had urged me to understand any such elements merely as examples of western, Christian influence, but I was not happy with this. In the first place, since the time of the first western penetration of Africa a much greater emphasis had been placed on the New Testament than on the Old. Old Testament motifs and ideas would not necessarily therefore have been channelled through missionary teaching. In addition, as the South African ethnographer Van Warmelo wrote, 'It cannot be assumed, even if some tales from the Old Testament had been often told to natives, that those tales should have taken such a hold on their fancy as to cause them to be woven into the traditions of the tribe.'

As far as Jewish influence, or indeed any influence, was concerned, I would have to keep an open mind. But this discovery of William's was not 'authentic'; nor, it seemed to me, was his style. It was rather the style of charismatic Christianity, and it was in the style of an evangelist that he was now praying:

'O God of Israel,' he intoned, 'the God of Abraham our

father, the God of Isaac and Jacob, give us one mind and one heart. Go with this white man in the journey to sojourn with the Lemba. Protect him against the *wasenzhi* – the gentiles. May he find the true Lemba who will guide him faithfully to Sena.'

Outside it was cold and grey. The gusting wind was whipping up the dust and smoke of Soweto into a low, noisome cloud. Just in front of the hut a group of ragged teenagers were huddled around a fire. In a half-hearted gesture of violence one of them threw a stone which landed at my feet. 'Come on, Prof,' said Ephraim, 'it's getting late. Got to keep you safe.'

He took me to his bungalow in the police residential quarters in New Canada, a drab suburb on the edge of Soweto. Everything inside his house was provided by the police force. It was clean, polished and smelled of Lifebuoy soap. There was brown lino on the floor, the walls were painted an utilitarian green. As far as I could see he had only two personal possessions in the house: a razor in the bathroom and a pineapple in a wicker basket on the table in his sitting-room.

'You haven't got much stuff here,' I said, pointing around his room.

'No. This is not my home. My home is in the north. I'll soon be retiring. I'll go back to Venda. Never come back here: thirty years is enough. If you were going next year I'd use my savings and come with you. This year I can't go.'

'I'm sorry. I would have liked that,' I said.

He stared hard at his big, tough hands for a few minutes.

'No, I can't go,' he muttered. 'And now, I'd better take you back to town. You got to keep safe. You got to find the city of God.'

2

The Gubbins Library of the University of the Witwatersrand possesses a unique collection of maps, manuscripts and books on southern Africa. The day after my visit to Soweto, I went to the Gubbins to see what I could discover about the Lemba. I did not expect to find much in the way of early records. There is much less documentary evidence even on the general history of the interior of East Africa than might be supposed, let alone on the Lemba. It is true that from the beginning of the sixteenth century the Portuguese were active on the east coast and before them the Arabs. But neither Arabs nor Portuguese left much in the way of eye-witness accounts of what went on in the interior. 'All that we know,' wrote my eminent colleague, the historian Roland Oliver, 'and that only in part, is what the peoples of the interior have themselves handed down or imagined about their own past.' Because of the interest the various monumental stone ruins of the Zimbabwe plateau – particularly those of the so-called Great Zimbabwe – had for white settlers and others, the picture here is a little different: here at least there has been a century of archaeological work which has yielded important results. But for the most part, as far as tribal histories are concerned, we must rely on three main sources: contemporary oral traditions; oral traditions recorded in the past by missionaries, administrators and ethnographers;

and the eye-witness accounts of the likes of Livingstone, Stanley, Moffat, Chaillu, Speke and Burton. It is fortunate that some of the early ethnographic and travel accounts have something to say about the Lemba: fortunate because some traditions recorded earlier this century have by now disappeared.

Perhaps because the library does not have many foreign visitors I was treated with somewhat greater consideration than is normal in university libraries. I was even invited to meet the Chief Librarian.

She asked me what I was working on. I told her about the oral traditions of the Lemba and how they claimed to be Jews, to have helped build Great Zimbabwe and to have come originally from a city called Sena. I think all of what I said was new to her: the Lemba are barely known in South Africa.

'It's an exciting story,' she said, 'but dangerous. Take the issue of Great Zimbabwe, it's been political dynamite for the last hundred years. A great deal hangs on the question of who built it. A lot of people will say that any work trying to show that outsiders built Great Zimbabwe is essentially racist.'

'What I am saying', I replied, 'is that the Lemba *claim* to have participated in it and the Lemba are black Africans!'

'Yes, but you say that they are influenced from the outside, from the Semitic world. That's diffusionism,' she said, 'a dirty word. You know the fashionable idea these days is that ancient Egypt, ancient Greece – in fact, world civilisation – is all derived from African models. You must have read Martin Bernal's *Black Athena*. There are American colleges where you get fired if you even question the Afrocentric view of history. If you even whisper that Great Zimbabwe, for instance, was affected by outside, non-African influence, you'll get yourself hung, drawn and quartered.'

'The trouble with Martin Bernal and his theories,' I said, feeling my way with some care, 'is that he takes things too far. To say that ancient Greece was influenced by the ancient Near East and by Egypt is fine, but to say that the ancient Greeks were black Africans is over-doing it. I remember a few years ago someone wrote a book somewhat along the same lines which argued that Greek was not Greek at all but a form of Hebrew. Well, that's nonsense. But without question Greek was influenced by Near Eastern languages. The fact is that hardly any language or society in the world has not been influenced by others.'

She appeared not to be paying any attention and, muttering under her breath, ushered me out of her room. Despite that, for many days she kept me supplied with rare maps and books from the closed shelves. One day, in a state of some agitation, she invited me to the rare map room. 'Didn't you tell me that the Lemba call themselves among other things "the Good Men" and that their sacred mountain near Great Zimbabwe is sometimes called "the Mountain of the Good Men"? Well, I've just found something fascinating. I have been checking references to the city of Sena on the Zambezi, which you told me may be one of the cities of Sena they built on their way down through Africa. Now look at this!' She put in front of me a beautifully bound copy of Livio Sanuto's *Geografica* published in Venice in 1588 and turned to a map of Africa. Pointing at the Zambezi River she said, 'Look, there's Sena and you see the river, it's called "*signorum bonorum fluvius*"; well, surely that means "the river of the good men". That could be your Lemba.'

My heart raced with excitement and it was a few moments before I remembered that *signorum bonorum fluvius* in fact means 'the river of good signs' – *Rio dos Bos Sinais* being the name given to the Zambezi by Vasco da Gama when he first came upon it in 1498. Research is no stranger to such moments. But fortunately there are other moments, like the occasion some months later when I found out that another area not far from the Zambezi, perhaps somewhere in the vicinity of Cape Correntes, had indeed been named by da Gama 'the Land of the Good People' – *Terra da Boa Gente*.

A few days later the librarian invited me to an inner sanctum where she had laid out dozens of ancient maps. A table covered with maps such as these, I thought, must have marked the beginning of many a Renaissance voyage of discovery, but could they help me with my journey? Could they help me find Sena? As I pored over these treasures I located two Senas: one was situated on the Zambezi River and was frequently drawn as a fortified European city with turrets and battlements; the other, not far away, was somewhat to the south, on the coast. Were these the latest cities of the Lemba? But where were their earlier cities: the various Senas which some of them claimed to have built as they came down through Africa? Was the first Sena Sanaa in the Yemen? Could it have been the ancient city of Senna, capital of the Persian province of Kurdistan, the ancient seat of the *walis* of Ardilan? Did it refer to the Axumite kingdom of Zion – the New Jerusalem of Ethiopia – built, according to Ethiopian tradition, at the order of Christ with its own Calvary, Golgotha and Jordan? Or was it perhaps the early mediaeval Muslim Funj kingdom of Sennar in the eastern Sudan?

Looking at the maps made me even more aware of the vast distances which separate Arabia and the Horn of Africa from the areas of Lemba settlement in southern Africa. It seemed improbable that there could be any connection between the Lemba and Ethiopia or the Middle East, or indeed between the Lemba and the Falashas, no matter what the Lemba claimed. Yet I remembered that when the Falashas were first discovered by Europeans and before their traditions had been contaminated by normative Jewish tradition, they explained their origins like this: 'We came under Solomon,' they said, 'we came by Sennar and from there to Axum, we came under Solomon.' Was the Sennar of the Falashas, the Sennar of the Funj, also the Sena of the Lemba? Did this phonetic similarity provide any support for a connection between the Lemba and the Falashas? Or was it just coincidence? And how about the Sena on the Zambezi? Was it mere coincidence that the mediaeval Arabic name for this Sena is taken to be Sayuna – the Judaeo-Arabic form of Zion?

The librarian left me to myself and for a long time I sat staring at these precious old African maps. What could they tell me? Until the nineteenth century they had been the product of rumour and guesswork as much as anything else, hence Swift's sneering lines: 'So geographers in Afric maps with savage pictures fill their gaps and o'er unhabitable downs place elephants instead of towns . . .' Indeed, on these maps there were plenty of exotic beasts and fairy-tale castles and not many gaps. In fact, there were more empty spaces on contemporary maps. It was clear that if I wanted to plot the march of 'the Good Men' across Africa, I would have to use a different map from these, the map of memory – but a collective memory which had been corrupted and attenuated, and which was now a dim recollection of old people's stories.

Through the open window a golden afternoon light brought with it the smell of honey. There was a jacaranda tree outside, but not in bloom, and although I inhaled vigorously whenever I passed the tree, I was never able to locate the source of the smell. The golden peace of the campus was only slightly disrupted by a white student shouting uncertainly into a loudhailer. Despite the noise, I dozed off over the maps and dreamed briefly of a turreted, ivory city of Sena. It was a dream of travel and motion in which this magical city reproduced itself endlessly on the slopes of a deeply ravined Zambezi. I was woken up by a girl shaking my shoulder. 'Telephone from Pietersburg,' she said, 'Professor Mathiva.' I followed her out of the map room and into the librarian's office.

'Hello, Parfitt,' said Mathiva, 'I hear you come safely. I'll see you at the University of the North on Saturday. I've been waiting for someone to take an interest in us.' And he put the phone down. Mathiva, the spiritual head of the South African Lemba, was prepared to talk to me. It was a start.

Over the next couple of days I read through the small body of ethnographic literature on the Lemba and was confirmed in my belief that no proper scholarly work had been done on the subject of the Lemba's origins. Ethnographers' conclusions on the Lemba's claims were tentative and at variance with one another. I hoped that the journey that I was about to undertake would provide some answers. I would follow the route preserved in the Lemba's oral tradition – the route they had taken through Africa, the route that should lead to Sena.

3

Many former colonial outposts have fine imperial railway stations. Johannesburg does not. This one, built in the 1960s, was monolithic, clean and, as far as I could see, empty. The grey night train to the north was standing in its bay. As I walked down the platform, bag in hand, there was no one in sight except a South African Railways guard. He made a jerky, resentful gesture of respect, not quite a salute.

My compartment was dimly lit, smelled of disinfectant and was intolerably over-heated. The hard, upright benches were upholstered in green plastic; everything else was mustard-coloured formica covered in a sort of 1960s cuneiform. I switched on the reading light and opened up my notebook. The brown-shirted SAR official returned to ask me for my ticket. He sat down.

'From England. On business?'

'No. I'm not a businessman. I'm just travelling. Going north.'

'So what d'you think? Not so bad, eh? These trains, you could set your watch by these trains. Best in the southern hemisphere.'

'Why don't whites travel on the trains if they're so good?'

'That's a very good question. They all reckon it's more

convenient to drive. But the good thing is, it's here if they want it. We South Africans are very proud of our trains. So what d'you think of our country?' he insisted, peering at me, ingratiating, suspicious, his dark eyebrows concertinaed in concentration, full of the spurious conviction for which Afrikaaners are noted. They think that if the outside world would only listen to their side of the story, it would support them to their last breath. And yet, from experience, they also know that not everyone from the outside wants to listen. Anyway, he was not going to get a political conversation out of me.

'Have you heard of the Lemba tribe?' I asked him.

'Yes, as a matter of fact I have. We had Lemba working on my dad's farm when I was a boy. North of Louis Trichardt. They're a peculiar lot. My pa used to call them Kruger's Jews. President Kruger discovered them prancing around and praying the way blacks do. But he was pretty surprised when they finished their prayers with the word "Amen". They'll tell you they are Israelites. We've always accepted that they are connected to the Jews. And Kruger believed so and he was no fool.' He paused and looked out of the window. 'I've heard it said that the Lemba brought the Ark of the Covenant from Israel at the time of King Solomon and that they hid it in the Soutpansberg Mountains. Something to do with King Solomon's Mines. I don't know if there's any truth in it.'

The train shuddered to a halt at an industrial siding: hundreds of black faces and the burnished side of an ancient steam-engine were caught in the dull, red glow of an open furnace. Then the silence was broken by a sound which I had almost forgotten, which shunted away everything but the excitement of being on the move: the irregular, slow, potent growl of a steam-engine. I ran to the corridor, jerked down the window and drank in the smell of childhood holidays. My journey had started.

The train pulled into Pietersburg at six o'clock the following morning. The rented car I had ordered was waiting for me at the station and a portly white woman with a faint moustache was sitting in it with her daughter. She wore her Avis jacket over a crumpled pink tracksuit.

'Why did you come by train?' she asked. 'Nobody travels by train. Nobody. Absolutely nobody. And look at the time! Avis tries harder, but you're pushing it!'

Black passengers from the train surged past the car and joined the crowds on the street. The town was full of black people coming in from their locations. I guessed that many of them were domestic servants. In the street makeshift stalls lit by kerosene lamps were doing a brisk trade in tea and buns. The Avis girl drove me to my hotel, gave me the keys and wished me a good stay.

'Won't you come in and have a coffee?' I said.

Thank you,' she replied, surprised. She picked up her child and followed me into the hotel. The girl was a chocolate-box beauty. She had gold ringlets down to her shoulders and was dressed in a faded pink velvet dress. I have never seen such beautiful children as among the Afrikaaners.

'Would the little girl like something to eat?' I asked.

'Yes. It'll save me having to make her breakfast when I get back.'

Mrs Pretorius walked to the breakfast counter and returned with a plate piled high with food, which she set in front of her daughter. When the child had polished off her steak and eggs, she was given a baby's bottle full of milk.

'What do you think of Pietersburg?'

'I've not seen much.'

'There's not much to see except for the museum,' said Mrs Pretorius.

'I was surprised to see so many people out on the street at six in the morning.'

'Oh, the blacks. Yes. I know. It's terrible, no? They're the ones with the money, you know. They come in early to do their shopping and they always get the best stuff.' Her face was tired and puffy, as if she had spent the night crying.

'But the shops are closed,' I said. 'I imagined they were just on their way to work.'

'No, they weren't. Absolutely not. They were out shopping. They're always buying food, always eating. They don't work Saturdays.'

'Today is Friday.'

'Well, they were working if you say so,' she said, pressing her thin lips together. 'They come in here from the villages: they're all after the big city life. They leave their villages and come and live around our towns. What can you do? We built them a university, which is more than we've got for ourselves. They've got the best hospital in South Africa. But it's not enough. They never stop complaining. We're the ones that should complain. And you should see the black girls,' her eyes narrowed and she paused for a moment before continuing. 'You know the Bantu women usually have these huge bottoms sticking out back like a hump. They're disappearing. The humps. The way they dress now in tight trousers, slender and slinky like, walking around the streets like they own them.'

I wondered for a moment what Mr Pretorius was getting up to.

'I guess you're going to the Kruger National Park,' she said.

'No, in fact I'm spending a few days here and then I'm going on to Vendaland.'

'There is nothing, absolutely nothing in Vendaland. But if you insist on going there, what can I do? Anyway here's a map – you may need it.' She pulled a serviceable-looking map of Vendaland out of her Avis bag.

'But before I go up to Vendaland I've got a meeting at the University of the North. Is that the black university you were talking about? Where is it?'

'Go straight out of town. You'll get to a black location called Nobody. Drive straight past Nobody and you'll see it. You can't miss it.'

Pietersburg is connected with what the Boers view as the heroic phase of their history – the period of the Great Trek. Between 1835 and 1848 thousands of Dutch farmers fled the constraints of British rule in the Cape Colony and settled vast tracts of land in Natal and the Transvaal. The most northerly town built by the Voortrekkers was Schoemansdal, constructed in 1849 in the shadow of the Soutpansberg Mountains. Eighteen years later it was sacked by the Venda chief Makhado (a man much influenced by Lemba tradition) and the Boers moved south again to escape the hostility of the Venda and Lemba tribes. The Schoemansdal settlers founded Pietersburg in 1886 as a centre for gold mining, hunting and the reconquest of the northern Transvaal.

The first Boer church to be built in the new town now occupies a commanding position in the centre of town. It is surrounded by immaculate lawns, which were being raked over by black gardeners. It was in this pretty white church that the museum was to be found. In fact, the museum boasts no more than a permanent exhibition of photographs of the town's past. There are many photographs of British concentration camps at the time of the Boer War and there was one large, blown-up photograph of a group of local worthies dressed in serge suits and stiff collars standing in front of the *minisipale slagpale* – the town slaughterhouse. It was here that their cattle, often stolen from neighbouring black tribes, finished their days. They looked proud of it.

Today Pietersburg is a completely square grid town; towards its edges emerald green sports fields defy the burnt sienna of the surrounding high veldt. In one small square of the grid a dozen matrons in starched whites were playing bowls in the Pietersburg Rolbalklub. The streets were lined with jacaranda and coral trees, the gardens full of geraniums in pots and vivid creepers. This is Boer heaven: one section of this dull, little town was called Nirvana, another Superbia. Boer history was retold in all the street names: Hans Van Renberg Street, Voortrekker Street, Kruger Street, Joubert Street.

From the museum I wandered over to the Great North Road Hotel. Solomon Sadiki had advised me not to stay there and I wanted to know why. It was soon clear. The Holiday Inn where I had booked in had a lot of black clients; this one had none. It was an Afrikaaner stronghold in which the Lemba had imagined I might feel uneasy. A short hairy man wearing a stained bush jacket was sitting in the bar. He was drinking whisky and chain-smoking. He wanted to talk. He introduced himself as Jock MacKay and told me that he had moved down to Pietersburg from Rhodesia after independence. He had been born in Scotland during one of his parents' home leaves, but had immediately been taken out to Africa.

'My dad came over from Scotland and settled in Rhodesia when it was still called Mesopotamia.'

'Mesopotamia is in the Middle East,' I said.

'Don't you go contradicting me, lad. You've only been here five minutes. You're still wet behind the ears when it comes to Africa and canna tell me nothing about Rhodesia 'cos I've lived here over seventy years. Like I said, my old man came over here when it was still called Mesopotamia.'

Jock's voice had risen and his Boer cronies were looking at each other dourly. One of them laughed a short, contemptuous laugh. Jock downed his whisky and asked for another.

'I reckon you must mean Monomotapa,' I persisted. Monomotapa was a black, pre-colonial kingdom which existed from the fifteenth to the eighteenth century. Not only was Jock's terminology out, but his chronology too.

'Ay, that's the one,' said Jock without effort or, indeed, the slightest loss of face. 'They were out there in Monowhatsit and went back to Scotland just long enough to have me. Mind you,' he prodded my chest with a leathery finger, 'I could go back to Scotland. I have a UK passport.' Looking round at his friends he put his hand on his chest, grinned and declaimed theatrically, 'Do na send me back to Blighty.' Turning back to me he talked of his brother, a millionaire in Worthing; of his son, who was sailing a yacht around the world; of his daughter in Australia; of his income from bonds, shares and pensions; of the book that he had written, but not published, which he wanted me, as someone in the business, to come round and have a look at; and of the time he had been dropped behind enemy lines. Finally Old Africa Hand dried up; the bar had emptied and I was not asking him any more questions.

'And you?' he asked. 'Been to Rhodesia?'

'I'm travelling up to Zimbabwe. Among other things I want to see the Zimbabwe ruins.'

He looked delighted at that and scratched his unshaven face with concentrated vigour.

'Ay, the whole bloody country is one big ruin since that

little bugger Mugabe took over. Na, but seriously, the ruins are mighty fine.'

'Yes, well I . . .'

'You know they were built thousands of years ago by King Solomon.' Pointing at the barman who stood a few inches in front of him on the other side of the bar he said, 'I've a lot of time for the black man, but they'll be the first to tell you, just you wait, that no kaffir ever built the old cities up there. They don't have it in them, you see. It was the Israelites and King Solomon.'

Promising to come and see me the following morning, Jock drank up and went home.

When Jock phoned up to my room, it was barely daylight. I dressed quickly, went down to the lobby and found him standing, ill at ease, in an alcove near the reception desk. Today he was wearing a light grey suit and had shaved. He looked smaller.

'I've got the old jalopy outside. Come back to the house. We can have a beer or two and I'll show you my book. *The Rape of White Africa*, I'm calling it. It's about my life and times. You're doing a book too, aren't you? That mean you're a writer?'

'Sort of,' I said.

'Paperback?'

'Some of my books have been published in paperback.'

'Anyhow, I thought you could tidy *my* book up a bit. Correct the spelling here and there. Put it in shape. You could even stay at our place for a night or two and then maybe you'd take the manuscript back to your publishers in the UK.'

'I've not got the time, Jock. It's kind of you, but I've really got to be going. I've got a long journey.'

31

The expression on his face was not very friendly.

'Ye canna go just like that. I've asked a few of the lads from the old country round for a jar later on. We do na get many visitors from back home in this Afrikaaner hell-hole. Anyway, I need you to fix up my biography.'

'Sorry, Jock.'

'Well, come and say hello to the missus anyhow. She's out in the car. She's a great reader. Wanted you to meet her.'

I looked out at the car park in front of the hotel and saw an old woman, wearing a fawn coat with a fur collar, leaning with crossed arms against a battered Morris 1000 backlit by the gold of an African dawn. We walked outside and I shook hands with his wife.

'Good morning, Tudor,' she said with a cold intimacy. 'So you're the writer. Hard work, isn't it? Why do you bother? It's the money and glitter I suppose. I hear you're from the UK.' She had a lot of bright red lipstick on, applied with little reference to the shape of her mouth.

'Ay,' exclaimed Jock, 'UK is a wonderful place, right enough.'

'When we met yesterday you said you'd rather be thrown to the sharks than go back there.'

'Let's not talk about that, it was nothing, just for the lads in the bar,' he muttered, glancing at his wife. 'In fact, we were in UK for the old lady's eightieth.'

'You don't look eighty,' I said, smiling politely at his wife.

'Not her, you stupid bugger, she's only sixty-nine. I mean the Queen Mum. We had dinner at the Charing Cross Hotel. Saw her live on telly and in the flesh after dinner. Best day of my life that was, wasn't it, mum? And it's the best place in the world, London is, after Scotland.'

'Did you get up to Scotland on your trip?' I asked.

'Na, I dinna have the time. I've never been to Scotland. But London's a great place too. I will na hear a word against it.'

With that, Jock and his wife climbed into their Morris and drove off. Above the radiator, firmly attached by a piece of string, was a sprig of purple heather.

4

At noon, the road from Nirvana to Nobody was like a reel-to-reel tape looped insecurely over the hills. The land was uncultivated and melancholy. Large, ungainly birds surveyed the wilderness from ragged outcrops of crumbling stone. The place has always had a bad reputation. Mrs Pretorius had told me that in the days of the Voortrekkers, the Boers were reluctant to stop here at all: the veldt was known to be infested by spirits. Nobody lived here. Hence the name of the shantytown where thousands of black people now lived: Nobody. A few men were sitting on old tyres in a dusty space between the Nobody Bar and Lounge, which consisted of two tin shacks, and the Nobody Bottle Shop, a sturdy brick building with iron bars over the windows. The dried-out plain beyond Nobody was dotted with black bushes. A tarmac road crossed it leading to the small town of Mankweng. In the far distance the mountains had lost all colour of their own: they were the point where the ochre of the land stopped and the pale blue of the sky started.

The University of the North dominates Mankweng. It is another grid town, a very much drabber version of Pietersburg. The university is functional red brick; the dormitories and lecture halls give the impression of having been shoved together, to save space. Weeds grow around the barbed-wire perimeter fence; the space around the buildings, unlike the lawns of Witwatersrand, is beaten red earth. The only entrance to the university, and the only gap in the fence, is a monumental brick arch, the university's sole adornment.

The mud road went around the university and on past a new, red-brick supermarket, a bottle store and a few wooden stalls set up at the side of the road. A group of students were sitting on the ground near the stalls. They told me where I would find Professor Mathiva's bungalow. I drove on and arrived at the house. Pushing open the wooden gate, I crossed a well-tended garden with a lawn, fruit trees and vegetable plot, to where Mathiva was sitting in a rocking-chair on a red, polished *stoep*. He stood up and beamed, clapping his hands in the Lemba greeting. He was wearing old grey flannels and a red cardigan. He was a big man with a thick, smooth neck; the shaved dome of his head was covered in a frosting of white stubble. A peculiarity of his upper lip, which was permanently turned up, gave him an expression of delighted surprise.

He ushered me in. One end of his sitting-room was piled with books, most of them encyclopaedias. The walls were painted in shiny bright blue, obscured in part by dozens of photographs of Mathiva's wedding and graduation, his sons' graduations and certificates of his inclusion in the *World Who's Who of Intellectuals*, and of his and his sons' degrees and diplomas. On one chair I noticed a stack of pamphlets from the Lemba Cultural Association marked with the elephant inside a Star of David. He apologised for the mess; he had retired as vice-rector of the university and was shortly moving back to Venda.

When the University of the North had been founded, he told me, nearly all the teaching staff had been white, but now there was a substantial body of black lecturers. Mathiva's own position in the university had not been easily achieved.

'You know,' he said, 'the worst things for me have always been the petty things: the fact that we used to have two common rooms, one for whites, one for blacks, the fact that it used to be illegal for a black to shake a white's hand,' and he mimicked the gesture of proffering his hand and its being rejected. He did it so well that I smiled.

'No, it's not funny. Every black man lived with humiliation every day. It seems incredible: we used to regard the white man as a sort of messiah – someone who would lead us towards education and enlightenment. In fact, when the whites first came to this area we called them the sons of God – the sons of Mwali – the sons whose ears shine in the sun. And under the British it was really like that. Enlightenment was the bridge to acceptance. You could qualify for anything, even the vote. But the Boers blocked all that.' He beamed at me. 'But there is no place for despondency. There's still time to solve the problems. I don't think the Africans are a vengeful people. Look what happened in Zimbabwe. The whites always said there would be a blood-bath if the blacks won the war, but not so. The sky has not fallen in: the whites are still in control of lots of things up there. And this is very amazing because apartheid was much worse on that side. I remember that blacks were not even allowed to go into whites' shops – they had to be served through the window. If redemption and peace can come to Rhodesia after years of one of the bloodiest wars, it can come here.'

While he was talking his plump, elderly wife entered the room and stood by my side holding a round, blue plastic bowl. She smiled, curtseyed and said that I should wash my hands. When I had finished, she took the bowl to her husband and knelt in front of him while he washed.

'It's one of the customs of the Lemba. We are a particular people: we wash before food, after food, before bed, after bed, before bodily functions, after bodily functions, before prayers, after prayers. You can read all about it in the Bible. Part of our Jewishness. Now it's before eating.'

His wife brought in a meal of grilled chicken, cold baked beans from a tin and a gelatinous corn porridge, *rokweza*, which is the staple food of black South Africa. Throughout the meal Mathiva talked about Lemba history, pausing from time to time to eat. What he spoke of most was the Lemba's involvement in the Great Zimbabwe civilisation, the civilisation whose ruins have intrigued archaeologists since their discovery just over a century ago.

'I thought no one really knew who built Great Zimbabwe,' I said. 'Isn't your claim somewhat controversial at the very least?'

'It's not a claim, it's a fact.'

'But I think the Venda and the Shona, for instance, also claim to have had something to do with it.'

'Just claiming,' sang Mathiva, his voice rising.

'But what proof do you have that the Lemba built it?' I asked.

'The chief proof is that our fathers told us it was so, but there are also artefacts.'

'What sort of artefacts?'

'Circumcision instruments, pottery, gold articles. What they have found in Great Zimbabwe, we have. We still have all those old things hidden away.'

'The best-known archaeological discovery in Great Zimbabwe was the soapstone birds,' I said. 'Do you have that?'

'We have it! We have it!' he cried, clapping his hands, and went out into the hall, doubled over in his haste, returning with a small, soapstone bird. The Zimbabwe birds were among the most intriguing finds at Great Zimbabwe, not least because they were unlike anything which had ever been found in Africa. There were eight birds carved in a soft, local stone, which formed the top of pillars some five feet high. It is not clear what these birds represent. An early idea suggested that they were hawks somehow connected with the Egyptian deity Horus. Others claimed that the birds represent the crowned hornbill. According to Lemba traditions collected by two French anthropologists, at least some of the birds represent the African fish eagle. It has also been suggested that the stone pillars crowned with the birds were memorials to distinguished ancestors. I looked hard at the small, carved bird which Mathiva laid carefully on the table.

'But this is modern,' I said; indeed, I was later to discover that it was the sort of thing which could be picked up for a few pennies in any tourist shop in Zimbabwe.

'Yes,' he conceded, his eyes crinkling in a smile, 'it is modern, but we used to have them like that. We put them in water and gave the children that water to drink against illness.'

'Does anyone have any of the old soapstone birds?' I asked.

'Maybe in Zimbabwe. Here I think they've gone the way of all flesh. The bird', he said, pointing at the replica, 'is an eagle, which was an important bird for us: the medicine man would send out the eagle, which can fly very high, and it would spy out our enemies.' He was a perfect mimic and for a moment became a hooded eagle, hunching his shoulders and peering evilly down his nose. 'The birds on the stone columns at Great Zimbabwe were doing the same thing: they were protecting the Lemba against their enemies.'

'One of the Zimbabwe birds has a crocodile climbing up its plinth. Does that mean anything to the Lemba?'

'Yes, it was like this. In those days the candidates for the great chieftainship had to swim in a pool infested by crocodiles. If they came out, they could be considered for chief; if

38

they didn't – well, if they didn't, they couldn't. So the crocodile stands for courage and endurance. Whatever you come up with from the Zimbabwe ruins, you will find that there is a connection with the Mwenye, with the Lemba.

'A final proof,' he continued, 'is the fact that the Tovakare family, one of the Lemba clans, is still up there keeping an eye on the old place. They used to stay a bit nearer, but the Rhodesian Government made the place into a reserve and pushed them out. The Tovakares have been there for a hundred generations. Their name is used only by the Mwenye; the full title of the family is Tovakare Muzimbabwe, which means "the ones that built Zimbabwe". They are still there, not far away, keeping an eye open.'

'Why do you think the Lemba left Zimbabwe?'

'The ten Lemba tribes were gathered there and one of the tribes committed a grave offence against the god Mwali. They gave in to temptation and ate mice. These animals are unclean. Neither the Lemba, nor anyone else, has been able to live there since. But our god Mwali sent a star and our people followed it south to Mberengwe around the Mountain of the Good Men. We stayed together, more or less, until the whites occupied, what d'you call, Rhodesia. It was the coming of the whites which spread us far and wide.'

During the war against the Boers, he continued, the chief of the powerful Venda tribe, Mphephu, had two outstanding generals: Milubi, a Lemba, and Funyufunyu, a Venda. They retreated across the Limpopo into what is today Zimbabwe to regroup and get reinforcements. Another Lemba chief, Ndouvhade, was left to fight the Boers alone. The Boers were defeated in one engagement with Ndouvhade, and the British promised to replace the tribesmen's old muskets with modern weapons if they would hand them all in.

'The British collected the muskets,' said Mathiva, 'but in

their sly way they failed to keep their promise. We are still waiting for those guns. When we lost our arms, we lost our independence and later we lost many of our traditions. What we are left with is a memory of some things and a curiosity to know more. Only barbarians are not curious about where they come from, how they came from there and where they are going to. We are called Mwenye, but we do not know what it means. So we have lost our name. We are from Sena, but we do not know where it is. We have lost the print of our foot on the earth.' He was silent for a long time.

'My friend,' he continued, 'let me, how d'you say, recap. First we Lemba are Jews. There are many of us. Maybe one hundred thousand in South Africa and Zimbabwe. In some ways too we are like a secret society. We have passwords, we are to be found everywhere, everywhere here among all the tribes as well as in Zimbabwe. Everywhere. Like other Jews, like the Freemasons. We are a very secretive people. You will find this a real stumbling-block. Many Lemba will not want to speak to you. And you will not know they are Lemba. But these are the signs: like the Jews we practise circumcision; we bury our dead like the Jews; we offer animal sacrifices like the old Jews; like the Jews the first day of the new moon is sacred; like the Jews the seventh day of the moon is sacred; we have forgotten, what d'you call, the Sabbath, but the number seven is sacred for us like the Jews; like the Jews we keep kosher. In fact, in the old days when a Lemba went on a long journey, he would take with him a little flock of chickens so he could eat kosher meat on the way. We cut the throat of animals like the Jews; like the Jews we keep ritual purity; like the Jews we do not marry the *wasenzhi* – the gentiles. Like the Jews', he smiled, pointing at the framed diplomas on the wall behind him, 'we are professors and our sons are doctors and lawyers – and in the past all the doctors were Lemba; like the Jews we are in, what d'you call, the diaspora; like the Jews we keep apart from the gentiles.'

The ethnographic literature devoted to the Lemba often mentions that they refer to other Africans as *wasenzhi*. When the hopelessly corrupt and impure nature of these 'gentiles' is to be particularly stressed, they use the fuller and more abusive term, *'wasenzhi – vali va nama ya vafu'* – *'wasenzhi* – the eaters of dead meat'. The word *wasenzhi* is probably a Bantuised form of the Arabic Zanj, which is a collective noun commonly used in mediaeval Arabic texts to describe the black, non-Muslim Africans that the Arabs found on the coast of Africa. Almost certainly the term *wasenzhi* comes from the distant coast. Could it be, I wondered, that the Lemba's sense of exclusiveness reflects an ancient sense of superiority: the sense of superiority of 'the white men who came from Sena' towards the negro Zanj?

Mathiva picked up a blue velvet cape embroidered with the Lemba's Star of David and slipped it over his shoulders. Closing his eyes, he made a sacerdotal gesture, stretching his hands in front of him as if in a blessing. Stroking the air with his fingertips he said, 'Once we had a book, but it was lost. This is one of the most important memories we have. We don't have much – the British took away our guns and our history. The Boers took away our self-respect. Perhaps if you write a book you can give it back to us. Now I will tell you what is permitted. What I *can* tell.' He started to chant, shuffling his feet slightly in time with the words:

'We came from Sena, we crossed Pusela,
We rebuilt Sena.
We moved to another Sena.

In Sena they died like flies.
We came from Hundji, to Chilimani.

From Chilimani to Wedza.
The tribes went to Zimbabwe.
They built the walls and lived on the hill.
Mwali sent the star.
From Zimbabwe to Mberengwe. From Mberengwe to Dumghe.
We carried the drum. We came to Venda.
Solomon led us.
Baramina was our ancestor.'

'Baramina,' he repeated and sat down heavily, beads of sweat on his forehead. 'This is what I know from my father and my research.'
'Who were Baramina and Solomon?'
'I do not know, really. Lemba leaders long ago.'
'And how about the drum and the star?'
'I do not know more,' he replied.
'And what about Hundji?'
'We came from that place. From Hundji.'
'If I understand you correctly, you are saying that Jews left Israel hundreds or thousands of years ago and they came down through Africa, building two cities called Sena as they went and eventually built the greatest stone-built construction in the whole of sub-Saharan Africa. I mean, this is a fantastic story!'
'That's right,' he smiled, 'except maybe it wasn't Israel. We know that we left Sena, but we do not know where Sena is. Some believe it is Israel, some believe it is Yemen or Ethiopia, some believe other things. We built Sena Two and Sena Three. These were in Africa. We do not know where Pusela is. I think it means the sea. "We came from Sena, we crossed

Pusela." But it is a strange thing. There is a town not far from here called Tzaneen. Before the whites came there used to be a lot of Mwenye there and their name for the place is Pusela. Near Tzaneen lives the Rain Queen – the Mujaji. It used to be said that the Rain Queen knew our secret words, and that is how she defeated us. Even if you cannot see the Mujaji – usually whites are not allowed to see her – you could send a message to try and find out. Listen. There are many mysteries. Many things we have forgotten. After you've seen the Queen, you'll have to keep going north. You'll have to try everything.'

Out of his pocket Mathiva drew three smooth white stones. Placing them on the table he spread out a map of Africa. Two of the stones he positioned towards the east coast. 'Sena Two and Three must be around here,' he said. 'But our original Sena is lost.' And he tossed the third white stone into the Indian Ocean. Muttering that he would like to come as well, Mathiva scribbled the address of the Rain Queen on a piece of paper and then typed an open letter of introduction which I could present to the Lemba I met further north. He also said that he would telephone a friend of his in Harare, a former cabinet minister and a Lemba, who would be able 'to open doors'.

As I drove back to Pietersburg I wondered about the value of the oral traditions which the Lemba had preserved. A people's story, after all, is not its history. Oral traditions in the Transvaal and Zimbabwe, no matter which tribe they come from, are complicated by the fact that, unlike some African societies, there was never a professional historian attached to the chief's *kraal*. As a rule the only societies to maintain reliable traditions are centralised ones, particularly those with special castes whose function it is to recall and transmit tradition. But it must be said that the fact that the endogamous Lemba did not marry with other tribes and had a sharp sense of their own particularity would tend to make their traditions more reliable. A similar group, the tiny endogamous caste of Benei Israel in West India which I had visited some years before, maintained oral traditions about their Jewish origin for the best part, probably, of two thousand years, even though they had forgotten almost all of their Jewish traditions and all of their Hebrew except the one word '*Shema*' – the first word of the elemental Jewish prayer, 'Hear, O Israel'. In any case, if I were to unravel the mystery of the Lemba's unrecorded past, I would have to rely on their sagas. Perhaps they were rubbish, perhaps they weren't, but there was nothing else.

It was getting dark. Near Nobody hundreds of rusty cans and paper wrappers stuck in the wire mesh fence dividing the location from the road were catching the dying rays of the setting sun. They looked like burning candles against the darkening sky, small beacons lighting the way. Even rubbish looks good in the right light.

5

The road from Pietersburg to Tzaneen goes through what John Buchan called the land of the silver mists. But that is not how it appeared to me: in the harsh morning light the round, brown rocks visible above the heat haze looked like steaming heaps of horse dung. It was wild, desolate country. Mathiva had told me that the Lemba had come this way and had established themselves as master builders and iron smelters at Magoro's Kop, a conical hill rising out of the Letaba valley. They built stone walls, dug grain pits and reservoirs and, for a while in the nineteenth century, dominated the whole area.

Somewhat before the arrival of the Lemba there had been another southern movement of people. According to legend, the daughter of one of the sons of the Monomotapa – the ruler of the great black kingdom to the north – was seduced by her brother and conceived. Fearing the anger of their father, the couple fled south, taking with them the prized rain charms. They became the founders of a new tribe. Their descendant, the sacred king Mugadu the Outcast, Mugadu-of-the-neck-with-great-folds-of-fat, decided to put an end to male succession, which always gave rise to bloody periods of internecine fighting. He committed incest with his daughter, Mujaji, and, when she gave birth to a daughter, he followed the ancient tradition which required a sacred king to end his rule by ritual suicide. Mugadu died – in the local idiom he crept into the horn of a cow – and Mujaji became the first Rain Queen. Female succession brought peace and the Rain Queen was worshipped by her tribe as a goddess. The focal point of her cult was a sacred mountain covered with prehistoric cycads, Mujaji palms.

For the warlike Zulus, Mujaji was the queen of drought and locusts, the most powerful magician of the northern lands, the immortal transformer of the clouds, who could send or hold back rain.

Europeans had a different version. João Albasini (1813–88), the Portuguese adventurer who became the *de facto* ruler of the northern Transvaal, was convinced that the Rain Queen was an abducted child. In *She*, Rider Haggard claimed that the Queen was of pure Semitic ancestry. Others said that she was a white woman sold into slavery. It was forbidden for whites to meet her. On the rare occasions when outsiders were allowed into the inner sanctum, the Rain Queen sat in the darkest corner of the hut, her face hidden. Those who believed that she was really a white woman claimed that her hair was shaved and her face darkened with charcoal.

In the time of Albasini the Lemba, who were unique in not fearing her magic, attacked the villages of the Mujaji and stole her cattle. The Rain Queen pleaded for help from Albasini, who sent fifty of his best Shangan warriors. Taking advantage of the morning mist the Shangan, disguised as Lemba, waited for the herdsmen who were coming down the hillside to pasture their cattle in the valley and massacred them in the thick mist. They took the fortified hill without opposition and annihilated its population. Although Lemba were found there at the beginning of this century, this marked the end of organised Lemba settlement in the Letaba valley.

*

Tzaneen is a small town whose ugliness is masked by ubiquitous banks of bougainvillaea. The jewel in its crown is a Kentucky Fried Chicken shop. The day I was there no one was buying fried chicken and no one was in the streets. I drove on to Duiwelskloof. It was a good road, a First World road: routes connecting 'white' towns are tarred; African locations and villages are usually connected by dirt roads. And indeed, a few miles after Duiwelskloof the tarred surface came to an abrupt halt. Duiwelskloof means the valley of the devils: this was the entrance to Mujaji territory.

A bright red dirt road cutting through dusty blue gum plantations stretched into the distance. As I drove in the steaming heat of the afternoon, I imagined the road to be a muddy river in full spate, not very interesting in itself, but with potentially interesting banks. I was not, therefore, surprised when two girls like kingfishers in their bright blue uniforms and polished black shoes darted out from the verge, their thumbs raised high. I pulled up and asked them if they wanted a ride.

Mumbling in what I took to be an appreciative way, they climbed into the back of the car and, after a few minutes, started to talk each other in the local language, Lovedu. After another few miles we passed into open country. Round thatched huts were dotted evenly over both sides of the valley, but from time to time the symmetry of the terrain was disturbed by a rectangular concrete house or bottle shop. I stopped at one. It was guarded by a breeze-block wall, in front of which stood a still line of red flowers on tall stems uncluttered by leaves growing straight out of the red earth. They were so perfect that I felt sure they were artificial, but when I stooped to touch them, the bottle-shop man shouted that I should not pick them. The girls were having an animated conversation which they interrupted to laugh at me.

'Don't you speak English?' I asked.

They giggled, but said nothing.

The sky was clouding over and a few large drops of rain made a thick orange paste on the windscreen.

'The Rain Queen is at work,' I said.

Again they said nothing.

'The rain in Spain falls mainly in the plain,' I said, enunciating the words carefully, for no real reason other than to say something.

'In Hertford, Hereford and Hampshire hurricanes hardly happen,' they replied, with childish solemnity. It was a breakthrough and we continued to swap rhymes and tongue-twisters all the way to the Mujaji's village. 'I saw Esau' was particularly successful.

A middle-aged black guard dressed in khaki fatigues and a peaked hat stood beneath a dripping blue gum tree in the centre of the village. With an ostentatious movement of his wrist he looked at his watch. It was five-thirty.

'Why you late? Close up at five-thirty. Why you not telephone? Do you have permit? And your passport?' He started writing on a pad. 'And your telephone number. Yes, in London, isn't it?'

One of the two girls disappeared into the village. The other, whose name was Maria, stayed by the car, smiling at me and the guard in turn. The guard did not take his eyes off her.

'Cycads,' he said. 'All shut now. Holy trees belong to Rain Queen.' The man's eyes still did not leave Maria.

'I would very much like to meet the Rain Queen, if it is possible,' I said. 'You look as if you are an important man in the village. Perhaps you could help?'

'You ask her uncle,' said the old guard, scowling at me.

'Perhaps *you* could ask him – is he a friend of yours?' I persisted.

'No!' he said. 'I am her friend, Maria's friend. Her uncle . . .' he did not finish the sentence, but spat on the ground.

Turning to the girl, I asked: 'Well, can I see your uncle?'

Jutting out her full breasts Maria said, 'My uncle is my friend, but now maybe he is sleeping. But I can show you the cycads if you want to see.' She started up the hill towards the grove of ancient trees.

'Who *is* that man, the guard?' I asked.

'He is my uncle.' She led the way over the brow of the Mujaji's hill and into the grove.

'Holy trees belong Rain Queen. No one touch; not grow other place.' She gave one of the holy shrubs a resounding slap.

'Sorry,' I said, 'I'm confused. Why did your uncle tell me I should talk to your other uncle? Why couldn't he help me?'

She laughed. 'All my uncles love me. This one jealous other uncle. They both want marry me.'

It was raining heavily now and we took shelter for a few minutes under a dripping cycad. She told me that once Jan Smuts's daughter had been forced to take shelter from a storm in the village and became one of the first white people to meet the Mujaji. Later the Smuts family and the family of the Mujaji became friends.

'Do you think there is any chance of *my* seeing the Rain Queen?' I asked.

Ignoring the question she said, 'Tell me "I saw Esau",' and started walking back to the village. She marched in front of me, head high, impervious to the rain, her soaked dress clinging to her body. My jacket held over my head I waded after her, reciting 'I saw Esau sitting on a seesaw, I saw Esau, he saw me'.

The huts of the village were decorated with beige, ochre and white geometric lines. There was no one in sight. We entered a gate set into a fence of long, peeled stakes, driven deep into the ground.

'This is the *kraal* of the Rain Queen,' she said, removing her shoes as she stepped on to the red mud. I removed my shoes and rolled up my jeans. She pointed at a ramshackle bungalow on the other side of the *kraal*. It had a deep, colonial-style veranda and a thatch, black with holes.

'Rain Queen house,' she said.

Near the bungalow Maria stopped in front of a beautifully painted rondavel with concrete floors and glazed windows, the Boer adaptation of the original African thatched hut, now back in its original habitat.

'Rain Queen have many houses.'

'Where is the Rain Queen?' I asked.

She pointed towards a muddy field sloping away from the back of the village. It was surrounded by cut thorn bushes. Elderly women were crawling on their hands and knees through the mud towards a circle of women in the middle of the field. In the centre of the circle sat the Rain Queen. As we got close to her I could see that the Queen was an obese black woman wearing a tight, wet T-shirt. She was drinking beer from a bottle. Stretched over her breasts were the words 'Letaba Town of the Rain Queen'. This sluttish woman's not very distant ancestor had been the Four-breasted Goddess of the North, feared by the Zulus and the other great tribes of the south. The courtiers had nothing of the Queen's girth: they were short, thin and very dirty. One of them said something to the girl. The rest looked at me without much interest.

'What is it?' I asked her.

'Before you talk to the Rain Queen you must give her a present,' she murmured. I remembered that no one was allowed to talk to her distant ancestor, the Monomotapa, without giving him a present too.

'I don't have anything here,' I said. Indeed, a foray into my jacket pocket produced only a one pound British coin, which I gave to Maria. She accepted it with cupped palms, curtseyed and passed it to the Queen.

'British coin, you know. That's *our* Queen,' I said, pointing at the head of Queen Elizabeth II.

The women cackled and, clapping their hands, broke into song. They clearly thought my gift most inadequate, but the Queen examined the coin with interest.

'What's the song about?' I asked the girl.

'It is a song for queens and for women.'

'What are the words?'

'The words are about women who make love and play with lowcaste boys. It is a song for the Rain Queen.'

She gave a throaty laugh. Whites, I remembered, had always imagined the court of the Rain Queen to be a hotbed of orgiastic decadence.

The women started whispering again. The girl told me that they expected me to give another present to the Queen. The pound was good as far as it went, but it was not enough.

'What would the Queen like? Perhaps I could send something when I get back to England.'

'A white dress,' said the girl, having conferred with the Mujaji.

'I'll send one, I promise. What size?'

'Sixteen,' said Maria, but she was interrupted by the Rain Queen, who uttered the only words I heard her say in English, and in perfect English: 'No. Size eight. I always take size eight. Eight English size.' I suppressed a smile. Vanity is universal. No part of the Queen would have fitted into a size eight.

The women who had been crawling through the mud had now reached the centre of the field and formed a second circle around the Queen, still on their knees. They were singing and clapping their hands in homage. The Queen asked me if it was customary for English people to sing songs to their Queen.

'Yes,' I said, 'I suppose it is.'

'So sing a Queen song,' she commanded.

It was raining hard. Water was trickling down my back and red mud was oozing up between my toes, which looked unnaturally white. The Queen's courtiers were scowling at me and I imagined that they thought that, as a man and particularly as a white man, my song was unlikely to be up to much. None the less, I pulled my shoulders back and sang 'God Save the Queen' for all I was worth. My audience was appreciative. They clapped their hands and one or two of them shouted out the Lovedu word for male lion. With this praise-name ringing in my ears, I felt sufficiently encouraged to ask the Queen to tell me what she knew of the Lemba.

'They used to live near us,' she said. 'They had beards, they knew magic and their heads were wrapped in clouds.'

'In clouds?' I asked.

'Yes. We defeated these bearded ones and sent them away. They were white men. They came from far away.'

'Where is Pusela?' I asked.

'The Lemba came from Pusela,' she said. The Queen's small eyes were clouded by beer. Her body swayed, she closed her eyes and seemed to fall asleep. I waited for a few minutes but it was clear that the audience was over. Maria pulled at my arm, I bowed deeply in the direction of the old ladies, and we left.

On the way back through the village I asked the girl if she knew anything about Pusela, if the word meant anything to her.

'I have heard stories. This place around Tzaneen is sometimes called Pusela, but the Lemba brought the name from the north. I think it is a secret word. You cannot know it.'

She darted into a hut and emerged carrying a decorated earthenware pot.

'This is present,' she said, smiling.

'Thank you. That's very kind of you. Can I give you a present?'

'Yes, please. Write on paper, "I saw Esau". I can forget it.'

We sat in the car for a few minutes as I wrote it out for her. The rain was torrential now and at the bottom of the Mujaji's hill I could see that a mist was forming in the valley. Before I drove off I asked the girl a question which had been puzzling me: how was it that she, a mere schoolgirl, had been able to take me, a white man, to see the Rain Queen?

'You can be surprised,' she murmured. 'You see, I am the next Rain Queen. I am Maria, the daughter of Queen Mokope, the great-granddaughter of Mugadu, the First Man, and the great-great-granddaughter of the God Mwali.'

6

I drove off towards Venda. The little I had gleaned from the Rain Queen had only deepened the mystery of the Lemba: a strange race of men from the north, 'their heads wrapped in clouds'. Now, as I drove, just about everything was wrapped in clouds. I could see nothing through the windscreen because of the mist and rain and the car was slithering out of control in the mud. It was impossible to drive on and it was too far to walk back to the village of the Mujaji. With some difficulty I got the car out of the ruts and on to a grassy track and drove into a forest. There was nothing for it but to wait for the rain to stop. So I climbed into the back of the car, wrote up my diary and spent the night neither awake nor asleep, thinking of the journey that lay ahead.

The next morning I followed the grassy track through a forest of tall, blue gum trees tinged pink by the dawn and soon found myself on a good tarmac road heading for Venda. The road from Letaba to Venda passes through the Boer heartlands. The great expanses of uncultivated high veldt are broken every few miles by worked fields and small whitewashed towns, which look as if nothing ever happens there. The last Boer town before the turnoff for Thohoyandou, the sleazy, modern capital of Venda, is Louis Trichardt, named after the Boer Voortrekker leader who arrived at the frontiers of Venda with the pioneers of the Great Trek in the 1830s.

Venda is a rugged territory, much of it covered by the Soutpansberg Mountains and their foothills. The majority of the population of Venda are BaVenda, black tribesmen who are thought to have come long ago from Central Africa in a southern migration which extended over many centuries. Although Vendaland had been united under a king at certain times in the past (the stone ruins of Dzata had been his capital), by the nineteenth century the territory was divided among a number of powerful chiefs.

Some of the Venda clans, helped by the Lemba, held out against the whites longer than any other tribe in South Africa. Many Venda worked in the Kimberley diamond mines; with their pay they were able to buy guns, which were used to good effect in defence of their mountain strongholds. But the Boers besieged their fortresses, dynamited the caves where they had always taken refuge in the past, and burnt their crops. Finally, in 1898, the Boer leader General Petrus Joubert, with 4,000 Boer troops along with their Swazi and Tonga allies, stormed the stronghold of Mphephu, the last Venda chief to hold out, and forced him to retreat across the Limpopo. In 1899, Vendaland was placed under white administration and a great deal of its land was expropriated for white settlement. In 1979, 2,500 square miles, a fraction of the original territory of the Venda, was designated the independent Republic of Venda by the South African Government.

Mrs Pretorius, the Avis representative in Pietersburg, had given me a colourful map produced by the Venda Ministry of Tourism on which the Republic of Venda was called 'Land of Legend'. Pictographically it showed 'Kokwane' (prehistoric footprints), the Sacred Lake Fundudzi, the Sacred Forest and, in the centre of the map, an enticingly drawn big baobab tree. But there was no mention on my map of the extraordinary history of the Lemba.

The wooded slopes rising to the Soutpansberg Mountains were crossed with rivers and streams; the land was red and fertile. Pale, thatched, conical huts on the hillsides blended with the woods which cover all but the highest peaks. The recent rains had turned the fields into bright green squares slashed with scars of livid red earth.

I knew that sizable groups of Lemba lived in some of these villages, always existing as a minority among the more populous Venda. As I drove along I remembered a passage from the authoritative book on the Venda by H. A. Stayt, who wrote of the Lemba: 'The life and customs of this peculiar people are strangely reminiscent of the wandering Jews of mediaeval times.'

The Soweto Lemba had told me to speak to Wilfred Phophi, an old Lemba whose long association with the Department of Native Affairs, and particularly with the distinguished ethnographer N. J. Van Warmelo, had made him an authority on Lemba history. He lived in Tshifudi, a village in a remote part of Vendaland, about forty miles from Thohoyandou.

I arrived in Tshifudi in the early afternoon and was shown to the house by a crowd of children. Phophi's tin-roofed bungalow was on the edge of the village, which otherwise consisted of round grass huts. The bungalow was set in a large compound surrounded by a rickety wooden fence. As soon as we got to the fence, the children fled back into the village screaming and laughing. The gate set into the fence was closed and propped shut from the inside by a walking-stick. A white enamel bowl full of soapy water, a razor and a piece of shaving soap on a flannel had been left on a low concrete wall near the gate. From these signs I guessed that someone, probably Phophi, was not far away. Indeed, at that moment, a tall, well-built old man, with grizzled hair, wearing a rust-coloured sweater, grey trousers and sandals, turned into the lane.

'Excuse me, I'm looking for Mr Phophi,' I said.

'I'm Phophi,' he roared, eyes milky with cataracts and bulging with rage. 'Who the hell are you?'

'Good morning. Tudor Parfitt from the School of Oriental and African Studies, London,' I replied, offering my hand to be shaken.

Ignoring it, Phophi said, 'I've been waiting for you people to get in touch with me for years. We've got to get moving together. Things to do.'

'I'll be happy to take back any suggestions,' I said, giving him a card with my university address on it.

'I've been waiting many years, many years, many years,' stuttered Phophi, in what might have been a clever parody of English donnishness, as he put my card, unread, into his back trouser pocket. 'About time you got here. I can be dead any minute.' He let out a staccato laugh. Unlike most of the other Lemba I had met, Phophi had a small, effeminate nose. There was nothing Semitic-looking about him at all.

'I hope you're not one of those who thinks we're Arabs,' he bellowed and, without waiting for a reply, leaned over the gate, seized the stick and brandished its ebony knop in my face.

'What?' I said.

'Why did you come?' he shouted. 'To prove we're Arabs?'

'I came because I wanted to speak to you. The Soweto Lemba told me that you are an authority on the subject and that you are respected throughout Vendaland.'

'I am respected throughout the whole of bloody South Africa,' screeched Phophi.

Using the end of his stick, the bellicose old man pushed me through the gate and into his bungalow and ordered me to wait for him. 'You'll see,' he said, disappearing into another room.

Phophi's bungalow looked as if it was going to collapse around my ears. Picking my way through the debris, I went into his sitting-room. There were three rickety armchairs around a coffee table. I sat down and glanced at the battered books piled against the wall. They were not books one would want to be marooned with; the third volume of Churchill's *History of the Second World War*, *Know Your Own Mind* and a dozen old copies of *Reader's Digest*. Phophi returned flourishing a piece of paper. It was a faded Gestetner copy in fuzzy purple print which had been prepared for his diploma ceremony from the Tshisimany College of Education.

'Look at that,' he said, stabbing his finger at the first paragraph: it was a citation from Dr Van Warmelo, Chief Ethnologist in the Department of Native Affairs. Phophi read it out, but I think he knew it by heart.

'No other example of such devotion', he paused, glaring at me, 'and thorough research', he raised his finger in the air, in admonition, 'over a period of thirty-five years', he paused again and then bellowed in my ear, '*exists in Southern Africa.*'

'Most impressive,' I murmured.

'*Where* am I respected?' asked Phophi.

'In southern Africa,' I said.

Phophi glared at me and took a swig at a bottle of beer he had brought in with him.

'I wonder if I could have a cup of tea?' I asked. 'It used to be the case that Lemba would refuse to speak to strangers until they had offered them water,' I said, smiling.

'Nothing to do with your tea. That was just a way of us

keeping up our purity. We did not want unwashed gentiles contaminating us so we gave them water *to wash with*.' He glared at me again.

'No tea now, we've got work to do. Right ho! Now have a look at this.'

I was uncomfortably aware that the house was being taken over. Termites had undermined the floor, lizards darted among the mouse droppings, dozens of small birds flew in and out of the broken windows, the invasion of branches and creepers went unchecked, and gigantic webs festooned the corners. But Wilfred Phophi did not seem to notice these intrusions of nature for he was writing a book. In his hand he held a synopsis of the work – his life's work, he said – a history of the Lemba. He pushed the grubby pages in my direction, but, before I could read anything, snatched them back.

'What I am writing', he declared, 'is a first-hand historical novel about the Lemba, for the whole world. Before finishing it I wanted to talk a bit to you fellows, to expand my horizons. What are you going to tell me?' He frowned and, in an absent-minded way, started reading his synopsis.

'You are the expert on the Lemba, Mr Phophi. I came to learn from you.'

'Right ho!' he shouted. '*This* is the origin of the Lemba. *This* is how we came to be sojourning in this wretched land of the gentiles. Solomon sent his ships to get gold from Ophir, that is Zimbabwe. Some of the Jews who went on those boats stayed in Africa. *That* is the origin of the Lemba. Our name means "those who avoid eating with others". *That* means Jews. The others we did not eat with were the *wasenzhi*. *That* means gentiles. And for all this gen do not think that I am relying on the dictum of old Mathiva,' he said, banging his hand on the table. 'My father could read and write. I got it all from him. He told me things that Mathiva will never know. Right ho! What *else* do you want to know?'

I was not at all sure how to proceed with this querulous old man, but I stumbled on.

'I've been wondering about the God Mwali,' I said. 'I know the Lemba maintain that Mwali is exclusively a Lemba god and is the same as the God of Israel, but many African tribes worship Mwali. I thought that the centre of Mwali worship had been among the Shona of the Matopos Hills near Bulawayo.'

Phophi nodded in agreement.

'So, is it not possible that the Lemba borrowed the concept of Mwali from African culture? In fact,' I continued, 'at least one book on Mwali worship does not even mention the Lemba.'

'*No, no, and no,*' shouted Phophi, clenching his fists. 'The Lemba introduced the worship of Mwali to African blacks. Before we came the blacks worshipped stones and trees. It is true that Mwali was worshipped in the Matopos, but that's because the Lemba sojourned in that place with the *wasenzhi* on their way down from Great Zimbabwe. We brought the worship of Mwali from Great Zimbabwe, from where it spread throughout the area.'

'Well, how about circumcision? The Lemba say that their circumcision rituals make them special, but many African tribes circumcise.'

'Yes, I know that,' said Phophi, 'but without doubt they got it from us. We brought circumcision into southern Africa. Look, I'll show you something.' He went to another room and came back with a book by I. Schapera, *The Bantu Speaking Tribes of South Africa*. He opened the book and read out: 'It is also said that the Lemba were the first to introduce circumcision. Lemba men certainly do often take a leading part in these rites.'

In fact, as I was to discover, most ethnographic accounts of Lemba life agree on this. Schlömann (1894) wrote, 'They are the only African tribal group in this country which practises circumcision. Other African groups who now practise it have almost invariably been influenced by the Lemba.' In 1936, Stayt wrote: 'Every MuLemba boy must be circumcised at puberty ... I tentatively suggest that the BaLemba introduced circumcision to all the tribes in the Transvaal.' A. A. Jacques (1931) wrote: 'They play a prominent part as surgeons and medicine men in the circumcision ceremonies practised by the Venda, Tonga and Suto of the northern Transvaal...'

There seems little reason to doubt that the Venda were introduced to circumcision by the Lemba. The Swiss missionary and scholar, H. A. Junod, remarked that his informant was convinced

> that the Balemba have brought it into the country, and that the Suto and even the Tonga have borrowed the custom from them. It is true, at any rate, for the great BaVenda tribe. When Ramapulana, the grandfather of the present Venda chief, was living, he strongly objected to the *ngoma* [circumcision lodge] being introduced amongst his people. But his son Makhado got into a circumcision lodge, and was initiated. His father said: 'He has become a Mulemba, kill him.' But the people had pity on him, and when he became chief the nation adopted the new rite.

It is sometimes argued that circumcision was introduced into Africa by Cushitic groups in the north-east of the continent, but at later periods Islamic influence must have had some impact. The Tongas of the south-east coastal areas, for instance, acquired their circumcision traditions from what appear to be Muslims. In the sixteenth century Dom Gonçalo da Silveira wrote: 'Circumcision is a feature of Tonga life, which, they say, was left with them by a distinguished Moor who came to their country some time ago.'

I mentioned to Phophi that as Jews circumcise on the eighth day and Muslims more or less at puberty, the Lemba traditions seemed to suggest Muslim antecedents rather than Jewish ones.

'No,' said Phophi. 'Not at all. In the past it *was* the eighth day. And then, in remembrance of the eighth day, we circumcised in the eighth year. Then the influence of the other tribes' initiation rites became very great and we started doing it whenever there were enough boys to make up a group big enough for an initiation school.'

I told Phophi what I knew of the Tonga tradition and of the Moor who may have influenced it. Pursing his lips and spacing his words carefully, as if he were talking to a child, he said, 'The Lemba were once Moors. And the important Moor you talked about was certainly a Lemba. But please do not think these Moors were Muslims. They were, of course, Jews. And in any case, long before the Portuguese came, we were doing circumcision at Great Zimbabwe. They've found phallic stones there. You know what phallic stones are? And guess what? They're circumcised.'

This reminded me that Thomas Huffman, the respected Professor of African Archaeology at the University of the Witwatersrand, had explained a good deal of the organis-ation of structures at Great Zimbabwe in terms of circumci-sion and initiation schools. His argument is that as such schools exist now among the Venda – a tribe more likely than any other in his view to have had something to do with the Great Zimbabwe culture – such schools must have existed at Great Zimbabwe. Using the same argument, one could conclude that as the Lemba were a circumcising caste among the Venda, they may well have played a similar role in Great Zimbabwe. This, clearly, was Phophi's view.

I was scribbling all this down in my notebook.

'You are writing a book?' asked Phophi, peering at my notes.

'I'm hoping to,' I said.

'It's no matter,' said Phophi. 'There's room for two books. You can write with my fullest permission for your people back in London, but', he raised his finger once more in warning, 'my book will be for the whole world. I am writing the history of the ancestors.' He picked up his battered synopsis and went back to reading it.

'Are the ancestors as important for you as they are for other African religions?'

'They are indeed very important for us. I can give you an example taken from life. At our annual *Utungura* ceremony – which is a sort of harvest festival – we can recite the names of our departed ancestors from the recent times to the distant, distant past. The spirit of one of these ancestors has the job of keeping the names of all the rest just in case we forget one or two. He has to bring the names of all of them before Mwali. While we're getting ready we take a special brew of sorghum and pour it on the ground as a, what d'you call, libation. Then we recite the names.'

In order to show me what he meant, he poured the dregs of his morning tea on to the termite-infested boards, closed his eyes and started chanting. As he did so, he shuffled across the room until he was standing directly over me.

63

'And what *are* the names?' I asked, sensing that here perhaps lay the answer to the mystery of the origin of the Lemba.

Phophi lowered his face until our noses were almost touching. He had the distinct and not altogether disagreeable smell of old age.

'That's enough. You're asking me too much. For fifty years I have been answering white men's questions. *Questions. Questions. Questions.* I'm retired now. I'm *old.* Don't I get any rest? I was offering you this as water to quench your thirst, but you're asking far too much. Leave now. Bugger off.'

'Look, I'm sorry,' I said. 'Why don't you have a rest?' But Phophi, glaring wildly, had already left the house, slamming the door behind him.

I let myself out and went off in the opposite direction, hoping to find someone who would give me something to drink. Outside a hut, not far away, I found two women who introduced themselves as Mary and Martha. They had been pounding millet in a wooden mortar, but they stopped work to offer me a swig of beer from a yellowing calabash lying in the shade of the hut. *Chibuku*, thick maize beer, is something like an alcoholic porridge, which is not at all bad, but what I really wanted was tea. Putting a handful of small coins and a packet of cigarettes on the ground in front of them, I begged Mary and Martha to make me some. They laughed; one of them gathered up the money and the other boiled up some water. As I drank my tea, I told them that I had been to see Phophi. At the mention of his name they rolled their eyes and looked uneasy. They spoke very little English, but managed to convey that Phophi was a very important man in the village and that he had a famous temper. I finished the tea, thanked them both and wandered back through the tree-lined lanes in the direction of Phophi's bungalow.

On the way, I passed a very short Venda, a dwarf, sitting on a low mud wall in front of his hut, next to a woman of normal height who was holding him in her arms. His stunted legs were tucked out of sight. Two children sat on the ground directly beneath the dwarf, their heads reaching the top of the wall. It was a *tableau vivant* of an Egyptian First Dynasty sculpture I had seen years before in the Egyptian Museum in Cairo: Senab, Chief Dwarf of the Clothing, supported by his beautiful high-breasted wife, his diminutive and invisible legs represented by his two sons. I nodded at them and they nodded back in unison.

Further down the lane I came upon Phophi deep in conversation with a very tall, thin man wearing a black suit. The two of them were standing under a great mango tree. Phophi was looking seraphically happy.

'This is my friend,' said Phophi, putting his arm around the very tall man's waist. 'When I quarrel with my wife, he makes the peace. Samuel the Peacemaker I call him. He's coming now to make peace between you and me.' He smiled and screwed up one eye in a comic grimace of apology.

Walking back to the house he showed me his orchard of citrus, figs, lychees and avocados. Phophi talked with enthusiasm about his trees, how he had crossed strains and created an irrigation system to keep them alive during the years of drought.

'I'm sorry for getting angry,' he said, pausing at the gate to his compound, 'it's the thought that you blokes think that we are Muslims that makes me angry.'

'But I've not said that!' I protested.

'No, but most university people do. I've met many of them, but they do not have good arguments. Just look at the differences. One of the most important elements in our tradition', he put his hand on the bony knee of the tall man and smiled up at him, 'is that we once had a book, but it was lost. If we were really Muslims, we could always have got hold of the Quran. *This* is a good argument. There were Muslims all down the coast of Africa from Mogadishu to Sofala. And in any case anyone can become a Muslim. You get circumcised, accept Muhammad. That's it. But you cannot become a Lemba like that: you can be a Lemba only by birth or, in the case of a woman, by initiation and marriage. And if you need further proof that we are not Muslims, it is that we are not vindictive. We're a peace-making religion. And finally, old fellow,' he beamed at me, 'we have always said we're Jews. We are Jews now, we were Jews in Sena and we were Jews in Great Zimbabwe.'

'Have you ever been to Great Zimbabwe?' I asked.

'Yes, in the olden days. We used to go in a bus belonging to the Lemba, but it broke down. And now we cannot go to Zimbabwe because of all the restrictions made by you whites,' he said.

'But it is a black government up there now.'

'But who introduced the whole bloody concept of pass-ports? That's not part of black culture.'

'Nothing specifically white about it either,' I said. 'In the ancient world . . .'

'*Get out,*' he snarled, his face contorted with rage. Samuel laid a restraining hand on his head and nodded at me.

'He's my only friend,' said Phophi, now smiling at me. I did not find his admission impossibly difficult to believe, so I nodded and said nothing.

Samuel the Peacemaker stood up and, stooping over me, placed a hand on my head. He then mimed that Phophi should sleep, that I should sleep, as well, and that at some time in the future we would eat together. Perhaps then Phophi would answer more questions. Perhaps he wouldn't.

As Phophi watched the pantomime, his face wore the untroubled smile of a sleepy child.

I sat under one of Phophi's mango trees, wrote up my diary and made a list of the questions I still wanted to ask him. The irascible old man had chosen a good place for his retirement. Tshifudi is a big village, full of fruit trees, occupying a crescent of high ground at the end of a valley. It is protected on three sides by wooded mountains, their peaks covered now by a slight haze. A mountain eagle lazily circled over the village. A late cockerel crowed. From the old man's cooking-hut the smell of cooking meat and woodsmoke wafted into the orchard and mixed with the sweet smell of dried dung. I fell asleep.

I was woken up by a young girl who was carrying a bowl of water. Kneeling in front of me, she held it for me to wash my hands. Our food was waiting under a lemon tree: a fragrant chicken stew, boiled wild spinach and mealie porridge.

'You like to have some meal?' asked Phophi, his face crinkled in an apologetic grin. 'Lemba food is Jewish food. Kosher food!'

Over dinner Phophi explained the Lemba's 'kosher customs'. His account tallied with what I had pieced together from the early ethnographic accounts. First and foremost pork was never eaten and any animal 'resembling pig', such as wart hog, hippopotamus or elephant, was forbidden. So were most others: lions, tigers, cats, jackals, dogs and mice. 'We eat only ruminants with cloven hooves,' said Phophi. They would eat beef, goat, venison or mutton, certain birds, but not vultures or owls, and were particularly fond of chickens. Phophi claimed that the Lemba had introduced chickens into the Venda areas. Only animals or birds which had been properly killed by a Lemba slaughterer were permitted. The slaughtering ritual – *shidja* – consisted of cutting the throat of the animal and letting the blood flow while certain blessings were uttered.

'What are the blessings?' I asked.

'I cannot tell you that. That is a Lemba secret. Secret words no one else knows. *Sacred* words.' Muttering to himself Phophi wandered off into the orchard behind the house. A few minutes later he came back with a pile of oranges, which we ate while the girl made tea.

'The blessings are our secret, but the cutting anyone can see. This cutting is more important than anything. No other African tribe does this. It is Jewish.'

In the past, he said, the *shidja* had been performed by a special tribal functionary, a sort of priest. It was *shidja* and circumcision more than anything else which had set the Lemba apart from the *wasenzhi*. It was because the *wasenzhi* ate unclean food that they were unclean themselves, that along with their uncircumcised penises. *Shidja* could now be done by any male Lemba, but an animal slaughtered – even correctly – without the blessing would still be forbidden. Without the blessing dead meat is unclean, and only the Lemba have the words which make it clean. In the past they preferred to go hungry, even risking starvation, rather than eat meat slaughtered by a non-Lemba. They refused to cook with pots and pans used by the *wasenzhi* and to eat with them. If a Lemba were found eating an unclean animal such as a wild pig, he was put to death.

There is an interesting passage in the journal of the extraordinary Scottish missionary Robert Moffat, who by dint of his singular dourness came to have an iron hold over Mzilikazi, the warlike Ndebele paramount chief, whom he visited five times between 1829 and 1859. Moffat described the reaction of a Lemba doctor working in the *kraal* to the gift of a goat from the great chief some time in the 1850s:

> The standing dish among the Matabele is animal food: this they prefer to everything else ... but the ... doctor and his suite never taste an ounce of it because it is not slaughtered by their own hands. No one ... will eat of what another has killed or shot. I have observed when Moselkatze sent a goat to the doctor he instantly ran a spear into behind the shoulder and immediately cut the throat, and at the same time laying the windpipe open lengthwise ...

A special knife was used for *shidja*. According to an oral tradition collected by Phophi's mentor, Van Warmelo, 'Knives were first brought into this country by the Lemba: they called them *tshishizho*, i.e. an instrument for kosher-killing meat. Many people called it the knife of the Nyai – that which cuts everything.'

In the past, said Phophi, the Lemba preferred a diet based on fish and rice. In fact, some people have claimed that once the Lemba ate *only* fish and rice – an unheard of diet in the Transvaal and Zimbabwe, and one which is strongly suggestive of a coastal origin. According to Portuguese documents, we know that in the sixteenth century rice was cultivated in the Zambezi delta and around Sofala and was even exported to Indian Ocean ports. According to oral tradition, it was also grown in the past near Mberengwe, the area of Lemba settlement in Zimbabwe: 'The Lemba', runs one account, 'said they came from across the sea to the hill "Mberengwe of the Good Men". This is a beautiful hill standing alone in the plain, with many streams running down from it on all sides. Here they cultivated much rice, the plant of the white man.'

As for the Lemba's drinking habits, said Phophi, now-adays, like other black South Africans, they drink *chibuku*, kaffir beer, so-called. But in days gone by they preferred a drink of the low veldt, a wine made from the fruit of a kind of wild plum. And it was this which Phophi now brought out.

'Very strong. Don't drink too much. You'll get drunk. You've seen Muslims drinking this strong stuff, have you? Seen Arabs getting drunk?' He laughed a sardonic laugh and then, with a deep sigh of contentment, put his arm round Samuel's shoulder and for no apparent reason started giggling.

'Parfitt?' he exclaimed, still giggling.

'Yes?'

'You've read the Bible where it tells about the history of the Jews?'

'Yes, I've read the Bible.'

'Just look at those chapters which describe the old religion of the Jews. I'm not talking about the New Testament. I mean the old, old book.'

He went into the house and came out carrying a Bible.

'You know what I told you about our eating customs? Look what it says in the Bible!' He opened the Bible and started reading out aloud from *Leviticus* xi:

Whatever parts the hoof and is cloven-footed and chews the cud, among the animals, you may eat. Nevertheless, among those that chew the cud or part the hoof, you shall not eat these: the camel, because it chews the cud but does not part the hoof, is unclean to you. And the rock badger, because it chews the cud but does not part the hoof, is unclean to you. And the hare, because it chews the cud but does not part the hoof, is unclean to you. And the swine, because it parts the hoof and is cloven-footed but does not chew the cud, is unclean to you. Of their flesh you shall not

eat and their carcasses you shall not touch; they are unclean to
you. These you may eat, of all that are in the waters. Everything
in the waters that has fins and scales, whether in the seas or in
the rivers you may eat ... everything in the waters that has not
fins and scales is an abomination to you.

'An *abomination* – d'you hear that? Now, do you know that
the Lemba do not eat pigs, or hares or rabbits or elephants
or mice or camels or rock-badgers or any animal that is
forbidden to Jews and we do not eat any fish which does not
have fins and scales? We follow these rules *exactly*. Could
that possibly be a coincidence? This book says also that Jews
must keep away from impurity. When a Lemba woman has
menstruation blood she is impure and cannot be approached.
Her food cannot be shared. She cannot visit the cattle *kraal*.
She must wait for seven days before her, what d'you call,
relations can be resumed. And then she has to go to the river
and be completely cleaned. We are more Jewish than the
Jews!'

Samuel was still in attendance. Phophi poured wine into
our cups and downed his in one.

'Right ho!' he said. 'What else do you want to know?'

In a number of the early ethnographic reports I had read
about a macabre custom among the Lemba which has
nothing to do with the Semitic world. Just before he died, a
Lemba's throat was ritually cut by another male member of
the tribe – as if a Lemba had to be made ritually fit for death
in the same way as an animal is prepared for eating. I
mentioned this puzzling custom to Phophi.

He shook his head in an energetic parody of dissent.
'Listen! You whites have caused us too many problems over
this so-called cutting of throats,' he said. '*No*, *no*, and *no*.
Jews do *not* butcher their kinsmen,' he continued, his voice

rising. 'The explanation is this. You know the Lemba have short hair – they shave their heads every new moon. It is the custom that no Lemba male be buried with long hair. So we go to the dead man, either just before he dies or just after, and shave his head. Certain whites thought that this was in order to cut throats. But that was never done. If you want to find out about our burial habits, there is a Lemba funeral in a few days on the other side of Vendaland. You should go. You'll see. But the burying is only part of it. There's lots more too. But, as for killing our relatives, *fat chance*. You must remember that one of the big rules for the Jews is "Thou shalt not kill"; so it is for us too. It is an *abomination*!'

Phophi talked into the night about his years with the ethnographer, Van Warmelo, from whom many of his out-landish mannerisms, I suspected, had been taken, and about his wanderings throughout South Africa. Samuel, the silent guardian of his choler, stayed on, his long arm around the old man's shoulder. The glow of the cooking fire had been replaced by the silver light of a gibbous moon, which hung awkwardly over the hills. No one had any more to say. After a long period of silence Samuel left his seat and squatted on the ground, his elbows resting on his knees, and looked intently first at me and then at Phophi. When he was sure that the conversation had really finished and that his umpir-ing duties were over, he rose and walked off through the orchard. Phophi gave me a blanket and showed me to a hut in the compound. There was a straw mattress on the dung and mud floor.

'Sorry about the fighting,' said Phophi quietly. 'You know what we say, "When two lions meet . . .".'

Early in the morning Phophi's girl brought water and made tea. There was no sign of Phophi. He had disappeared. For the rest of the day I walked around the village, was entertained by Mary and Martha, and looked for the dwarf I had seen the previous day. But he, too, was not to be seen. I ate some fruit from Phophi's orchard and spent another night in his hut.

I woke the next morning to find the girl kneeling in the doorway with a bowl of warm water in her hands. As I washed, she jerked her head and rolled her eyes to indicate that someone was outside. It was Phophi, who was sitting on a chair in front of his bungalow. The sun had just risen. In its pale light he was again reading his synopsis. I asked him where he had been.

'In the hills', he said, 'talking to the ancestors.' He looked tired and lonely.

He glanced over his shoulder and whispered that there were a couple of things he had decided to let me know, after all. His father had told him that long ago, before the arrival of Europeans, the Lemba used to hold a fast once a year. On this all-important day, warriors went around the Lemba villages to make sure that no food was being consumed and that no cooking fires were burning. On this day, the notables wore white robes and the chief sacrificed a black ox, un-blemished in any way. Phophi closed one eye and looked at me quizzically.

'You know what this is, old chap? It's the Yom Kippur of the Jews. And there's something else I'll tell you – it's no longer a tribal secret because many years ago a Lemba wrote about it in a white man's journal – it's a prayer.' In a low voice he chanted:

> 'Let Moses return to us again.
> Man is evil.
> We'll not see a man like him again.
> Death is a journey . . .'

I was later able to confirm that both of these extraordinary pieces of evidence had been noted by early ethnographers. This suggested that they were authentic. Without doubt the existence of an annual day of fasting was reminiscent of Jewish practice. There is no obvious Muslim, Christian or African equivalent. Even more remarkable, I thought, was the revelation that Moses figured in the tribal tradition in a significant way – although clearly Moses legends could derive from many sources including Muslim ones. I asked Phophi if Moses was considered to be one of the Lemba ancestors.

'He was even before the ancestors,' he said. 'He was the father of all the fathers. We are descended from him. Some people say that our praise-name, *Mushavi*, comes from Moses.'

I had never heard of this explanation of *Mushavi*, although it is perfectly true that in Arabic a normal designation of 'Jew' is *Musawi* – a follower of Moses. *Mushavi* is usually connected with the Bantu root *shava* and is taken to mean trader. Earlier suggestions connecting the word with Sheba or Sabean are no doubt fanciful. Phophi's idea perhaps had more substance. I wrote down what he had told me and asked him some more questions about Moses, but he had said all that he was going to. I had the feeling that he was already regretting having said so much.

'Off you go now, young fellow,' he said. 'They are waiting for you at the funeral, I sent a messenger yesterday. A young man will be waiting for you at the garage just south of Louis Trichardt. And tonight you should sleep in the Cloud's End Hotel near Louis Trichardt – we have Lemba men there who will keep an eye on you. But', he roared suddenly, 'come back *soon*. We must talk about *this*.' He waved his manuscript in the air and saw me to the car. 'Don't forget,' he shouted as I drove off. 'Don't forget. We're not Arabs!'

7

A young man was indeed waiting for me at the Bridge
Service Station. He was wearing a light blue suit,
highly polished black shoes and a broad smile.

'*Mamuga*,' he said, clapping his hands together. 'I am
Reuben Hamisi.'

'*Mushavi*,' I replied, getting out of the car to shake hands
with him. 'Tell me, what does *Mamuga* mean?'

'Ah! It is a word from our ancient Lemba language. I only
speak Venda. That is the only Lemba word I'd learn, isn't it?
You say this word when you meet a very old man. Like this.'
This time he dropped to his knees on the garage forecourt,
clapped his hands and repeated the greeting.

'But I'm not a very old man,' I protested.

'If we respect you a lot you become a very old man,' he
said smiling, still on his knees. After further compliments, he
got into the car. We soon came to wide dirt roads bounded
on both sides by wire fences dappled with scraps of plastic
and paper. As we drove, Reuben analysed the Lemba's social
position.

'Anti-Semitism is our big problem,' he said. 'The *wasenzhi*
are persecuting us because we are Jews. The other nations go
up and we stay down. When we were young, whether we
were Lemba or not was not important. We thought that the
old peoples' stories was, what d'you call, superstition, isn't

it?' He exposed high pink gums in an engaging smile. 'Our concentration was not on our history,' he explained. 'Also, we lost our language and we will never find it again. And this is why we was ashamed of being Lemba – in fact, sometimes the young ones said they was Venda peoples or Pedi peoples. But now in these days the Venda peoples, our neighbours, are always promoting plenty Venda things, Venda societies, Venda this that. So now the Lemba are concentrated in making plenty Lemba history, Lemba societies and Lemba this that. Fighting back!'

We reached a grim shanty town about twenty miles south-west of Louis Trichardt. We left the car and walked to the cemetery. A cold wind was blowing off the veldt. Hundreds of Lemba were huddled around a freshly dug grave. On the far side of the hole were the men, dressed in old suits or overcoats. And on my side, like a legion of scarecrows, were the women, bare-legged, feet encased in high-ankled baseball boots, with woollen blankets around their shoulders flapping in the wind. The graves in this cemetery were rectangles of raised earth with crude lumps of uncut granite placed on top. They had rough angle iron and plastic headboards. I closed my eyes and listened to the music: the Lemba were singing a densely harmonic song. Sometimes it was snatched away by the wind, only to soar and dance above it.

A tall man in a greatcoat, a light coloured scarf tied loosely around his neck, left the graveside and strode towards me. He had a shaved head but his face was unshaven. He raised his hand in a clenched fist salute. From his fist emerged a long finger, which he pointed at my nose.

'My name is Mberengwe,' he spat. 'I give you some facts. Ah yess. I am Mberengwe from Tshifudi, Mberengwe is our holy mountain. Ah yess. Me Mberengwe, I'm from Phophi's place. Old man sent me last mght. Ah yess. We is united man. We Lemba is one holy nation. Yess. You want the facts?'

'Yes, well I am interested in what happens at Lemba funerals,' I said.

He grinned at me in an unfocused sort of way, seized my arm and led me over to the grave. The deceased was wrapped in a blanket and laid on a rough earthen shelf; one arm protruded from the blanket and pointed north.

'That hand pointing to Sena,' said Mberengwe.

The singing had stopped and the Lemba were drifting in the direction of a group of huts on the corner of the location. Mberengwe, Reuben and I joined the line of mourners filing through the wire gate. Cooking fires were burning in the yard and the men were sitting in groups waiting to be fed. Two goats were hanging from a tree, watched by a circle of cats. A fat woman, a sister of the deceased, walked up to us, carrying piles of sliced bread and a pot of tea on an aluminium tray. She poured me a cup of thick brown tea and gave me a piece of bread. White pre-sliced bread, a symbol of urban poverty in England, was a luxury here. We sat next to a woman with enormous hams who was squatting on the earth floor stirring a steaming mess in a black pot. She ladled some into a bowl and handed it to me: it was a strongly flavoured goat stew. Most people were sitting on the ground, but Mberengwe made me sit on one of the few chairs.

'I am afraid to tell you just what I heard about this nation,' he said grinning. 'Ah yess. I do not like to feed you with rumours. There is many mysteries. We came from Sena, but we do not know where that land is. After that we went to Zimbabwe and built cities. Then Mberengwe. Ah yess. After that my family came there,' and he pointed northwards at the hard, glittering rocks of the Soutpansberg. 'That is Ndouvhade. That was the last town with a Lemba chief in

South Africa. In history Ndouvhade fought against the Boers. You finish your goat and we'll take you to Chief Ndouvhade. He's dying now, too.'

Some of the Lemba pointed at me and whispered to each other; others pushed through the crowd to shake my hand. Finally, Mberengwe pulled me away and we left.

We walked down the dirt track to a group of mud houses on the other side of the location in which the chief lived with two wives, their children and the rest of his family. It was Ndouvhade's grandfather who had been the last Lemba chief to hold out against the Boers. Reuben and Mberengwe pushed open the door of the largest building of the compound – a tin-roofed mud shack. In the middle of the otherwise empty room stood a wooden table covered with a green oilcloth. There was one window obscured by a rusty mosquito screen clogged with dead insects. Next to the table sat an old man reading from a Venda translation of the Bible. A rug depicting the Last Supper was pinned to the wall behind him. He was a square-shouldered, big-boned man wearing a white vest and brown trousers. He clapped his hands together in greeting, but immediately put his hands up to his shaved head. He had pains in his head, in his chest, in his legs and in his back. He had once been a very strong man; his muscles now hung in dimpled sacks from his arms.

'I wish I could help,' I said.

'If you have any help, you can help, isn't it?' he said. 'You're a doctor, aren't you?' he said, peering at the letter of introduction Mathiva had written for me.

'Not that sort, I'm afraid,' I said.

'Well, you can pray for me, isn't it? I'm a Jew. I'm a Christian. Everyone, everyone can pray.' He prodded the Bible with a calloused finger.

'I don't pray much,' I said.

'You should. Are you married?' he added.

'No.'

'You should be married. You not like women? You like men?'

'No, I like women. I have a girlfriend.'

'No, girlfriends is bad, isn't it? What you doing here? You should stay in England. You must marry, you must take care of woman. You must live with your woman, your children.'

His face was a patchwork of different colours, grey, ebony, bruised violet. He looked disapproving.

'You can't live with woman and look for lost cities of Sena at one and the same time. How about you? Do you have a wife?'

He nodded, I thought a shade uneasily.

'Just one?'

'No,' he said, 'I got four wives: two up-country wives here and two town wives in Soweto. I used to work down that way as a spanner boy in mechanic's shop. Even now I look after these women,' said the old chief.

'But I thought you said you were a Christian,' I said.

'I met these girls before I met Jesus,' he thundered. 'What do you want me to do with them now? Do *you* want to decide which ones I am going to divorce? I made a deal with the minister. He said I could keep the wives if they became Christians too. Like that, he said, it was like converting a whole village: four wives, twenty alive children, thirty-three alive grandchildren.'

I laughed and the laughter broke the ice. He grabbed my arm and made me sit down next to him. To start with he told me the story I had heard from Mathiva about his ancestor who had held out against the Boers while Milubi and Funyufunyu joined Mphephu, the Venda general, across the Limpopo.

'We beat the Boers – we Lemba. We had old muskets which we bought from the Portuguese, but the British tricked my grandfather and we lost the guns. Then we lost the war. And some years ago we lost our land. That's where we were – at Ndouvhade,' he pointed through the window. 'That's where we came from. That's where I want to be now!'

As one of his up-country wives served us tea, I told the old man that I would like to see the ruins of Ndouvhade.

'I've not been near the old place since I'm sick,' he said. 'If you have a car, you can take me too.' I could see that the thought put new strength into him.

He hauled himself to his feet and shouted something in Venda. A young woman came in carrying a thick overcoat and an ebony knobkerrie. Ndouvhade led the way out of the house and, wielding his stick, made his way through the location back to the field near the cemetery where I had left the Avis car. By now the grave had been filled in and bits of debris blown by the wind had already started to cover the fresh earth.

Ndouvhade pointed over the dried-out scrub of the veldt at a low mountain caught in the crook of an encircling span of jagged peaks. This hill was called Mberengwe after the sacred Lemba mountain in central Zimbabwe which the South African Lemba had left long before. 'On that mountain,' said the chief, 'on Mberengwe, God gave his power to man. The star which brought us there settled on the mountain.' The young man named after Mberengwe flexed his muscles and grinned at Reuben. 'Because of that,' the chief continued, ignoring him, 'the Lemba used to be the best nation around. We had the best towns. We made the best weapons and ornaments from iron and gold. No one could beat us because of this iron, isn't it?' The others nodded in agreement. We got into the car and drove off. A few miles outside the location Ndouvhade said, 'I'll show you some Lemba iron from the old times. I brought it out of the old village when we were thrown out.'

He guided me off the main road to a smallholding down a track. Bits of scrap metal, most of it from agricultural machinery, were strewn over the sandy ground which surrounded a small fenced-off bungalow.

'Press the hooter,' said the chief.

Reuben jumped out of the car and strode towards the gate. A sexy blonde in tight jeans and a white T-shirt opened the front door of the house and started shouting at him in Afrikaans. Seeing the car, she walked towards the gate, her face twisted in anger, her arms crossed over her breasts. I got out of the car.

'Oh, hello,' she said, her face softening, but it hardened over and stayed hard as soon as she realised that, though white, I was a stranger and a foreigner.

'You're trespassing,' she said. 'Get off my land and take your boys with you.' Her sallow faced husband had joined her.

'Get going,' he said grimly, jerking his thumb.

The old man was still in the car. He wound down his window and spoke directly to the Afrikaaner.

'Do you remember that press I sold you a few years back? The one that came from our old village? It used to be under that very tree,' he said, pointing at a heap of rusting junk under a coral tree.

'I remember,' he replied. 'I sold it for scrap a few months ago.' Turning to me, he then said, 'Clear out. I don't like the look of your face.'

'Is that a fact?' I retorted. 'It's a pity about the press. I represent an American museum and we're collecting pre-colonial iron African artefacts. I'd have paid ten thousand US dollars for a Lemba bangle press.'

The man looked around him in panic. His wife gave him a poisonous look.

'Is that true, master?' said Reuben, as we drove off.

'Certainly not,' I said, 'but they were so bloody rude I thought I'd spoil their afternoon.' The three men laughed so hard, clutching my shoulder as I drove, that it used up their desire to talk.

We turned on to a single-track drive. After a mile the way was blocked by an iron five-bar gate, which was locked. When the village of Ndouvhade was destroyed and its Lemba population evicted, the land around it was bought by a white farmer who built himself a country retreat at the foot of the hills. This was his gate and he had the key. To get to the village we would have to leave the car and walk a couple of miles over the veldt.

'Are you sure you can manage it?' I asked the old man. 'I can drive you back or you can stay here in the car.'

'I will walk,' he said. 'It will be the last time in my life I visit the resting-place of my father.'

The plain was flat savannah, broken by white-needled thorn bushes. The mountains towered over the plain, casting long shadows into the bush. Hundreds of tracks criss-crossed the land. We walked in single file behind old Chief Ndouvhade, following a cattle track. The chief shuffled along in pain. Reuben stopped from time to time to wipe the dust off his shoes with his handkerchief. We made slow progress.

Occasionally the old man stopped to rest and would tell us something about the history of the village. Some Lemba had been encouraged to settle here by the great Venda chief, Ramapulana, and his son Makhado. Before Makhado's death, he gave the Lemba a large tract of land around Ndouvhade, where, in the shadow of the Mountain of Mberengwe, they were able to practise their iron-making and pottery without interference.

Until 1972 there were over six hundred Lemba living here – it was probably the last village inhabited exclusively by Lemba in South Africa. From this sheltered and well-watered place they were transferred to the shanty town in the middle of the plain where they lived along with Venda and other tribes. The white man very rarely visited his weekend farm.

As we got nearer to the mountains, great boulders and dense clumps of yellow-tasselled thorns littered the plain. A hornbill flapped its noisy way through the bushes.

'That bird is bad luck,' said Mberengwe, shooting anxious looks into the bush. Rolls of thorn hedges marked the border of the old village.

We passed some twenty-foot-high boulders and came across a shaded patch of land surrounded by a stone wall, at the centre of which stood a concrete cube.

'This is the chief's *kraal*,' said the old man, 'and that is father's grave. I used to come here very often. Sit here, remembering.' He leaned to catch his breath against the tomb.

'Was it usual to put blocks like this over the graves?'

'No. This is cement. We did not used to have cement. We make this like this to make a permanent reminder that the Lemba were once here. Usually the Lemba are buried lying down, on a shelf, the head towards the north, facing Sena.'

Most of the early ethnographic accounts agree on the Lemba's burial procedures. The body was wrapped in an ox skin and laid on its side or on its back on a shelf excavated from the side of a grave six feet deep. All other tribes in southern

Africa buried their dead in a sitting position. The hoes of the dead man were placed along with him in the grave, but his assegais and axe were left for the oldest son of the principal wife. When a woman died, she was wrapped in cloth. Half her beads were placed above her head in the grave, the other half were distributed among her relatives. The pots of the deceased were placed on top of the grave. If a woman died in labour, she was carried out of her hut, not through a door, but through an opening made in the wall, and her stomach was pierced 'to let out the air'.

Despite what Phophi had said, it seems almost certain that in the past the Lemba had slit the throats of their relatives just before death, or, if they had been found dead, before burial. At the end of his initiation period, a Lemba youth was given a knife made by a Lemba smith. This knife became his most treasured possession and was the knife he used for the ritual slaughter of animals throughout his life. At the end of his life, as one ethnographer put it, 'When he was becoming very weak and the end seemed near, a relative held up the precious knife, so that the dying man could see it, and then brought it close to his throat. This action was repeated three times, and if he gave no sign, the third time his throat was cut. I have been unable to discover a parallel rite among any other African tribes.' It is worth mentioning that similarities have been found between this Lemba knife and knives used for slaughter in Ethiopia.

The relatives of the deceased used to shave their heads and mourn for seven days, during which time they were not permitted to work; on the seventh day a feast was held at which an ox, a sheep or a spotless goat was sacrificed. The blood of the animal was sprinkled over the heads of the assembled men or was drunk. The priest prayed to the ancestors, calling on them by name. The prayers ended with the word 'Amin'. Later the men all knelt and the word 'Hundji' was called out. According to a Lemba informant in 1931, Hundji was supposed to be the Lemba's country or place of origin. Mathiva had said much the same. Was it another name for Sena? In addition, the Ndinda song was sung, celebrating the history of the Lemba. This seventh day was the day on which it was believed a man's soul returned to his body. Mathiva and others had told me that the soul goes on to Sena. As Phophi had said, 'To die is to go on a journey.'

Phophi had vehemently denied that the Lemba had ever slit the throats of their dying or dead. In view of his conviction that the Lemba are Jews and, given his knowledge that the Jews had never practised such a rite, his denial of it was understandable. Perhaps for the same reason Mathiva had written in an unpublished article that the whole matter was no more than 'debatable'. It seemed to me that the throat cutting ceremony was a vestige of the notion of ritual suicide for divine kings, and had its origins in ancient African, not Semitic, rite. Had the 'white men who came from Sena' once been a privileged caste at some African court where, as a caste, they had taken on some of the attributes of divine kingship?

Slowly Chief Ndouvhade showed us around the ruined kraal. The huts had originally been built to a certain height in stone; the upper parts had been made of mud and thatch; stone walls, often connecting great boulders, surrounded the domestic areas.

'Before they came here,' said Chief Ndouvhade, 'the Lemba lived in Dzata, before that in Mberengwe, before that in Great Zimbabwe, before that in Israel, in Sena. I went to Dzata and Great Zimbabwe with my father when I was a boy. Those places are like this place. We were the only people who knew how to build in stone. We built for ourselves and we built for the Venda. When you see the Zimbabwe ruins, you will see it is like Ndouvhade – every little detail same. When we left the north we crossed those hills and went to Dzata, and then we asked the Venda chief to give us this place because it reminded us of Zimbabwe and Mberengwe. Maybe Sena was like this. I don't know where it is, but it was a golden place. A perfect place. I'd like to go there now. It was a golden world we were forced to leave long ago in the time of Solomon.'

'Who was Solomon?'

'He was the king of Israel long ago and our leader when we were in Sena.'

'What else do you know about Solomon?'

'He married the Queen of Sheba and gave the Lemba the Ark of the Covenant. My father told me that. And he told me this too: Solomon was the one who brought us from Sena. Solomon is the father of the Jews!'

'And how about the Ark? Where is the Ark? What is the Ark?'

'They say it's hidden somewhere in the mountains, but I do not know what it is or where it is. For us Jews it is a very holy thing.'

'But you're a Christian!'

'I am a Jew. Recently I became a Christian. Like Jesus: he was a Jew who became a Christian!'

He wandered around the village, stooping to touch stones and examine trees and bushes. He sat for a long time inside a ring of stones which marked the site of the hut in which he had been born. Then he rose and made his way to the chief's *kraal*, where he stood by his father's tomb. He closed his eyes for a few minutes. When he opened them, they were a deeper yellow, wet with tears. He lifted his knobkerrie above his head in a gesture of defiance and, with great tenderness, whispered, 'I want to sleep here with my father. We will sleep together in the bosom of Abraham, isn't it? At the least I think they will let me do that last thing.' I hoped that he would be allowed to be buried here. I hoped so very much.

Walking back to the car, I told Chief Ndouvhade of my plan to retrace the steps taken by the Lemba to discover where they had come from. He had no doubt which way I should go: from Ndouvhade to Dzata, from Dzata to Mberengwe, from Mberengwe to Dumghe Mountain, from Dumghe to Great Zimbabwe, from Great Zimbabwe to what he called Sena Three, from Sena Three to Sena Two, from Sena Two to Sena One. There were still Lemba in Zimbabwe and possibly, he thought, elsewhere in Africa, in the north.

'And where do you think Sena One is?' I asked, as we reached the car, suspecting that I knew what he would say: that it was meta-geographical, something from a fabulous past, infinitely remote from life, place and time. A smooth, white stone tossed into the Indian Ocean.

'I know what it is,' he said, 'it is a perfect lost place. But where it is nobody knows, except it is beyond Pusela. But you will find it, and when you find it you must let me know. Ah! Sena, Sena. Remember, I am the Chief of the South African Lemba, so let me know what you find. But please be quick. I don't have too long.'

8

Cloud's End Hotel is set in a small copse of jacaranda trees in the middle of a meadow sheltered by the foothills of the Soutpansberg. It is just off the main road which leads from Louis Trichardt north to Messina and the Limpopo. Phophi had been right: it looked a good place to spend the night. I walked into the small reception area and asked for a room.

'Sorry,' said the Indian receptionist. 'If you've not booked, we're full right up.'

Wearily I carried my bag back to the car and was about to put it in the boot when a bald, lean, black man, who had been standing in the shade of one of the jacaranda trees, hurried up to me.

'You Parfitt, baas?' he asked.

'Yes. That's right. How did you know?'

'*Mamuga, Mamuga,*' he whispered, bringing his hands together in the usual greeting. 'You writing us the Lemba's book, so you stay here in this hotel,' and he picked up my bag and carried it back to the reception room.

'This Mr Parfitt,' he said to the Indian. 'We've been waiting for him.'

Phophi had sent a message from Tshifudi to one of the Lemba workers in the hotel to say that I might be coming and a small wooden bungalow had been reserved for me with a view over the mountains. A family of bickering blue-bottomed monkeys scampered off the roof as I walked in. I unpacked, put my books on a shelf and contemplated with some satisfaction the comfortable bed and the desk in front of the window. 'Dop en dut' was the motto of the hotel and was printed on the beer mats, glasses, china and just about everything else. It means 'snooze and booze'. After the last couple of days, I was ready for both. I walked over to the hotel bar, which was full of Boer farmers from the area around Louis Trichardt out on the town with their wives and girlfriends. It was a good bar, full of bottles, smoke and noise. I ordered a whisky and tried to get into conversation, but the farmers were not easily drawn: they seemed uncomfortable in English and embarrassed to be talking to a stranger. After a while I gave up and found myself a table in the wooden Alpine dining-room, which was decorated with stags' heads and a great stone fireplace. My attention was drawn to the sheer size of the Boers and the seemingly endless number of courses and astonishing quantity of food they were managing to consume. The man next to me was wearing shorts; his legs were twice the girth of mine and he was not fat; he was eating everything on the menu. I, too, had a good meal. After some cold fish, roast kudu and a bottle of Cape wine, I was getting ready to leave the dining-room when the bald Lemba hurried up to me and said, 'Not eating? No soups? No puddings? No cheeses? No savouries?'

'No thanks. I've had enough.'

'You eat like a black man, baas – *Mamuga, Mamuga*,' he beamed and made a movement as if to clap his hands.

The Boer farmer next to me who had overheard this exchange yelled at the Lemba to shut up and to bring him another bottle of wine and some cheese. Without hurrying himself, the waiter returned to the kitchen, a smile on his face.

The next morning, with mounting disbelief, I watched the same farmer eat his way through the breakfast menu: orange juice, porridge, two kippers, bacon, sausage, kidneys, scrambled eggs, steak, toast, marmalade and a good deal of coffee. I was sharing a table with a slightly anarchic, white Johannesburg lawyer, who watched my fascination with some amusement.

'Your national food consumption must be incredible,' I said.

'Don't forget the blacks eat next to nothing.'

'I'm sure the Boers more than make up for it.'

The lawyer smiled and told me the following anecdote. Not many miles north of Louis Trichardt, on the way to the Beit Bridge, there was a Boer farm called Little Africa. The owner of the farm had a keen interest in the science of eugenics: it was rumoured that he really wanted to experiment on people, but for the moment had to content himself with dogs. He set himself the task of recreating the original African Dog, but in the process bred a monster: an enormous dog, dangerous and half-mad. This animal conceived a passion for a sack of potatoes and several times a day endeavoured to enjoy sexual congress with it. One day, exhausted, the dog went down to the farm pond and drank, and kept on drinking, until its stomach burst.

'What a horrible story,' I said. 'Is it true?'

'Yes, it's true. Even if it were not, the symbolism is clear, isn't it?'

'Not to me.'

'Don't you see?' he said, giving me a sharp look. 'Apartheid was one very big, very disgusting racial experiment and, it was always going to finish up with a very big, very disgusting bang.'

The hotel had a small collection of volumes on the early history of the Transvaal. After breakfast I settled down on the veranda, hoping to find something about the Lemba. Instead, my attention was drawn to the extraordinary exploits of the Portuguese adventurer, João Albasini.

Albasini's father, Antonio Albasini, was a wealthy sea captain and ivory merchant, who had left his native Tyrol in 1807. His son was born in 1813 on board ship in the Bay of Oporto and was granted Portuguese nationality on the strength of it. In 1831, João Albasini arrived in the Portuguese colony of Mozambique with instructions from his father to open up trade routes into the still unexplored heart of Africa. It was not long before Albasini and his band were captured. While his four companions were being eaten, so the family legend runs, Albasini was tied to a stake and instructed to wait his turn. But as soon as he was untied, the stockily built, bearded little man barked, fell on all fours and pretended to be a jackal. Suspecting a ruse, the blacks put him to the test by making him fight an African hunting dog barehanded. Howling maniacally Albasini throttled the animal and scampered off into the bush. The terrified tribesmen let him go.

Having recovered his supplies and equipment, he continued on his mission and some days later came across a large group of emaciated and starving Shangan tribesmen. He shot them an elephant, which they stripped to the bone and devoured within minutes. He soon acquired a great reputation as a hunter and provider, so much so that over a hundred years later Shangan mothers were still singing this song to their children: 'We ride horses/The horses of João/Father does not come back/We will still eat bread/The bread of the white man/ *Kikigi Kikigi/Kikigi Kikigi* .'

Sometimes, to impress the Shangan, Albasini turned great vats of water into blood using permanganate of potash. The Shangan came to look upon him as a god.

With the help of his bedazzled hunters he tracked down elephants and slaves. He traded beads and cloth for black and white ivory. His Shangan carried the merchandise back to the coast by way of the elephant trails. These routes were ideal for the heavily laden porters – elephants never climb gradients of more than one in three. With his trade routes established Albasini created a permanent base in the foothills of the Soutpansberg and linked up with the Voortrekkers who had arrived from the south. But he soon found the Boers' company intolerable and moved to Piesangkop, where he built a fort. By now Albasini was the paramount chief of the Shangan and from this power base he set himself the task of destroying the power of the Venda and the Lemba of the northern Transvaal.

After wiping out a number of minor chiefs, he turned his attention to Makhado, the son of the Venda chief, Ramapulana. Makhado, known as the Lion of the North, had been the first Venda chief to be circumcised – the ceremony had been conducted in a Lemba circumcision lodge near his neighbour Chief Mashao's *kraal* – and subsequently the circumcision lodge had become a revered institution in the royal Venda *kraal*. As a result, Makhado was sometimes called the Little Lemba. It was he who had given the land to the Lemba at Ndouvhade.

Makhado's *kraal* was built in an impregnable position near Hangklip. But Albasini's Shangan managed to breach the defences and put the great village to the torch. According to legend, Albasini led the attack, but as he was about to deliver the *coup de grâce* and put an end to Makhado, his wives fell on his body and, in the confusion, he was able to escape.

Chief Mashao was less lucky: Albasini established a camp in front of the chief's *kopje* (hill) and started making elaborate preparations for a frontal assault. But in fact he attacked Mashao at dead of night from the back of the hill. In the moment of Albasini's victory an event took place which was to be held against him for the rest of his life. An account of this incident was provided by one of the books in the hotel library – a short pamphlet written by João Albasini IV, Albasini's great-grandson. In order to impress the Venda, Albasini had gone to war in the dress uniform of a Portuguese naval officer. But Chief Mashao was not impressed: even after his capture, he remained insulting and defiant. So Albasini drew his sword and, in Albasini IV's words, 'prodded Mashao in his extremely big stomach. Somehow, probably through excitement and movement of the warriors, the sword penetrated further than was intended and Mashao squealed like a pig when his entrails and fat bubbled out.'

Not everyone believed this version. Many whites suspected that Albasini had deliberately murdered a defenceless man and at the time, even among the Boers, this was thought to be going a bit too far.

Overnight the hotel had filled up with former white Rhodesians returning to Zimbabwe. The small car park was full of old Austins and Morrises, relics of the old Smith régime. The tables at breakfast were taken up by thin middle-aged couples with English accents, poorly dressed by comparison with the prosperous white South Africans. They were in South Africa to buy the luxuries no longer available in Zimbabwe: shaving soap, hand lotion, dish-washer detergent, whisky. They seemed to have little desire to return, things had gone downhill after the war, they said. But they had no alternative because their money, homes and possessions were in Zimbabwe; if they left the country, for South Africa for instance, as many had done, they would have to leave everything behind.

On the sunlit terrace outside the breakfast-room I started to talk to two elderly women who were huddling together out of the fresh wind which was blowing down off the Soutpansberg. The older of the women was wearing a cheap flannel coat and carpet slippers, her companion was wrapped in a leather jacket. I took them to be Rhodesians. It was an error which did not go down well. They were both fourth-generation South Africans and the older woman was not slow to tell me that she was descended from one of the first white men to settle in the Transvaal. Her name was Maria Eyssell Albasini.

All her life she had worked the farm which her famous ancestor had founded in 1832. The farm had not prospered. Indeed, none of the Albasinis had had any money sense, she told me, and she was no exception. She was now living in reduced circumstances in an old people's home in Louis Trichardt and her presence in the hotel today was due only to the generosity of her more affluent friend, whose gleaming black BMW was the showpiece of the parking lot.

I told her of my interest in the Lemba and of the role Albasini had had in their downfall. Family tradition maintained, she said, that Albasini had feared the Lemba more than any other tribe. They were much cleverer than the other blacks. Because he had feared them, he had treated them well; he had in fact treated all the kaffirs well, not that he had got any thanks for it. But Maria had things to say to her friend and excused herself. Feeling that I would like to hear more from her, I went back to my room.

94

I did see Maria again. The following day she telephoned me and asked me to join her for coffee in the Great North Road, Louis Trichardt's best-known restaurant. One of the few remaining Jews in Louis Trichardt was sitting there beside her. Maurice was in his late eighties and had an interest in the Lemba. He was convinced that they were Jews. He was able to cast light on one thing which had perplexed me – how the Lemba had come by the six-pointed star, the Jewish *Magen David*. I had seen it in Soweto and in Mathiva's sitting-room. The Star of David had only become a Jewish symbol in the late Middle Ages, so it could hardly be seen as the vestige of some ancient Jewish migration. It had presumably been picked up in recent times. I said as much to Maurice.

'You're right there,' he said. 'A neighbour of mine, a religious Jew, used to employ a number of Lemba servants. Years and years ago. Long before the war. He had *Magen Davids* all over the house. It just so happened that a fellow called Mtenda, one of his servants, was a founder of the Lemba Cultural Association. It was Mtenda who designed the logo of the Association – an elephant inside the Star of David. I know for a fact that he got the idea from his master's house. They never had it before.'

I could see that Maria was pleased that I had got some useful information from her guest, but I could also see that she wanted to talk too.

'Your great-grandfather Albasini was quite a character,' I said.

'He certainly was that. He was a great man. He kept the white man's flag flying here at a time when there was no one else to do it. Without him we would have lost the northern Transvaal. The stupid Boers had got into trouble with the kaffirs. They kept stealing their cattle – you can do just about any damned thing to a kaffir, but you can't steal his cattle. Well, the kaffirs got sick of it and rose up in a big way, with the upshot that in 1867 the first Boer settlement up here – it was called Schoemansdal – was evacuated. This place, Louis Trichardt, was only founded in 1898.

'After Schoemansdal João kept the kaffirs at bay for all those long years until the Boers got back. By rights we Albasinis should own all this land. I'd settle for half!' She gave a bitter little laugh. 'Anyway, João did great things here.'

'I must say I have read some pretty terrible things about your ancestor too,' I said.

'Yes, I know that there was always a lot of bad talk about him,' she replied, making a dismissive movement with her hands. 'Most of it was nonsense. He used to have a trick of building what we call *kaffirtjies* – little wooden nigger boys on pulleys that you could shoot down, then pull back up again – and, as a result, he was accused of shooting real live piccaninnies as target practice. As far as I know he never did that. At another time Cecil Rhodes asked him to recruit some of his Shangan men for the Kimberley mines and paid him one pound and ten pence for every head he sent. So people said that he had sold them as slaves. But they went of their own free will. There was a lot of jealousy. But the truth is he was a good man, a good, noble, brave man. He died a pauper, not a penny. But he was rich in spirit.' With a serene smile she turned towards Maurice, who nodded in agreement.

'As it happens I have just been reading a book written by a relative of yours, all about Albasini's attack on Mashao, the Venda chief.' I said.

'Ah, yes, the Mashao episode. Well, you know João needed to take Mashao's *kopje*. He brought up his troops and as the bugles played he paraded them all afternoon and evening in

full view of the village. But secretly he sent a strong detach-
ment to the other side of the *kopje*. The Venda hurled insults
at João until the early hours of the morning. And then, as
soon as the kaffirs fell asleep, João attacked. The chief, a big,
fat man, was caught and dragged down the hill, all tied up in
ropes. He was in a terrible rage. When he got close to great-
grandfather, he spat at him full in the face. It was the worst
insult you can imagine – a nigger spitting in a white man's
face.' Her soft, dimpled face broke into a reproachful smile.

'So what happened?'

'Obviously it was a question of honour. Great-grandfather
took his sword and cut his stomach out.'

9

Two mornings later a white chauffeur-driven Mercedes drove up to the hotel and I was handed an invitation to visit Mr Moeti, one of the Lemba leaders most active in political affairs. The Lemba waiter followed me to the car.

'I'm going to see Mr Moeti. He's a Lemba,' I said.

'He's not of the BaLemba and he is not of the BaVenda. He's of the BaBenzi,' he said, laughing and pointing at the Mercedes.

I followed Moeti's Mercedes in my rented car and an hour later I was in his office. Moeti looked too big and muscular for his suit and made his office furniture look like toys. His shaved bullet-head sat surely on big shoulders. He mumbled a greeting, dismissed his assistants and closed the door behind them. They were BaVenda, he told me, as if that explained everything. In a hoarse whisper Moeti told me about his career. He had headed four Venda government departments over the previous eight years. He was too powerful to dismiss, but as a Lemba he was considered too dangerous to entrust with the same job for too long.

'As long as everything goes just fine, my being a Lemba does not matter one damn. But as soon as things start going wrong, it is attributed to my Lemba origin.'

Moeti's secret ambition was the creation of a Lemba

autonomous zone in the western part of Venda, near Louis Trichardt.

'The South African Government seemed to be about to recognise us some years ago, but now they do not distinguish between Venda and Lemba. And then in Venda in 1982 we tried to get our own tribal authority, but without success. It's not easy, being a Lemba here.'

I was about to say something when Moeti held up his hand and silenced me.

'I don't want to talk politics. I asked you here to talk about the Lemba. You are going up north? You'll find plenty of Lemba still there – in Zimbabwe certainly, and maybe further north, so I have been told. You see, we started in the north and we travelled down, some of us, along with the BaVenda, to the south. In fact, we led the Venda here. We were the carriers of the drum and they followed us everywhere. We knew the country well because our traders and metalworkers had travelled here before. We knew the whole of Africa, inside out. It's this fact which explains our whole relationship with the Venda. Our history informs even our present.'

I asked him to explain what he meant.

'We first met the Venda tribe when at Great Zimbabwe,' he said. 'Soon after the Lemba nation split into two main groups. Some stayed around Mberengwe, some came south with the Venda. With the Venda we were an elite group. We were the ones who guided them and told them where to go. In addition, we carried into battle the sacred drum – the *ngoma lungundu* – which was a sign of religious and political power. And we carried our own secrets – the secrets of magic, of healing, of metal-working and mining, of pottery and stone-building. We were the generals in the Venda armies right until the end, when finally we were beaten by the Boers; two Lemba generals, Milubi and Ndouvhade, led Venda and

Lemba armies. When we got to Vendaland we built the stone city of Dzata, which is just a few miles away. Now it is in ruins. You see, in those days we were light-skinned – white men really – and the Venda treated us like a sort of upper class, almost like gods. We were the elite. Like the Chosen People. We did not have to do the things normal people did: we did not work in the fields of the king, we did not build the king's huts. The only work we were required to do was to supervise the building of Dzata, as we had supervised the building of Great Zimbabwe.

'You know, when I was a boy I used to go around the Venda villages selling pots which my mother had made, and sometimes I saw Lemba masons pecking away at stones. And those stone-peckers, I used to think, were keeping up our traditions; more than anyone they were holding on to the thread which takes us back to the days of our glory in Great Zimbabwe when we were white and powerful – the thread which links us to Sena!'

Moeti was no longer whispering, he was bellowing – and his eyes burned as he recounted the history of his people and described the ring of hammer on stone in the mountains of Vendaland which was the echo of their past.

The rather extraordinary picture painted by Moeti is, in fact, amply confirmed by early ethnography. About fifty years ago a Lemba informant maintained that the Lemba had been considered an extension of the royal Venda court. It was even the custom of Venda princes to choose their wives from among the Lemba womenfolk. Princely tastes were gratified by the Lemba production of cotton cloth and gold and copper ornaments – prestige items which were in demand in royal *kraals*. Lemba men were prized medicine men: no war party would leave the *kraal* without first being doctored by a

Lemba medicine-man-of-war. And when the fighters returned triumphant but exhausted, they would be soothed by Lemba musicians, for, as one Venda account put it, wherever you went in Venda at that time, there was Lemba music in the sky.

Many local traditions agree that the Lemba and Venda came south together. One day by chance, I met Chief Revelele, an elderly member of the Venda royal family. He told me that when the Venda came from the north, they had been led by a Lemba vanguard: he was not sure whether they were chosen because, as traders, they knew the routes south or on account of their magical powers. Perhaps the latter because, as they marched, the Lemba had the honoured role of carrying the *ngoma lungundu*, which was filled with magic objects and which protected the people on their journey and made their armies invincible. This was, as one writer put it, 'the sacred drum which was borne along on their wanderings like the Ark of the Covenant'.

According to some sources, the original Venda decision to move south had been taken because the Venda paramount chief of the time had a dream in which his dead father told him that the Lemba would be able to lead his people to peace and plenty. When the tribes finally arrived in Vendaland, they settled in the Nzhelele valley. It was here that the Lemba claim to have helped build the magnificent stone construction of Dzata – the most impressive pre-colonial structure in the whole of South Africa.

But there was a darker side. As metal-workers, the Lemba were viewed as masters of the magic arts, and as medicine men and traders in magical wares they were considered to be dangerous wizards. In addition, their custom of throat-slitting before death often terrified their neighbours. Chief Revelele told me that the Lemba had been held in such fear that there were only certain parts of Vendaland in which they were permitted to reside: a sort of Pale of Settlement.

Also, what of Moeti's repetition of what I had already heard in Soweto – that the Lemba were once white men? As I had already discovered, nineteenth-century travellers to Vendaland and Mashonaland had cited the local tradition that white men had once inhabited the interior. In *Twenty-Five Years in a Wagon in the Gold Regions of Africa*, Andrew Anderson wrote: '... the natives state that the gold was worked and the forts built by the white men that once occupied this country whom they call Abberlomba...' At about the same time Karl Gottlieb Mauch, the German explorer credited with the discovery of Great Zimbabwe, noted that, 'It is firmly believed that in former times white men had lived in this area.' Anderson's Abberlomba are clearly the Lemba; it could be that Mauch's 'white men' are too. In any event, at the beginning of this century, notwithstanding their dark colour, the Lemba were still commonly known as *valungu* – white men. A further connotation of the word *valungu* has some bearing on the status of the Lemba: it means spirits of the dead, or even gods.

As I left Moeti, I began to feel that the historical importance of the Lemba was much greater than I had imagined. Their history was remarkable in itself, linking as it seemed the Semitic and African worlds. What kind of role they had played at Great Zimbabwe remained to be considered, but in Vendaland, a more than probable successor to the mysterious Great Zimbabwe civilisation, tradition maintained that they had been an elite whose position derived from a status they had had before their migration south.

From Moeti's office I drove back through the hills past the ruins of Dzata. The ruins are situated on a low hill next to a stream. It was raining hard and it was cold. The aromatic smell of wood fires wafted over the site. The only people in view were two women hurrying home with great bundles of brushwood tied to their backs. The ruins cover about three acres and consist of an outer wall built of local stones and an inner structure made of quite different, more evenly shaped stones. According to Venda legend, these stones were carried from the other side of the Limpopo River by vassal tribes as Thohoyandou, the great Venda chief, was afraid of using local stones for the centrepiece of his new capital.

That evening at dinner the Lemba waiter asked me what I thought of Dzata.

'How on earth did you know I was there?' I asked, making no attempt to keep the surprise out of my voice.

He laughed and, in the kindest possible way, said, 'There is Lemba people watching over you all the time, baas. We is keeping you safe. You been see Mathiva. You been see Phophi. You been see Chief Ndouvhade. We are sorry you're going to Zimbabwe. In Zimbabwe you will be alone.'

PART TWO

The Mountain of the Good Men

10

The next day I continued northward on my journey. If the mystery of the Lemba were to be solved anywhere, I felt sure that it would be around Mberengwe and in the villages of Chief Mposi. The only way to get north to Zimbabwe from Louis Trichardt without a private car (rented cars are not allowed over the border) is by bus. There are three a week which leave the pretty little square in front of Louis Trichardt's railway station terminal at a quarter past four in the morning.

The passengers were mostly white Zimbabweans returning home. A few young men, a crate of South African beer between them, were singing along to a guitar: 'I feel so broke up,' they sang, 'I wanna go home. I feel so broke up, I wanna go home.' But you could tell their hearts were not in it.

For a few minutes the fact that I was the only passenger getting on at Louis Trichardt and that I was English caused a ripple of comment throughout the bus. 'Welcome to Zimbabwe – Paradise on earth ... Nothing to see from the Limpopo to Bulawayo ... It's a dust bowl ... May as well sleep. Most beautiful country in the world ... No rain for seven years. If the blacks don't ruin our country the drought will! ... Murdering bastards ... What a country we've given them! Hospitals, clinics, the best farms in the world. They've made colonisation a dirty word, but where would they be without it? Heading for Mberengwe? The only thing there is the emeralds. Never buy 'em uncut. Otherwise...' The speaker pressed his wrists closely together and clicked his tongue against his teeth to suggest the snapping shut of handcuffs.

The sun was just rising as the bus rolled into Messina. The copper mine which dominates the small border town was glowing red in the dawn light. Indeed, everything in sight was within the red spectrum: the roofs of the miners' dormitories were covered with azalea and bougainvillaea and everything else was coated with a thick layer of coppery orange dust.

According to Lemba tradition, Messina was the mine of the Mwenye, established long ago by the clans of Hamisi and Sharifu. Here their ancestors made bellows of animal skin and blew the flames until they turned blue and the ore melted like water.

It took some time before the Lemba, always a secretive people, imparted their skills to other tribes. An old Lemba copper miner, William, whom I met in Ndouvhade's location, had spent his life working at Messina, and his father before him. He was reluctant to tell me what he knew of pre-colonial mining methods: these things were tantamount to tribal secrets, as precious in their way as the secret incantations said at circumcision or at the slaughter of a sacrificial beast. It took Mathiva's letter and a couple of beers before he opened up. What he had to say was fascinating.

Their system of mining was to sink a shaft thirty yards or so into the earth. In the evening a fire would be lit at the bottom of the shaft against the metal-yielding rock. The next morning water was poured on to the heated rock-face and, when it cracked, the ore was removed with a special stone hammer and an iron pick.

The copper ore was placed inside a clay kiln between alternating layers of charcoal. The kiln was embedded in an open fire, which was blown red-hot by animal-skin bellows. Once it melted, the copper dripped through the charcoal to the bottom of the kiln. It was made into ingots by pouring the molten copper into moulds of damp sand.

There were two types of ingots: commercial and ceremonial. The commercial ones were cylindrical or rectangular and came in varying sizes. On the top of each ingot were studs which indicated how much copper was to be found in it. Each stud represented about a quarter of a pound of copper. For purposes of trade one stud was worth an iron hoe; two studs were worth a goat; twenty studs were worth a cow. The largest ingots, boasting many studs, were so heavy that two men were needed to carry them. The ceremonial ingot was a curiously shaped instrument about two foot long, very much like a hoe, with a variable number of short rods sticking up out of the base. No tradition has come down to us to explain the bizarre form of this ingot. Its value, however, is known: one bought a cow, five bought a wife. If the Lemba ingot does indeed represent a hoe, which it seems to, it may well have some connection with the small silver-handled hoe which was part of the royal regalia of the Monomotapa and which symbolised fertility and peace.

As we have seen, the Lemba craftsmen were highly skilled: the Venda called them 'the people who can make everything'. Their greatest skills it seems were reserved for their copperwork. They had two special tools: the *magogo* – a piece of perforated iron, and the *ngwenya* or 'crocodile' – an iron pincer. Molten copper was poured into a mould formed in sand by a long reed. This produced a copper rod, which was pulled through the largest hole in the *magogo* using the *ngwenya*. It was then drawn through the smaller holes until the desired thickness was achieved. The finest copper wire was wound around lengths of oxtail hair to make *busenga* – the copper bracelets which were prized throughout southern Africa. They were so prized among the Venda that the only women allowed to wear them were those of the royal *kraal*. But Lemba women had the right to wear them too.

Many of the stone ruins which are to be found in Venda-land and Zimbabwe are situated near ancient metal-workings such as Messina. One theory has it that the metal-workings came first and the stone buildings followed. A more comprehensive version of the same idea is that in Africa and elsewhere, it was itinerant metal-smiths who were the essential carriers of culture. Certainly they achieved a mythical, almost supernatural, status in the traditions of many African societies. It is curious that both the Lemba and the Falashas of Ethiopia, who after all have so many other things in common, should both be metal-working castes. In addition, they both suffered as a result of their association with metal: both groups were regarded by the peoples among whom they lived with fear.

At the beginning of the century instruments similar to those used by Lemba craftsmen, as well as great quantities of copper beads and *busenga* wire, were found at the Great Zimbabwe ruins and elsewhere, particularly in areas connected with ritual. Is it possible that Lemba smiths played some sort of religious role at the courts of one of Africa's greatest civilisations?

In earlier times the Lemba participated in and perhaps controlled the gold trade between the interior and the coast. It was this trade which was responsible for the prosperity of the Arab settlements on the coast and later for the profits made by the Portuguese. Splendid mosques were built in the legendary coastal city of Kilwa out of this trade; while the monstrance of the Sacred Host in the Church of Belem in Lisbon was built of solid Zimbabwe gold.

Lemba traders travelled far and wide to sell their gold and metalware. They bought brass, glass beads and cloth from the east coast and sold copper, tin, ivory, skins and ostrich feathers, as well as gold. They took their metalware and trade goods throughout what is today Zimbabwe, the Transvaal and hundreds of miles to the south to the Zulu areas.

In the 1930s, a Lemba told the story of one of his ancestors called Mbalanyika, whose nickname was 'Gumboyi', which means 'leg'. He acquired this name because he was a trader and travelled a great deal. When people mocked him because he did not plough the land or even possess a hoe, he would say, 'Gumboyi badza, masango nda feza' – 'My leg is my hoe, I walk about to every country.' Any trader's objective was to return with cattle; a goat was all right, but a cow was much better. A Lemba song recorded in 1931 reflected this preference: 'The best traders are those who bring the cattle home/Those who bring back goats are nothing.' A somewhat similar song noted by a Portuguese missionary, Father Fernandes, in 1561 in what is today the Chopi area expressed much the same thing: 'The cow has leather for shoes/The goat has no leather for shoes.'

There are no longer any Lemba practitioners of their ancient metalworking skills, although William told me that a few traditional Lemba smiths were still active in the 1940s. The period of fierce inter-tribal warfare in the first half of the nineteenth century, the *mfecane*, when the Ndebele successfully invaded what came to be known as Matabeleland, brought to an end much local mining and metal-work. Mzilikazi, the Ndebele warrior chief, forbade gold mining in the territory he had occupied; miners in the eastern parts of Zimbabwe were wiped out by Mzila, a Shangan chief, in the

1860s; at the same time Ramapulana, the Venda chief, prohibited gold and copper mining in his territory.

None the less, in 1867 Karl Mauch reported of the Lemba that, 'Apart from the growing of crops, they also know how to work metal and the great part of the tribute they have to pay is in the form of metal: assegais, knives, bracelets and anklets, which they decorate with designs.'

But within a few years whatever metal-working activity survived was rendered completely unprofitable by the activities of the early white trader settlers who usually stocked rolls of machine-made copper wire and iron hoes from Birmingham in their native trading stations. Even before this commercial onslaught had begun, the detritus left behind by European pioneers was being used by black tribesmen as an interesting ornamental alternative to the bangles which they had hitherto bought from the Lemba. In the *Ruined Cities of Mashonaland* (1892), J. T. Bent described how the round ends of discarded bully beef cans were pounced upon by native bearers for use as ornaments, while the cylindrical cans were considered fine bracelets.

The general impression given by the first white settlers in the northern Transvaal and Rhodesia was that metal-working and mining had long since ceased, even though we now know that it had been in full spate until the 1860s. Andrew Anderson, the intrepid prospector I have already cited, remarked that in the 1880s, 'no African of these parts ever built these strongholds or took the trouble to make such extensive excavations in the earth as we find all over the country'. Anderson and others relegated such activities to a distant past. The truth is somewhat different. Even if many Lemba miners had been killed in the *mfecane*, as Lemba oral tradition maintains, there were none the less pockets of Lemba miners and smiths active until late into the nineteenth century and to a lesser extent into the first few decades of the twentieth. The temporary cessation of large-scale activity caused by the *mfecane* and its aftermath coincided with the arrival of the whites in Zimbabwe and the northern Transvaal and contributed to the myth that no local black peoples were capable of mining, metal-working or, indeed, anything else.

As the bus passed the copper mines of Messina, I remembered a curious encounter I had had the morning I drove back from Phophi's village. Crouched in front of a gaily painted *rondavel* of the Venda Development Corporation Craft Centre near Thohoyandou, I had noticed a white man photographing a number of wooden figures positioned in front of a piece of black plastic sheeting. He was a Belgian anthropologist working at the University of Venda and the figures, in red, blue and green, had been carved by a Lemba sculptor.

'It's quite absurd,' he said; 'we whites killed off their old material culture with our imports and cast-offs and now we are persuading them to go back to it, but in a way which suits our own cultural and economic interests. After all, who buys all this stuff?' He pointed at the pots, masks and hand-woven rugs which were piled up by the side of the *rondavel*. 'White tourists. And, you know, the people here don't see the point of making things without a direct practical application. That is particularly true of sculpture. It's complicated in this case by the fact that the sculptor was a Lemba – and the Lemba have always had the reputation among the Venda of having supernatural powers. So what happens is that the Lemba craftsmen who make these figures are accused of witchcraft and casting terrible spells. This sculptor was murdered: had his throat cut. He's the third this year. They're kind of caught between white and black. If you're looking for a symbol of the death of Lemba material culture, there it is.'

A mile or so past the Beit Bridge which crosses Kipling's 'grey, green, greasy Limpopo river', we arrived at the Zimbabwe border post. The weather had changed from being cold and wet in the south to bright, hot sun. Black, uniformed customs officers searched our bags for contraband, while the returning whites grumbled about the import restrictions imposed by the Zimbabwe Government and the shortages which had sent them over the border in the first place. The words fabric softener, food processor, deodorant floated in the heat haze rising from the melting tarmac: western consumer items which had replaced local products. But these were not the words I wanted to hear or think about. Looking beyond the piles of luggage and the customs sheds, at the empty expanse of dry veldt, I imagined the southern march of the 'white men who came from Sena', with the Venda chiefs, carrying the sacred drum and beads, playing their musical instruments and 'making music in the sky'.

11

Bulawayo was once the undisputed industrial centre of Rhodesia. Now, as the chief city of the western, Ndebele part of the country, it has been allowed to run down by the Shona-dominated central government. The surrounding bush had been the scene of frequent attacks by Ndebele terrorists against both black and white targets. Over the previous three months 500 blacks and twenty whites had been killed in Matabeleland. In fact, Bulawayo was under siege.

That afternoon, however, the town looked prosperous and peaceful, the public buildings neat, the parks and tree-lined avenues well tended. The broad main streets (built wide enough to permit an ox-drawn wagon to make a complete turn without having to back up) lined with tin and wooden awnings and raised wooden walkways were deserted in the heat of the day. But the drought had taken its toll here too. The lawns in front of the suburban villas and bungalows were dust. The only green grass was on the ring of the Ascot Race Track.

From the Holiday Inn I telephoned Louis Bolze. Friends in London had told me that he was the only white man in Bulawayo who knew anything at all about local history. He invited me to come straight over to his office on Rhodes Street. A short, lean man in his sixties with a shrewd face,

Bolze loved to talk. He told me about his background: his great-grandfather had been a German mercenary, part of a contingent led by one Baron von Stutterheim, recruited by the British for use in the Crimean War. The Germans were assembled in a barracks in Colchester, but before they could be despatched to the front, the war had come to an end. Searching the globe for a spot where this German Legion could be deployed, the authorities hit upon the eastern Cape where the garrison had been depleted by the Kaffir Wars. Louis's ancestor, Johann, had married a girl from a shipment of impoverished Irish girls sent out as maids for the colony.

Louis had built up a publishing firm which specialised in reprints of nineteenth- and early twentieth-century books on Rhodesia. His office was lined with the leather-bound books of his Rhodesian Reprint Library. I took one of the series down from the shelves – Cullen Gouldsberg's *Rhodesian Rhymes* – and came upon something called 'Caravan':

> God gave the Heathen woes enough – but deep content as well
> Fashioning him from sterner stuff to bear a sterner hell,
> The soft skinned darlings of the West may cling to Fortune's lap –
> Our lot, perhaps, is still the best,
> Marching across the map.

Smiling, I read this out to Louis. His responding smile was a grim one. 'Terrible, what's happening,' he said. 'All my stock is viewed as subversive colonial literature by the present Government. It's impossible for me to trade. A friend of mine, a leading member of the Rhodesia Pioneers and Early Settlers' Society, has just been arrested for possession of *Rhodesian Rhymes*.'

But life, as he said, went on: the cultural life of the white community continued despite the Government. The previous day he had gone, as he always did on a Thursday, to the

Thursday Sandwich Club, a group devoted to discussing cultural and current affairs, and had given a talk on the South African statesman and writer, Sir James Percy Fitzpatrick, to mark the eightieth anniversary of the publication of *Jock of the Bush-veld*. He was also a member of the Rotary and the Bulawayo Club – a colonial institution whose land had been given by Rhodes himself and whose library, he told me, boasted a number of books donated by Kipling.

Louis refused to let me stay at the Holiday Inn and sent a car to pick up my bag. He drove me through luxurious white suburbs, stopping every now and then to introduce me to his friends. Not many visitors came to Bulawayo.

His house was constructed on and around a rocky outcrop under which, thousands of years before, Bushmen or Hottentots had painted their stick-like animals and men. Louis had built a library around one high, pointed outcrop of granite, whose peak pierced the room and served as a display area for his fine collection of African pottery. On one side it overlooked a pool, on the other an artificial lake, both empty because of the drought. We sat in his library, drinking a cane and tonic, and he told me that he would never leave; if he did, he would not be allowed to take his money out, and he would rather suffer the inconveniences of Zimbabwe than eke out a life in South Africa. Also, his friends were here – and not only whites. He told me about Mike Hove, a Shona who had served as High Commissioner to Nigeria in the 'good old days' in the time of the Federation.

'First friend I made over the colour bar, Mike was. Had him here to dinner. Told my friends. Unheard of at the time. Some disapproved. Others wanted to do likewise and wanted to know how to go about it. I've asked him round for a drink.'

Hove was tall, patrician, with English mannerisms. He had

retired from political life many years before and now devoted himself to writing. He had brought me a copy of his latest book: *Confessions of a Wizard: A Critical Examination of the Belief System of a People Based Mainly on Personal Experience.* I asked him if he believed in magic. 'You couldn't not believe in the supernatural in Africa,' he said. Louis nodded in agreement. I told them about the Lemba's reputation as magicians and sorcerers. The Lemba are scattered and keep to themselves and, as a result, very few Zimbabweans, black or white, have ever heard of them, despite the fact that there are probably around fifty thousand in the country. But Hove knew about the Lemba. Three or four generations back, he told me, an ancestor of his had moved with his tribe, the Mbangowa, into a new area near Mberengwe. Leopards kept attacking their cattle and it was not long before they came to believe that the leopards were the spirits of the Lemba ancestors who were punishing them for encroaching on their traditional homelands. So they decided to move back to their own areas, only to discover that another tribe had moved in.

'My forebears', he continued with a chuckle, 'asked those Lemba chaps who were very good in the use of bows and arrows and magic to give them a hand.'

The potions and spells of the Lemba proved irresistible, and Hove's Mbangowa and the Lemba people remained on close terms. But in recent times, he said, the importance of the Lemba had diminished. They were just one tribe among many. However, he was convinced that they had a great historical importance, not least because of their alleged connection with Great Zimbabwe.

'They certainly must have had a part to play in all the rituals and ceremonies, because even in my time they were considered to be a particularly religious people, actually a sort of godlike people, quite distinct and apart from us. They were fascinating – and the old folk were really dignified . . .', he searched for the words, 'they were Jewish sages.' But, he added, I would be lucky to find anything of their past, because the old traditions had largely disappeared. 'This was the worst aspect of the colonial experience. Take the Lemba – they were a very bright lot. Wanted education and were keen to go to the mission schools and get it. The first thing that happened was that they were offered pork to eat, so they were given the choice: western education or local culture; no one ever told them that they were not mutually exclusive.'

Some of the Lemba had subsequently become Christian and had completely forgotten their old beliefs and customs. But there were others, he thought, in the mountains beyond Mberengwe, particularly, in the villages around the *kraal* of the Lemba Chief Mposi, who still clung to their ancient faith. But he doubted if they would talk to me. They were a secretive lot.

Bolze was appalled that I was intending to visit these remote rural areas. He spoke at length about the security situation. The road to Victoria Falls could not be taken at all, the road to the Matopos Hills was only safe till mid-afternoon and the road towards Mberengwe could only be driven in convoy. Nine black people had just been killed in Nkazi and whites had been killed in Plumtree and Figtree. In one recent incident a black village had been attacked; the men of the village were rounded up and forced to dig a mass grave. At the point of a gun the women were made to decapitate their husbands, with an axe, and shovel them into the pit. Bolze suspected that the attacks on whites were government-inspired, calculated to get them to abandon their farms and their land, but he was not sure. Mberengwe area was particularly dangerous, he said; a Ndebele bandit by the name of Morgan was especially feared and the police, afraid to confront him, always followed his tracks at a leisurely pace and at a safe distance.

In addition to this, the country around Mberengwe was rough, said Louis, pushing himself deeper into his comfortable chair; there were hyenas everywhere in the bush. 'They go for your face and hold on like grim death, like a bulldog. Jim, my neighbour, lost his face that way.' He also told me to watch out for puff adders, whose bite is deadly unless you can isolate the affected part: 'Better to saw off a leg than die.'

Hove was more optimistic. If I were careful, I would get through. There were few wild animals around the villages and, in convoy, one was unlikely to be attacked by terrorists. But I would learn nothing from the Lemba. They were more like a secret society than a tribe. Even he, a local historian with strong links with these people, knew almost nothing, he said, not enough to fill a postcard. Nor did anyone else.

I did not have to leave immediately: Louis had a first-rate library of Rhodesiana – not only the complete sets of his reprint series, but also many of the original books of travel and exploration of the area. For a number of days, I sat in his garden close to the prehistoric rock drawings, reading my way through his library. When I needed a book he did not have, he would drop me off to spend the afternoon in the cool reading-room of the Bulawayo municipal library.

One day I hired a battered old car and drove out to the Matopos hills. Phophi had told me that this was one of the areas the Lemba had travelled through after they left Great Zimbabwe, and it was here, he said, that the Lemba introduced the Mwali cult to their Shona neighbours.

Most Lemba believe that the worship of Mwali by non-Lemba was due to their influence. Reading through Bolze's bound copies of the Rhodesian journal of local history,

NADA, I came across a number of articles which claimed that Mwali worship had originated to the east of Great Zimbabwe, that Great Zimbabwe had been the focus of the cult and that subsequently, for political reasons, the centre of the cult had been transferred to the Matopos. From the Matopos some of the cult members split off and moved across the Limpopo to Vendaland, taking with them precious cult objects. This seems so close to Lemba and Venda traditions concerning the Lemba's arrival in Vendaland that it is possible, even probable, that both traditions refer to the same series of events. Although no Lemba are to be found in the Matopos area nowadays, in the 1880s a German missionary, Knothe, noted that the chief of the Lemba in the Mberengwe area controlled at least twelve *kraals* in the Matopos, so it is more than likely that there were links at the time between the priests of Mwali in the Matopos and the Lemba. Roger Summers, the archaeologist, has connected the worship of Mwali with Great Zimbabwe. He added that the worship of Mwali is 'a local monotheistic religion associated with high places, with wind and with oracles in caves. In many ways it has Semitic connections.' There was plenty of traditional and other evidence, then, to support Phophi's claim.

In earlier times still, these humps of hills with gigantic boulders teetering on their summits had given shelter to Bushmen, whose delicate rock drawings are still to be seen. It is a place of extraordinary beauty. Stunted oaks and paper trees, their bark peeling like sunburnt skin, huddled in the slopes between the hills. Each hilltop was a monument to the magical or the improbable. It was like a giant games board, with great stone balls placed with consummate care in winning positions.

On the way back to Bulawayo I stopped to get something

to eat at the Churchill Arms, a red-brick, mock-Tudor hotel on the edge of town. The interior groaned with beams and gleamed with horse brasses. The red walls of the restaurant were hung with prints of Cotswold pubs and English hunting scenes. There were more hunting scenes on the table mats, and the black man playing 'Yesterday' on the piano was wearing a pink hunting coat. The only more-or-less African thing to be seen was the crocodile tail (coated in batter and served with chips) featured as a local speciality on the menu.

'You from the UK?' trumpeted a middle-class English voice. 'Come and have a drink. First tell that Johnny in the red coat to pull up a chair.'

I pulled up my own chair and sat down. This retired colonel was having dinner with a group of friends. The colonel wanted to know what I was doing in Bulawayo.

'Interested in the history, eh? Let me tell you – this lot don't have any ruddy history. There are ruins at Khami just a few miles away and at Great Zimbabwe. Christ only knows who built them, but it wasn't your bloody kaffir.' He laughed loudly and, in a stage whisper, informed me, 'Can't use that word. Put you in jail.'

He winked at the black waiter and asked me where I was staying. Not waiting for an answer, he said, 'All the hotels here are full of the enemy. But you've got the enemy in Notting Hill too, I hear. Can't get away from the buggers!'

'He's researching the kosher kaffirs,' the colonel shouted across the restaurant.

'The willy-snippers!' someone shouted back.

'Those that make the unkindest cut of all,' yelled back the colonel, his eyes twinkling with pleasure. 'Have an *Old Standbye*, old chap, the cane's better than the gin these days. Want to hear a good one? What's the difference between a kaffir and a cartload of spuds?'

'I've no idea.'

'You don't use a pitchfork on spuds. Spoil 'em! What's the difference between a kaffir and a bucket of shit? The bucket.' He laughed a good deal before returning to the subject of the Lemba. 'I've heard a bit about them. Met a Scottish laird, nice chap, called Gayre of Gayre and Nigg. Odd name. Worked in Germany after the war with the education outfit. Sound views on race – specially on blacks; picked 'em up from the Germans, I reckon. At least in that area Germans got it about right. Just look at what's happening back home now. Rhodesian Government got Gayre to write a book about Great Zimbabwe. Best book on the subject. Reckoned your Jew built it. Not Jews so much as Israelites. Well, you can be damned sure your regular kaffir didn't get off his arse to build anything better than a grass hut. Why not your Jew? Say what you like about the Jew, he's no fool!'

I had seen Gayre of Gayre and Nigg's book at the Bulawayo Public Library. For many years Gayre of Gayre had been the editor of a racist journal called *The Mankind Quarterly*, in which in 1967 he had written a short article on the Lemba. He then went on to write a book about Great Zimbabwe, *The Origin of the Great Zimbabwe Civilisation* (Salisbury, 1972). In it he argues that tribes such as the Venda and the Lemba which claim connections with Great Zimbabwe have Jewish cultural and genetic traits and that their 'Armenoid' genes can only have been acquired from Judaised Sabeans who settled in the area thousands of years ago. The book's clear objective was to show that black people had never been capable of building in stone or of governing themselves.

I returned to my table and, not for the first time, was assailed by the gloomy thought that if the real and somewhat complicated story of the Lemba were to confirm the racist prejudices of the likes of the colonel, it was perhaps better not to tell it. On the other hand, an essential ingredient of white attitudes is the idea, an idea articulated by the colonel, that black people have no history, that their past is a homogeneous block of time filled with subsistence farming, cattle raiding, inter-tribal slaughter and destruction from which they were delivered only by the happy advent of colonial rule. Instead, what I was learning about the Lemba revealed a richly textured past and an interesting history which needed to be told. With these somewhat conflicting thoughts on my mind I left the restaurant and drove back to the Bolzes through the *guti* – the local word for a light, almost imperceptible drizzle. I mentioned the colonel to Louis. 'Yes, there are a few Brits like that. Still living in the bad old racist Raj. Find it impossible to shrug off the toga.' And he left it at that.

It was time for me to get moving. Mathiva had suggested that I make contact in Bulawayo with Saul Sadiki, a Lemba policeman of the Sadiki clan, who would help me get the necessary permit to visit the remote rural areas beyond Mberengwe – the only areas in Zimbabwe or South Africa where the Lemba lived in exclusively Lemba villages under their own chief. But for security reasons, and because of the proximity of the emerald mines, foreigners were not normally permitted into the area. A telephone call to the police station revealed that Sadiki was on temporary duty at Victoria Falls. If I wanted to visit him, I would have to take the overnight train. I could not drive because terrorists had shot up a car on the Victoria Falls road just the day before.

12

The waiting-room at the Bulawayo railway station was full of tired, dirty soldiers returning from anti-terrorist duty in the bush area around the Wankie Game Reserve. Many of them were sprawled, exhausted, on the floor. There was nowhere for me to sit. I went back out on to the platform and stood for a few minutes admiring an antiquated steam-engine with its pre-Second World War wooden carriages newly painted in the livery of Zimbabwe National Railways. This I soon realised was the Victoria Falls train. I climbed on and made my way to my sleeping compartment. It was panelled in mahogany, there were worn leather straps on the window and shutters, and in the corner I noticed an ingenious metal basin made by Beresford of Birmingham, which folded away and was held by a sturdy catch which had been working for decades and would clearly carry on working for as long as it was required to. The walls were decorated with framed photographs of elephants, zebra and hippopotami. The attempt to convert Rhodesian into Zimbabwean rolling-stock had stopped with the paint job on the outside. Inside, everything was marked with RR for Rhodesian Railways, from the mirror to the blankets. RR was engraved on the armour-plated glass of the window and 'Armourplate RR' was stamped on the thick piece of steel which protected the area between the window and the floor. 'You'll be safe in here,' laughed the attendant, 'this is an old government car.'

As the train pulled out a garrulous white dentist told me that Zimbabwe Railways no longer kept up the old dining-cars where uniformed waiters had once served their white masters. What remained was a sort of buffet car with four or five loose wooden tables, where a few passengers, all white, were sitting down to brown soup, fried steak, boiled potatoes and overcooked cabbage. These ubiquitous relics of the East African Raj were meeting with universal approval. 'Say what you like, they've kept the standards up in the cooking department. You won't eat better than this anywhere in the world, not on a train,' said the dentist. A menu stood on the table unconsulted. That evening we should have been eating Braised Beef Moda Chef, Fish à la Orly, Vegetable du Jour, Banana Grumble. But there was great consumer resistance to fancy foreign food, said the dentist, and the chef knew better than to serve it up.

Every time the train stopped, which it did often, women with children tied to their backs and carrying sacks of onions, boxes of vegetables, long walking-sticks, bed-rolls and chickens, would file through the dining-car to the fury of the waiter-cum-cook. After several such invasions, he bolted the door, incarcerating around a hundred people in the corridor until a bellicose corporal threatened to break the door down with the butt of his rifle.

A couple of hours later I went back to the restaurant car for a drink. To the sound of Zambian rock music an English girl, on her way to join a safari group in Victoria Falls, was dancing with the by now spectacularly drunk corporal, whose rifle lay among the abandoned glasses on the bar. The corporal had one hand cupped around the girl's breast and the other clamped to her bottom. She looked pink, defiant and, perhaps, a little nervous.

I found myself a place at a table opposite an old man who was nursing a whisky. He was wearing a blue tweed jacket, an orange cap, a red kerchief around his neck, a beard and a monocle. He looked, and I suppose he was trying to look, like a prospector in an old American western. And he was a sort of prospector. He had recently been granted a concession on an old gold-working dump near Bulawayo which nobody else wanted because it was in dissident country. He was taking the old refuse, soaking it in a cyanide solution, and passing it over zinc shavings: 'and then, abracadabra, the cyanide dissolves the gold and conveniently the gold sticks to the zinc like paint'.

Oswald had been born in Kenya, had spent forty years in Rhodesia, and had never been to England. But he considered himself a Sussex man, a Horsham man, and spoke with indignation about the noise level at Gatwick airport and the destruction wrought by the M25.

'They should stay at home, the English, these days. Just look at that,' he said under his breath, jerking his thumb in the direction of the pink-faced girl. 'It's outrageous. Not just the behaviour – it's that she's only been out here three days and already she's feeling superior, and solving all the racial problems of Africa. The blacks don't like it, we don't like it, nobody likes it.' This was far from self-evident. The corporal and the girl were clearly having one hell of a good time.

To change the subject I asked Oswald why he was going to Victoria Falls. All part of a day's work, he told me. He was employed by Zimbabwe Railways and was on railway business now; the prospecting was just a sideline – moonlighting. His real job was spotting landmines or other impediments on the railway track. As we were speaking, the train came to a jerky halt and, waving his heavy-duty flashlight from side to side, Oswald disappeared up the line. After a few minutes he came back and got himself another drink. Every twenty miles or so the same procedure was followed. Around midnight I asked him how he knew that the many miles of track in between his brief inspections were clear of mines. 'I don't bloody know. It scares the daylights out of me. But what can you do? It would take for ever to inspect the whole line.' And, knocking back his seventh or eighth whisky, again he stepped out on to the track.

I did not sleep much. In the bright light of a full moon the bush rushing past the window was like a black-and-white film I could not turn off. From time to time the train would stop and I wondered if Oswald had found anything on the track. Then the film would start again: great expanses of bush, baobab trees, small villages and tiny stations, a nocturne of light and shade. Then, for a moment at dawn, the veldt turned the colour of old newspapers before losing all colour in the coruscating glare of daylight.

I saw Oswald as I was following a porter across the lawn to the Victoria Falls Hotel. 'How long you staying?' he yelled. 'Just check with the stationmaster before you go back. Just check I'm on duty. They've got all sorts of riff-raff checking the lines these days. You don't want to get blown apart!'

The central police station in Victoria Falls looked as if it were preparing for a siege. The windows were protected by iron mesh, thick iron bars and more iron mesh. I found Saul Sadiki in a dusty administration room in the back of the CID section. He was a nervous, broadshouldered, good-looking man and was delighted to have a visitor. I showed him my introduction from Professor Mathiva.

'What you want to know about the Lemba?' he asked in

excitement, investing the word 'Lemba' with a sweetness which in English could only be addressed to a child or a lover.

I said that to start with I would like to know how many Lemba there were in his home town of Bulawayo.

He whistled, laughed and then cooed in an extended ululation, as if to suggest, by means of these sounds, that the number of Lemba in Bulawayo was somewhat in excess of the sands of the sea.

When pressed for a more precise statistic, he started counting off names on his fingers and eventually said, 'Five hundred families. So many! Too much people! Too much Lemba every place.' Again he smiled in delight at the fecundity of his tribe. 'In Zimbabwe there are forty, fifty thousand, maybe more. But apart from that, I do not know much. I do not know the right history of these Lemba.' He spoke these last words slowly, his neck stretched out of his white collar, his tendons tight with regret and embarrassment at his ignorance. 'No one of the Lemba in Bulawayo knows the right history of the people. Only that we are Jews and we come from Sena. I do not know where Sena is. For the right history you must go to Chief Mposi in Mberengwe.'

I asked him about the recent spate of terrorist activity and whether I would be able to get a permit to visit Mposi's country.

'I can get you that permission,' he said.

'And it is not too dangerous to go there?'

He let out a deafening bellow of a laugh.

'What? Once the Lemba knows you is coming you cannot believe that you has anything at all to fear. The problem is', again his face contorted in a grimace of regret and embarrassment, 'it is difficult to let them know that you is coming. But

I'll phone CID Mberengwe to let them know you has this permission. No! Better – I'll ask the Super, he can do it uniform-to-uniform. I'm just a plain-clothes man in charge of finance.' He rubbed his fine, high-bridged nose with a finger. 'You know us black Jews!'

13

I took the train back to Bulawayo and some days later set out for the Lemba villages around Mberengwe in an elderly rented Ford. I left dull, comfortable, suburban Bulawayo with the sense that I would not feel intolerably misused if denied the opportunity to return. Yet at the same time I quite liked its long, straight streets alternately planted with mauve jacaranda, red flamboyants and white and pink baunenia; the park with its foxgloves and geraniums and small narrow gauge railway for children; its Haddon and Slim – a department store which still had its band, potted plants and a tea-room which served knickerbocker glories; the excellent reference library where an efficient English-born librarian, dressed always in cool cotton dresses, went to endless trouble to locate references; and Bolze's Bookshop, where Louis was strangely reluctant to sell me anything 'at the price I'd have to ask' and preferred to give or lend.

Louis had not been happy about my going. Just before I left, he told me more gory stories about recent terrorist attacks and insisted that I travel, if I was intent on leaving, at midday and that I drive in convoy with other cars. But in fact on the entire length of the road I saw no cars, only two lorries, driving fast in the opposite direction. I passed flat, featureless plains burnt brown and gold by the sun, and occasionally white farms – Hilltop, Sunnyside, Willowside.

And police roadblocks. President Mugabe was visiting Bulawayo, the police told me, to discuss recent, unreported killings.

It was with relief that I arrived at the Mberengwe police station. The compound was swept, the trees whitewashed to the regulation height, the painted stones bordering the dirt drive were dazzling white in the sun. The commanding officer was a very big man wearing brilliant black boots, an immaculate khaki uniform complete with leather belt, complicated with brass buckles and hooks. Behind his desk hung a shield quite credibly proclaiming this to be the best-kept police station in Zimbabwe. I told him I wanted to visit Chief Mposi. He asked to see my passport, which he examined for a very long time in silence. Eventually he spoke:

'The Mposi area is out of bounds to tourists and foreigners because of the emerald mines. People come here – it's very easy to get uncut stones – and then they take them back with them and make a fortune. So the best way is to let no one in.' He started cleaning his nails with a penknife.

'But I have had special authorisation from the CID at Victoria Falls. Hasn't the superintendent been in touch with you?'

'I see. That's you, is it? Ah! Yes, Parfitt, that's right,' he said, looking again at my passport. 'They telephoned to say a professor was coming. I was expecting someone different,' and he glanced at my jeans and plimsolls with amusement. 'You don't look much like a professor.'

'Well, I'm not actually a professor. I'm a lecturer,' I began, but he interrupted me and said:

'No matter what you are. I've had a telephone call from a former minister in Harare – a very important man – as well as from Victoria Falls. I've been instructed to give someone called Parfitt all the help that I can and also to keep an eye on him. For his own sake. But I warn you, anyway, to keep away from the emeralds. Now a couple of my plain-clothes people will ask you a few questions. One of them will go with you as a bodyguard.' I felt considerable gratitude to Mathiva, who clearly had got in touch with his Lemba cabinet minister friend as he had promised to do.

The commandant yelled something in Shona and two young men came into the room. One of them was a Lemba, the other a Shona. Putting his polished boots upon the table and lighting a cigarette, the CO let his detectives get on with their job. The Lemba was suspicious. He questioned me at length, but did not seem satisfied. There were many tribes in Africa, he informed me, with heavy irony, and the Lemba must be very interesting if I had come all the way from England to visit them. And it was convenient, was it not, that I should have come from South Africa and was travelling through sensitive areas of Zimbabwe using this pretext? How could I prove I was an author, and how could I prove that I had a *bona fide* interest in the Lemba? Well, I could. In my bag I had a copy of *The Thirteenth Gate*, a book of mine, which had just been published and which contained a few pages about the Lemba. I fetched the book from the car and handed it to the young Lemba policeman, drawing his attention to a photograph of a Lemba child in Venda.

His eyes devoured the book; his thin, long fingers gripped it so tightly that his knuckles turned light brown. And he was silent. After a decent interval I tried to prise the book away from him but he refused to let me have it. 'If a man is hungry', he said, his eyes full of reproach, 'and you have bread, you must give him that bread.' I explained that I intended to give the book to Chief Mposi and that in Mposi's *kraal* there were many hungry people. With obvious reluctance he handed the book back. The Lemba's complicated response was not lost on his commanding officer. Pointing at the young Shona policeman, he told him to pack and accompany me to Mposi's village. The Lemba was to stay behind in Mberengwe.

According to Lemba tradition Mount Mberengwe had two rather unusual features: it could set itself alight and it could roar like a lion. Its name is therefore explained from *yaka berengwa*, which means 'it was considered peculiar'. According to another tradition, 'two groups of Lemba first met at Mberengwe where they started counting each other to find out how many they were'. Hence the name Mberengwe, since *kuverenga* means 'to count'.

According to a Lemba tradition not deficient in sexual symbolism, the area around Mount Mberengwe was conquered by the great chief Nkalahonye. His success was achieved because the indigenous tribes were afraid of the supernatural powers of the numerically inferior Lemba. They went on to build a fortified stone settlement on Mberengwe called Munhungi. All the tribes in the vicinity came and paid tribute. And here, on the mountain, the Lemba were to stay, until the time of Nkalahonye's grandson, Shimbani, one of whose daughters married a local chief. A favourite of her father's, she had learned some of the secrets of the tribe and some of their magic potions. She knew for instance of Shimbani's magic pouch, which contained a white substance, prepared by the women, which protected the village from wild beast and human enemy alike. The girl was forced to steal her father's pouch and its potent contents. With the white magic substance at his disposal, her husband was no longer afraid of the Lemba. He launched a ferocious nocturnal attack against them which dislodged 'the Good Men' from their villages and from their mountain fortress.

The Mountain of the Good Men was, indeed, imposing. It was fenced off and no Lemba lived there any more. 'It's government property, private,' snapped Tagaruze, the Shona policeman, and refused to let me stop. From Mberengwe to Mposi is about forty miles. A narrow dirt track wound through mountainous country, criss-crossed by dried-out river-beds. For the first few miles we passed through white settlers' ranch lands, and then the closed-off fields gave way to open tribal country where the hillsides were dotted with round, thatched huts. Beyond the villages we drove through uncultivated mountainous country. Tagaruze, a slim, broad-shouldered man in his twenties, kept his gun on his knee and his eyes on the surrounding land: he encouraged me to drive fast as this was terrorist territory, Morgan territory. After about an hour we arrived at an overshadowed stretch of track from which wooded hills rose steeply on both sides. It was here that the mishap occurred.

At the darkest point of this closed-in valley the car started coughing, steam billowed from the engine and it stopped. A hose had split, the water had drained off, and the car could proceed no further. It was too dangerous, Tagaruze said, to stay overnight in the car and it was too far to walk back to the last village before darkness fell; but there was a village in the hills above the trees, a Shona village, where we could spend the night. So, carrying our bags, we clambered up the steep bank of the ravine.

During the half hour it took us to get through the woods to the open country beyond, night fell. There was no moon, but the first stars were so bright I could make out the outline of a small village at the top of the hill. It had never been much of a village, but now it was empty. Several of the huts had been burnt to the ground. Not far away jackals were baying. Apart from that, there was no sound.

'Village abandoned,' drawled Tagaruze, 'probably Morgan. Don't be afraid, sir, lightning does not strike twice.'

Whistling under his breath, he lit a fire. From my bag I produced dinner – chocolate, whisky and tinned sardines – and we slept in one of the least damaged huts. It contained nothing but a torn plastic sandal. I woke once. Tagaruze was sitting motionless and cross-legged by the opening of the hut, gazing out at the bare mountain top; the revolver on his lap gleamed in the starlight. You could almost imagine you were in the presence of a Zen master.

The following morning we returned to the car. Tagaruze pulled out the rubber overflow pipe and used it to suck water from the windscreenwash reservoir into the empty radiator, while I produced a pint from my water bottle. As he worked, he kept fingering the revolver stuck down the back of his trousers.

A pick-up truck pulled up alongside and a white farmer jumped down.

'If you drive it and it's overheated you'll kill the motor. Oh! It's rented,' he said, glancing at the Hertz sticker. 'Oh, then drive the shit out of it!' and, without a further word, he filled the radiator from his jerry can and drove off.

The car limped on for another few miles before stopping again. The cylinder-head gasket had gone. We could walk, said Tagaruze; the Mposi villages were only about twelve miles away cross-country and we would probably meet Lemba on the way who would give us water and food.

In fact, we saw no one. The beautiful highlands through which we walked were deserted. The grass was dun-coloured, closely cropped. The leaves on the trees were dry and barely green. There had been no rain for a long time. It was hot and my bag was heavy with books and cameras. After an hour, I could go no further and we rested in a wood in the shade of one of the huge boulders which litter the landscape. Later, once or twice, in the distance, I saw a village with a few slender columns of smoke rising from the cooking fires. But we saw no people. It was perfect terrorist country, said Tagaruze, and he pointed out caves and rock formations which had provided shelter to dissidents in the past.

Late in the afternoon, walking through a deserted valley, we passed a cliff-hung mountain. A pair of eagles were circling over its flat summit.

'That's Dumghe Mountain,' said Tagaruze. 'When the Lemba came here they made this their sacred mountain. It is like the one in Mberengwe. This one too they call the Mountain of the Good Men.'

Strange and mysterious things took place in this valley. There was a white lion which was sometimes seen. Occasionally wailing sounds were heard throughout the night, which people said were the Lemba ancestors weeping for the land from which they had come. At other times there were sounds like a moving car, but there was no car. If these sounds were heard over seven successive days, it would rain. But they had not been heard for years now. Most frequently of all, goats' heads were found on the paths, here in the shadow of the mountain. However, it was not leopards who had eaten them, but Lemba ancestors masquerading as leopards. People did not come here much, as a result, and no one ever dared to go on to the mountain. Even the police.

We were within 200 yards of the cliff-face, following a path which would cross the valley and take us into the low, wooded hills on the other side. On this side of the valley the path led through brittle, dried-out bush, but further away from the mountain were some barren-looking fields.

At one point the path curved towards the cliff to pass underneath a tree. In its shade was standing a tall, handsome man who was startlingly reminiscent of the violinist, Yehudi Menuhin. His skin was light-coloured and his eyes were remarkable: neither blue nor grey, but rather emerald – like the eyes of mariners who have spent their lives in the sun. He was a Lemba, said Tagaruze.

The man clapped his hands in greeting and invited us to rest with him in the shade of the tree. As Tagaruze explained the reasons for my visit, he gave us fruit from the tree – a *meshunah* tree – a dry fruit, fibrous like a rosehip, with the bitter taste of a fresh date. He listened with care and squatted on the ground in front of us. Looking at the desiccated ground in front of him where pieces of twig and *meshunah* fruit were mixed with the grey soil, he said in halting English, 'This is holy soil.' He picked up some dust and let it trickle through his long fingers. 'The whole of the land of the Lemba is holy. The land here', he jerked his thumb over his shoulder towards the great buttress of the mountain, 'is very, very holy. It is forbidden to all except the Lemba people – the Mwenye. Even in the war the Ndebele and Shona fighters knew they must not bring the war here. We are a peaceful people. Our spirit medium – the *svikiro* – told them they should not even bring their guns into our *kraals*. They obeyed her.' All except one group of Ndebele fighters who had planted mines near the villages and had then gone on to the sacred mountain. They lit a bonfire and caroused all night – the sounds were heard in the *kraals*. The following day in one of the many atrocities of the war, they were first tortured and then butchered by the Rhodesian army. Not one of them escaped.

The birds circling above us were eagles – '*shiri ye denga* [birds of heaven],' he said, nodding up at them in a meaningful way. They warn the Lemba of impending danger. It was the *shiri ye denga* which had betrayed the Ndebele fighters. It was the *shiri ye denga* which protected the Lemba now.

138

14

It was late afternoon when I saw the Lemba villages. The dried-out fields and thatch glowed golden in the setting sun. Perched above the expanse of the valley the conical brown mud huts looked somehow like the European domes and battlements you see on mediaeval maps of Africa.

Tagaruze explained that these days political custom in Zimbabwe required that we first pay our respects to the councillor, the local representative of ZANU. Combining in his office the new political and, as a relative of the chief, the old traditional functions, he was a force to be reckoned with. We skirted the village in search of the councillor and walked down towards a broad valley, in whose lowest point a residual moisture had left one or two faint, green patches of land.

The councillor's small *kraal* stood on the edge of the valley. His wife and daughters, stripped to the waist, their skin ruddy in the sunset, were separating wheat from chaff on a copper-coloured earthen threshing yard. The councillor, Dongijena, was working in the fields, and we would find him in the valley. The girls giggled when they caught sight of me. I could understand why. My face was red from the sun and exertion and a red spotted handkerchief, knotted at the corners, covered my head. In this remarkable evening light I must have looked like an intruder from the Red Planet.

We picked our way through the rock-strewn hummocks in the valley. The policeman strode ahead, shouting loudly over the fields for Dongijena, his voice mingling with the rhythmic ringing of the cowbells and the mournful sounds of a nearby owl. But there was no reply.

We walked into the village and entered the fly-blown village bottle shop. There had been a generator here once but it did not seem to be working now. No spare parts, Tagaruze surmised. It meant that the beer would be warm. He suggested that we go next door to the bar where there was sometimes ice in the ice-box. He led the way into an uninviting booth, where I ordered beer for both of us. We sat down at a table; a candle stuck into a rusty tin was shedding a flickering light on mud walls decorated with faded advertisements: Chibuku Beer for Good Cheer, Drink Strong it makes you Strong, Crack a Quart of Lion. At a corner table a dead drunk woman in a 1950s American cocktail dress was resting her head in a pool of vomit. She was a war widow and the village prostitute. I drank my beer and contemplated this drab scene without enthusiasm. As I did so two Lemba dandies swaggered in, perched on stools at the bar and shot me covert glances. One of them was attired in a white suit with enormous lapels. The other, hardly less striking, sported an electric-blue jacket and a boater. The other drinkers were clad in wretched worn-out suits, knitted bonnets and went barefoot. They were all drinking *chibuku* out of plastic bags.

Tagaruze went off to order dinner. Turning his head the white-suited dandy opened his mouth to say something but fell off the stool, fatally damaging his aplomb. 'You want to know about the Lemba?' he asked, picking himself up, and went on to explain that the tribe had come from Arabia via Tanzania, and that indeed his own name, an ancient Lemba name – Tainzana – was proof of this. Sheepishly he looked at me for confirmation. Vaguely mindful of anthropological practice I did not want to approve or disapprove. I simply pointed out that, in fact, Tanzania is a modern name made up from the first syllables of Tanganyika and Zanzibar.

'Black man very bloody ignorant, baas,' he said, with a broad smile. 'But with my friends I'm more interested in business than history.' With that he pulled a pretty handkerchief out of his pocket and, with considerable circumspection, revealed its contents – a few grubby looking stones. 'Emeralds,' he hissed. 'You can have all for five hundred dollars.'

'No thanks,' I said, and was glad to see that the policeman who had just returned did not seem to have noticed anything. He was accompanied by the cook, a very fat Lemba woman, who was carrying plates of *sadza*, a slab of corned beef, and bread. It was too late for cooked meats, she said; this would have to do.

She, too, wanted to put me right about the Lemba: they came from Israel, which was in South Africa, went to Egypt and America, and finally came to Mposi. She was evidently not a woman to brook contradiction, so this time I said nothing.

'Don't listen to her,' growled Tagaruze, 'the women here know nothing. These things are men's secrets. When they meet together to talk about the ancestors and the past, the women are not admitted. The women are allowed to bring the food and the beer and later come to collect the empty plates – that's all. That's the place of women in Africa.'

Some of the men were talking at the bar. They had a secret means of communication, said Tagaruze; they spoke a language called Hiberu, the Shona for Hebrew. But, as he had been stationed in this area for a long time, he was beginning to understand it. They were now discussing, he told me, the propriety of revealing tribal secrets.

A tall man, with a long, shiny forehead, left the group and looked at me over the guttering candle.

'We have never met,' he murmured.

I agreed that this was so.

'My name is Moses. You are welcome in our country,' he said with a soft lilt to his voice. But then, in a sterner tone, he warned me that the Lemba were a secret and dangerous people. They were not to be trifled with. For hundreds of years they had never been defeated. They had their own means of defence – artificial scientific defence he called it – through the age-old method of herbalism.

'During the Matabele wars no one harmed us. Even the Europeans failed to conquer us. We used to make bush fences around our villages, sprinkle that fence with powerful African herbs, and anyone who passed that fence dropped dead.'

He gave me a probing look, as if to discover how I had got through.

'Did I pass that fence today?' I asked.

'You passed that fence. But there is not herbs on it now. That custom is expired. The elderly people who had the secrets has died. Those who has not died has gone along with the missionary what-not.'

The fat woman shuffled in with the key to our room. She told the drinkers to clear out and ordered us to go to bed. On the other side of the yard, in a corrugated iron shack, was a row of small rooms. With some dignity she showed us the washing facilities, demanded payment in advance and bade us good-night. Tagaruze went out, 'on patrol', he said, and, covering myself with a dirty blanket, I fell into a sound sleep. Some time later I was woken by something on my stomach. I leapt out of bed and saw an animal scurrying across the floor. I was able to identify it later as *Aethomys Chrysophilus*, a variety of African rat. Afterwards, I could not sleep. I went outside and in the distance saw Tagaruze sitting under a tree, talking with the man in the white suit.

I went back to my room, smoked a cigarette and waited for dawn.

As soon as the sun rose, I sat myself at a plastic table in a sort of eating room attached to the bottle shop and wrote up my journal. It was 6.30 and already it was stiflingly hot. During the night, Tagaruze had recruited some Lemba to patrol the approaches to the village. He was now sleeping. The open window near where I sat had a ledge which was providing support for the chins of half-a-dozen Lemba youths who had already started indulging what appeared to be their major interest – drinking maize beer. They were gazing at my literary activity with interest. Beyond their heads, in the village square, the women were working: some were turning maize cobs on a threshing floor, allowing them to dry in the sun; others were carrying water in oil drums from the borehole; another group was carrying maize in baskets to the village miller. With meticulous care, the children were sweeping the earth between the huts. Through this Bruegelesque scene strode the short erect figure of a man who proved to be Dongijena, the councillor.

'Greetings, brother,' he said, sitting down at my table.

'Good morning, councillor.'

'What to do, comrade?' he continued. 'What to do?'

The problem was that Dongijena, who, as well as councillor, was also the headmaster of the village school, had recently been hoist with his own petard. In order to avoid military service in the civil war, he had exaggerated his age. Now, although he was only forty-three, the government records showed him to be sixty. Consequently, the Ministry of Education was demanding his immediate retirement. Dongijena did not have a birth certificate, so what to do?

After a number of digressions, he turned his attention to me and, not without protracted discussion of his own political views, gave his grudging consent to my presence in his area.

At Mathiva's suggestion I had brought with me from South Africa a white cotton shirt as a present for Chief Mposi. Dongijena thought that the gift could well be supplemented with a number of bottles of Bols brandy from the bar and with something for the chief to eat. I bought up the bar's stock of brandy and went in search of food.

In the square in front of the bar a group of women sat cross-legged in the shade of a tree. They had small, neat pyramids of dusty oranges, spring onions and shrivelled lemons. Five women sat in front of five identical piles of tomatoes. I took two from each of them, apparently to everyone's satisfaction, and wrapped them up in my handkerchief. Dongijena and Tagaruze were waiting for me in the bar. The councillor had been thinking over my request to study the Lemba. The matter was not as simple as it had at first seemed.

'You understand, comrade, I am the representative of ZANU, but not even ZANU can give the green light in questions of tradition. That is a problem for the chief. In the past, the chief would not talk about such things. In the past *no one* talked about such things.'

Another man had joined us: Hamandishu, a teacher and expert joiner, who had spent his youth in Natal.

'You cannot stop the winds of change,' he said. 'We did not believe, really, in the possibility of change during the war, but it happened. It is not the same country it was. More changes will come.'

'Yes, these days perhaps,' conceded the councillor, 'the comrade chief has the responsibility to let his people know where they come from and what they are. But it is difficult, very difficult.'

Sevias, Chief Mposi's oldest son by the first of his five wives, arrived. The old man sat down with us, clapping his hands and murmuring, '*Mushavi, Mushavi.*' His every movement suggested diffidence, but when he began to talk it was with a quiet authority.

'The Lemba are Jews and the Lemba are blacks,' he said. 'The other tribes have become white men of black colour. We have not assimilated. We are Jews and we are blacks. We slaughter our animals according to the law.'

The men clapped their hands and chanted, '*Mushavi, Mushavi.*'

'If a man is not circumcised, he cannot slaughter.'

'*Mushavi, Mushavi,*' they repeated.

'We do not eat the pig, the lion or the cat.'

'*Mushavi, Mushavi.*'

'Our totem is the *zhou* – the elephant, the holiest of the animals. Like the lion was the totem of the Jews in the Bible – the Lion of Judah.'

The councillor held up his hand. Nothing more could be discussed without the chief, who could not receive me immediately because he was ill. An appointment must be made, in the proper way.

'There is no hurry,' he proclaimed, his back straight, chin raised. 'We are after information, not time.'

But Hamandishu still wanted to talk. The Tovakare clan, he said, were the builders of the stone city of Great Zimbabwe.

'I saw those ruins,' he said. 'I doubted the tradition, but there is something in the blood to show you. In the same way, the descendants of hunters are still good at snaring animals. When I came back here to settle down, after my years of work in South Africa, I found myself building everything in stone like our forefathers; no one ever taught me how. We have not much tradition left – we are groaning under the weight of the people among whom we live' – both Tagaruze and the councillor looked uneasy at this – 'but sometimes we surface.'

This mildly seditious comment was enough for Dongijena.

'End of meeting, comrades,' he said, with an abrupt gesture and, pulling me up by the elbow, led the way out of the bar into the dazzling glare of the village square.

In the thin strip of shade offered by the building, half-a-dozen Lemba lay slumped together, empty bags of *chibuku* at their feet, swarms of flies on their faces and feet. As we crossed the square, other drunk men staggered across our path, coming too close and then lurching off, their faces vacant. If they all drink like this, I worried to myself, they'll have no memory of what they did last week, let alone any tribal traditions going back centuries. Not for the first time I wondered if my research into the Lemba could not be better conducted in the cool reading-room of some London library. In this age, how much can one learn by travelling? After all, even those traditions to which the Lemba did refer may well have been contaminated during the colonial period. Somewhat uneasily I thought of a senior colleague of mine who was fond of remarking that no self-respecting orientalist need ever travel further east than Leipzig, a university town noted for its library.

Dongijena led the way to his *kraal*, where his wife had cooked a midday meal. Full of pride, he showed me the stone grain bins behind his living huts, which were either full of produce or had vertical marks on the side indicating how many bags of cob corn had already been sold, one stroke for every ten bags. We went into a cool, dark hut to eat. After *sadza*, goat in peanut sauce and a succulent roast rabbit, a daughter, one of the girls we had seen threshing, brought us an enamel bowl of water, kneeling in front of each of us with head bowed. She was another war widow. Her husband and her four children had been killed on the banks of the Limpopo near Beit Bridge.

'By the whites?'

'No, by ZANU forces,' said Tagaruze, looking embarrassed. 'The whole family had a dispute with ZANU. They shot the rest down, but the girl escaped.'

'Were they collaborators?'

'Something like that.'

'A harsh punishment,' I said.

Tagaruze shrugged his broad shoulders and stared straight in front of him. The councillor contemplated the company and said nothing. He was taking no more chances.

15

Chief Mposi was dying. Everyone said it was good that I had come now and not later. His *kraal* lay a few miles away, up in the hills. We walked – Sevias, Dongijena, Tagaruze and I – in the half light of dusk and then in complete darkness. The only sounds were the scuffling noises of animals in the bush and the distant howl of jackals. As we arrived at the village the councillor took me through his version of tribal protocol: he would do most of the talking – and I would speak only when spoken to. This visit was to deliver my presents: any other matter would have to wait.

The village was lit by the glimmer of firelight which shone from the openings of huts, but the chief's hut was in darkness. One of his wives and a grown-up son were sitting in front of it. Deep groans came from inside. The woman lit a candle and urged us to enter. The chief was lying on the floor, covered in blankets, his face grey with pain. There was the stink of sickness in the hut. A younger wife brought us chairs, while the first wife attempted to rouse the chief. I protested that, as he was so ill, he really should be allowed to sleep.

'It is our custom that he gets up to receive his gifts,' said Dongijena.

'And it is our custom not to disturb the sick,' I said, rising to my feet.

One of the chief's sons lolled against the doorpost blocking my way. 'Chief is bit sick,' he sneered, 'but life goes on. We must not worry, be happy. Drink and be happy.' He jigged around as if to some pop group, snapping his fingers.

Again the chief groaned. I left my gifts next to the chief's bed, pushed the son aside with more force than was necessary, and left the hut.

'Sorry about the boy, *Mushavi*,' Sevias said later, 'he was drunk. Not a good boy. You made a great honour to chief by leaving your gifts and letting him sleep. I am sure he will make big honour to you.' From that evening all the Lemba called me *Mushavi* without fail.

We walked along a dusty track to Sevias's small village a few miles further on. Sevias offered me a hut for the duration of my stay: it was a simple affair, round and thatched; the walls were made from mud bricks and between the top of the wall and the thatch was a slight gap, to allow the smoke to get out and the breeze to come in. These people were obviously very poor. There was no furniture except for a mattress, but the floor was clean and swept. I asked Sevias if I could repay him somehow for his hospitality.

'In the city, in Masvingo,' he said, 'there are shops where you pay to sleep. This is not a shop. You do not pay. This is your house.'

Sevias's wife, known only as Mama, had prepared food – *sadza* and wild spinach – which we ate around a table in front of my hut. Sevias was renowned in the surrounding country as a healer. He talked about plant and animal extracts and the great care required in their use. To illustrate his point he took me to a large tree whose outline I could pick out against the brilliant starlight – it was a *mushava* tree covered by a luxuriant mistletoe. Sevias snapped off a twig and explained that normally the berries of the mistletoe were poisonous and were not to be used. However, the fruits of the *mushava* were edible, and therefore, a parasite mistletoe growing on a *mushava* would also produce useful fruit. But to use the wrong mistletoe would be fatal. He offered me one to try. Tagaruze took a handful and chewed them throughout the evening.

As we sat in the darkness under the tree, Sevias asked me about my job in England. I told him I taught in a university.

'A university is like a big, not religious church?' he asked.

'Yes, pretty much.'

'And lecturing is like preaching?'

'Yes, more or less.'

'And you are like a bishop?'

'No. More like an ordinary priest.'

'You not a big man?'

'No, not at all.'

'*Mushavi, Mushavi,*' he intoned. The others clapped and gazed at me with sympathy. Darana, Sevias's brother, had joined us.

'You teach Hebrew?' asked Darana. 'The Lemba know Hebrew too. It's called Hiberu – this is our secret language. But nowadays few people speak it. Even when I was a boy this language – which is a sort of Egyptian – had almost disappeared. But some people spoke it. Probably when Solomon, the old man, left Sena, he learned Egyptian in Egypt. Our language is really Egyptian, I think. The Israelites stayed in Egypt for some time and they picked this language up. Our language is Egyptian, a kind of Arab language, but we are the men of Sena. In fact,' he continued, beaming, 'when I fought the Rhodesians all those years, I was fighting for my mother country. But my real mother country is Sena.'

'You are writing a book?' asked Sevias.

'Yes.'

'Is it?'

'Yes,' I repeated, smiling.

'Only one?'

'Well, you know, one at a time.'

'So only one man can read it?'

'No. They make many books. Lots of people can read it.'

'So you are writing many books!'

'Yes, in that sense.'

'*Mushavi*?'

'Yes.'

'*We* once wrote a book. Anyway, we once had a book, but it was lost long ago. We knew how to read and write long before the white men came here. We used to read and write Hiberu . . .'

'How did you write in the old days? On what? And what do you know of this book?'

'The book was the Bible,' said Sevias, 'and we used to write on leather and on stone.'

Many Lemba talk of their lost book, but the suggestion that they wrote on leather and stone, and in Hebrew, I only heard from Sevias. If the Lemba had ever had any knowledge of Hebrew, there is no trace of it. The language which some of them call Hiberu is, in fact, an old form of Karanga, a Bantu language close to Shona. Within this language there are a number of Semitic words including some of the tribal names which seem to derive from Arabic, although some could perhaps derive from Hebrew. Every time I asked for concrete examples of Hiberu, my informant, no matter how venerable he was, would refer me to someone older and wiser.

The very fact that they call Hebrew Hiberu suggests that the name came from the English word 'Hebrew' (and not from Hebrew *ivrit* or Arabic *ibri*) and probably, therefore, from missionary sources. More to the point, there is no trace of any written language in Southern or Central Africa. There are a couple of references to what might have been an inscription at Great Zimbabwe and that is all. However, the question of this inscription is intriguing.

In the sixteenth century, the Portuguese historian João de Barros noted that certain Arab merchants had visited the African interior and the ruins of Great Zimbabwe, the stone city which the Lemba claim to have built. Above the doorway of the most imposing of the structures they saw an inscription in a script which they could not decipher.

In 1721, a letter from the governor of Goa to Antonio Rodrigues da Costa makes further mention of the inscription:

> In the court of the Monomotapa, there is a tower or a building of cut stone which appears not to be the work of the black people of the country but of some powerful, political nation like the Greeks, Romans, Persians, Egyptians or Hebrews, and they say that this tower or building is called by the blacks Simbaboe, and inside there is an inscription in unknown letters. And they say there are good reasons to believe that this land is the same as Ophir and that Solomon sent his fleets here ... and this matter could be resolved if the matter of the inscription could be determined – because no one can read it. If it were in Greek, Persian or Hebrew, it would be necessary to make a copy in wax or in some other substance which preserves letters or numbers. The inscription would have to be well cleaned too ...

It is generally thought that these and other accounts are confused references to the chevron pattern which adorns one of the walls of Great Zimbabwe. In the 1950s, however, a South African of right-wing inclination, the late Dr W. Punt, revealed that he had in his possession documents proving that an inscription on stone had once existed at Great Zimbabwe. This stone had been removed by a Boer hunter who allegedly found the ruined city in the 1860s. Forced to abandon the stone because of its weight, the hunter none the less described the inscription in some detail. The Boer's notes were allegedly in the hands of Punt in the 1950s, but I have been unable to discover more. I asked Sevias if he had ever heard of such an inscription, but he said nothing. Perhaps he thought I was sceptical about the Lemba's book. In any event, whenever I brought the subject up, and I tried many times, he would change the topic of conversation. And Sevias was a master of evasion.

The other subject of conversation that night was the infamous terrorist Morgan: there had been another hideous massacre, this time of blacks, somewhere to the south of the Lemba villages, and the gunmen were rumoured to be coming this way. Sevias with enviable *sang froid* enumerated their recent atrocities. When I showed signs of anxiety, he laughed.

'That Morgan is too much afraid of Lemba magic to dare to come near this place. Do not be afraid, *Mushavi*.'

None the less, that night Tagaruze sat on the threshold of the hut, gun in hand. Before I went to sleep I asked him who the man in white was that I had seen him speaking to the previous night.

'He works for us. He's an informer. He told me he tried to sell you emeralds. He was just trying you out, boss's orders. Nothing to worry about.'

I woke at 4.30. I had heard someone, or something, walking around and what I took to be voices beyond the *kraal*. Tagaruze was not there. Now, in addition, I thought I could hear muted singing, the chatter of women and children, and the crowing of a cockerel – not sounds to be afraid of, I decided, as I drifted in and out of sleep. I was woken up fully by Sevias, who was shaking my shoulder.

'*Mushavi*,' he whispered. 'I want to make an honour for you.'

Wondering what he was proposing, I followed him to an area behind the domestic huts, that part of the village which in Shona society is always reserved for private or ritual activity. It was cold and there was the good smell of dung smoke in the air.

A chicken bound with strips of wet bark lay on its side in a hollow next to a tree. Sevias picked it up and put it in my hands. 'This is the honour,' he said and, taking the chicken, cut its throat, muttering words under his breath as he did so. I thanked him and, as it was still more or less dark, returned to bed. But the singing that I had heard earlier had become louder; it was now obviously coming from within the *kraal*.

I went out of the hut and saw the youth I had met the evening before, the chief's son. He had a white sheet draped around his shoulders and was leading a large, fat-tailed ram. He beamed joyfully at me, and the women and children who were following him clapped their hands and broke into another song.

'The chief is sending you the big honour,' said Sevias, smiling a patient smile, rubbing his hands together in anticipation. 'This ram is a very dear animal to us,' he said. The big honour meant that I was a quiet, respectable, he searched for the word, gentleman.

Leading the ram to a boulder which shone in the first rays of sun, he tied its feet with bark strips and laid it down on the rock.

I stood with my back to the *mushava* tree and watched as the knife fell on the ram's throat and its life gurgled away. Sevias removed the windpipe and muttered a prayer over the animal – a prayer which might help to determine the tribe's origins. But I could not hear what he said, nor was I meant to. Sevias and his brother Darana, who lived in the same *kraal*, skinned the ram and took the carcass off to the cooking-hut. As soon as the first cut was made, the rock was awash with blood. The *kraal* chickens and a multitude of chicks darted forward, pecking at the thick liquid; within seconds a file of ants was plying back and forth between the rock and the roots of the *mushava*. Nothing was wasted; the skin was scraped clean and hung up to dry, the curved horns were put aside for later unspecified use and the liver, grilled over the fire, was served up for breakfast.

Indeed, nothing was wasted here at all. For the second-hand western clothes that finished up in the *kraal* it was the end of the road. When they could be worn no more, they became underclothes or cleaning rags. When the rags fell apart, the boys compacted them with string into footballs. Old tyres, cut up, became sandals and handles for buckets. There was no litter anywhere. The countryside around the *kraal* was like the world's best-kept park – except for the drought, which had balded the grassland and turned it to dust.

In the past, Sevias told me over breakfast, animal sacrifice, performed very much like his slaughtering of the ram, had been a frequent event among the Lemba. If you were building a new grain bin, for instance, you would sacrifice a sheep or a goat. For bigger festivals you would sacrifice a black bull, or sometimes a black goat. You used a special knife covered with medicine. You had to be very careful to ensure that there were no white spots or patches on a sacrificial animal. You would wash the goat from head to foot and make sure it was free of blemishes. If you could not find a completely black animal and the feast was upon you, then you would smear some dung into the white patch and hope for the best. 'But everyone knew the spots were really there,' he added gloomily.

After breakfast Sevias busied himself collecting waxy green mistletoe berries, taking care to select firm, undamaged fruit which he would prepare later for his sick father, the chief. Sevias told me that the Lemba had always understood the secret properties of herbs and that their trade in herbs and medicines took them throughout Southern Africa. Lemba doctors were so highly esteemed that they served in the *kraals* of non-Lemba chiefs too. Circumcision doctors attended to youths from other tribes and Lemba medicine-men-of-war had a great reputation in the magic arts of doctoring troops before battle. The Sadiki clan traditionally provided the medicine-men-of-war; the Hamisi clan had a special knowledge of fertility medicine. Such was the Lemba's standing with other tribes that the Shona word for doctor – *chiremba* – seems to refer to them. Sevias and the other elders were convinced that the Lemba had known more about herbal medicine than any other tribe in the whole of Africa. As Sevias talked, I was reminded of a passage in the journal of the missionary Robert Moffat which described a Lemba doctor – perhaps a medicine-man-of-war – at the court of Mzilikazi, the famous Ndebele paramount chief in the 1850s: 'He is one of the finest looking men I have seen among the natives. His head and face would do for Melanchton. He was among the Matabele practising as a doctor when his people came and took cattle from Moselkatse which rendered it dangerous for him to return.'

Long before, in the middle of the sixteenth century, a Portuguese trader reported that throughout the lands of the Monomotapa Moorish *ngangas* were the principal witchdoctors. It is almost certain that these were the ancestors of the Lemba.

But, notwithstanding his tribe's medical credentials and his own knowledge of herbal medicine, Sevias was anxious to know if I had anything in the way of conventional medicine. Medicine would be a fine gift in exchange for the ram. The chief was very, very ill, Sevias stressed. He was dying of tuberculosis, but, despite this, he would receive me later that day.

Tagaruze returned later in the morning. He had located a group of the army's Special Tactics Unit – an anti-terrorist group – which was hot on the heels of Morgan. Using their field telephone he had arranged for the Hertz Ford to be repaired and delivered to Chief Mposi's *kraal*. He also came with instructions from his commanding officer that we were not to stray from the Mposi villages. In view of the deteriorating security situation, police reinforcements were being sent in from Mberengwe.

At noon Sevias, Dongijena and Tagaruze led me back across the dusty bush to Mposi's *kraal*. The whole area was criss-crossed by dried-out streams and rivers: that was the reason the Lemba had settled here in the first place, said Sevias; they needed the water for their purification rituals. For a while we followed a dried-out river-bed. It had been a good river – there had been water even in the driest summers – but now it had slept for four years. We crossed a stone ford and stopped for a moment in the shade of a dead *meshunah* tree; in its branches was an unkempt coracle of black twigs – the nest of a fish eagle, said Tagaruze. When it comes back, murmured Sevias, the good days will have returned. As it was, the drought had taken its toll: the boreholes were almost dry, the earth was turning to powder, and most of the animals had been eaten or had died. The ram which had been slaughtered in my honour was the last of the chief's great flock. In the old days they would have sacrificed a black bull for rain – the black symbolised rain clouds – but they had all gone. The only things which carried on growing, said the councillor, were the ant-hills.

From the top of a small hill we could see the towering mass of Dumghe. I said I would like to visit the mountain. A white man, a missionary called Othenius, had once, sixty years before, nursed a similar ambition, said Sevias. He had been repeatedly warned by the Lemba that were he even to lay a foot on the mountain he would be put to death. None the less he persisted and one night he was found on the mountain by a group of elders returning from an initiation ceremony. What could they do? He was a very old man, a saintly man. It would not really have been right to kill him, as custom demanded. So they decided to circumcise him and turn him into a Lemba. They did it there and then.

'He was very interested in Lemba people anyway,' said Sevias, with a wry smile of apology. 'Othenius was almost a Lemba already. He wrote a book about us, about our ceremonies, but when he died his wife burnt the book and kept our secrets.'

'Is it possible, then, for a man to become a Lemba by circumcision?'

'Not really,' said Sevias, 'but for him we made an exception. You can be a Lemba by birth or, in the case of a woman, by marriage. In the past men were not allowed to marry into the tribe. And it was nearly impossible for women to become Lemba.'

'Do you know how it was done?' asked the councillor, who had paused by a great crumbling ant-hill at the side of the path.

'Yes,' I said, 'I have read that the woman had to crawl through a hole in an ant-hill.'

'That's right,' he said, scratching a hole in the ant-hill with his fingers. 'The idea was that the ants sting and suck off all the pig blood that this non-Lemba woman has eaten in her life.' A large ant crawled on to his fingers and was crushed for its pains. 'But that was not all. A fire would be lit on top of her which could burn the contamination, and then, just before she was roasted, they pushed off the branches and threw her into the river to get purified.'

'A baptism by fire,' said Sevias.

In some places, he said, another custom was followed: when a woman from another tribe was being admitted as a Lemba, an ox would be slaughtered and some of its meat, mixed with an emetic herb, would be given to the woman. After she had vomited, the impurities in her were deemed to have been removed. She was then taken behind one of the huts, where a hole had been made in the wall. She put her head through the hole and it was shaved. She then crawled through the hole and thus became a Lemba. Once she had undergone this ritual, she was never allowed to return to her native village unless accompanied by a Lemba lest she be tempted to eat forbidden foods.

'And if a woman died in childbirth, her body was taken out through a hole in the side of the hut,' I said. 'Is there a connection?'

'Yes,' said Sevias. 'If a woman died in this way, the child nearly always died too. The woman exists to bring Lemba into the world. If she is not successful, she is not a Lemba. When they take her through the hole in the hut, it means she joins the *wasenzhi*.'

'I don't suppose many women wanted to become Lemba if they had to go through so much to become one.'

'Not at all,' said the councillor, his chin raised proudly. 'Lemba men were the best husbands. We were much richer than the others. We were much cleverer than the others. We were whiter than the others and we were much more handsome.' The men all laughed and Tagaruze joined in.

We followed a goat track down the side of a hill. Once we passed the ruins of an ancient stone-built settlement. The coursing of the evenly shaped stones was perfect. It looked as though it might have been a very small fort. Sevias was sure that long ago it had been a Lemba chief's house, or perhaps a temple. Further down the track we passed a couple of small Lemba villages; many of the huts were painted in white and ochre patterns, smoke rose in lazy spirals from the cooking-huts, but no one appeared. The children were in school, and all able-bodied adults were engaged in building a road as part of the Government's 'Food for Work' programme.

The chief's *kraal* was situated on a flat, grassy plateau surrounded by wooded hills. The fields around the village were still green, just.

The chief's reception hut was empty; the cow-dung floor was swept clean; the walls were decorated with drawings of flowers growing out of rectangular boxes; clusters of sweet millet cobs hung from the blackened rafters to be used as next year's seeds. A small smoking fire kept insects away from the cobs, and flies away from us.

The chief hobbled in, supported by two of his wives. He sat on a low stool, black and polished with age and use, and was given a knobkerrie to lean on. He was wearing outrageously dirty grey trousers and an orange sweater. His feet were bare, swollen and shiny with age. He thanked me for my gifts, I thanked him for his, and for his son's hospitality. He told me that he had given me a ram because I had left my house to come to his. There was a pause. I murmured that my house in London was the chief's house. He did not think that he would ever come to my house, he said, but he had once been to London as part of a delegation of chiefs in Rhodesian times.

'When I tell people in Harare what to give me to eat, they do not understand. In England they understood Jews. In London I said, "Me Jew. No meat; me fish." In the old, old days Lemba eat just fish.' The chief smiled at his reminiscence, but, falling back into the present, groaned in pain. Did I have anything for TB?

All I had was a box of vitamins, which I handed to him. At the same time I produced the letter from Mathiva. The councillor took it from my hand, read it aloud in English and then translated it, for the chief's benefit, into Shona. The chief objected to this and started berating him: tradition, he said, demanded that hospitality precede business. The translating of Mathiva's letter constituted business and was an infringement of the chief's prerogative. Sevias, with some tact, pointed out that their guest would certainly be hungry and thirsty and that the argument could be finished later. The chief held up one hand and beat upon the floor with his stick. His wives returned, bearing a calabash of beer and a large aluminium dish covered with a cloth. The younger wife removed the cloth and, kneeling in front of me, offered a rounded pile of large, fried ants. Sevias told me that to catch them you make a sort of raffia tunnel, one end of which is connected to the ant-hill, the other end to a bowl of water. When the ants try to fly away, they fall into the water.

'Not as good as soldier ants,' said Sevias, munching away. 'The women catch those by putting a lighted candle in a special sort of bowl. Or you can get them by just pushing a piece of stick into an anthill: pull it out quickly and you can eat them at once. No need to cook.'

'The earth under these ant-hills is good,' said the councillor. 'The women, particularly, like to eat it as it is rich in iron.'

The women were sent to bring me some ant soil, which they gave me wrapped in a piece of paper. The ants were good, something like small fried shrimps.

Sevias started to talk. He explained my purpose in coming to see the chief and produced from his bag *The Thirteenth Gate* which I had loaned him. The chief showed great interest in the photographs and in the chapter devoted to the Lemba, which he could not read. He begged me for a copy of the book and I promised to let him have one before I left.

'This story of ours is not to do with politics,' he said, glancing at the councillor, 'it is to do with history. It is not to do with political parties, it is to do with our people's traditions. We must all bury our differences and contribute what we know to recover this history. Sometimes knowledge dies with a people. I have heard that in Egypt there are buildings which were built thousands of years ago which could not be built today. They have forgotten the knowledge.

'The same is true here,' he continued. 'We built Great Zimbabwe. Our ancestor, Ali Tovakare, built a very tall tower there. But we could not do it now. We have forgotten. But we must not forget any more.' Again the chief banged his stick on the floor. This time there was a long silence before he spoke again.

'We came from Sena,' he said. 'We crossed Pusela, we came through Kenya, Tanzania and from there to Mozambique. We came to Zimbabwe. Some stayed near Zimbabwe, some went to Veja.'

'Where is Veja?'

'That is South Africa,' explained the councillor.

'We are Israelites,' said the chief.

'Are you sure?'

'Yes. We came from Sena.'

'When did you come from Sena?'

'I cannot remember. It was long before I was born.'

'Would it be possible', I asked, 'for you to tell me the names of the ancestors, starting with the oldest?'

Tagaruze translated my request. There was a pause, followed by an outburst from Dongijena, directed at the policeman.

'He is a local man from Gutu,' explained Dongijena. 'If he knows our secrets, the whole of Gutu will know them.' In addition, he argued, the chief did not have the right to reveal tribal secrets such as the names of the ancestors, or the route the ancestors took, or the words which were used in the ritual. Only the people had the right to reveal these secrets.

'You can write a history if you like,' he continued, 'but you cannot be given tribal secrets. Because only the people has the right authority to let you have those secrets. And who is the people?'

There was silence. Then the chief spoke, only occasionally raising his gaze from the dirt floor.

'How was the world created?' he asked me.

'I am not at all sure,' I replied with a smile.

'We have often wondered about this. When the missionaries came – when my grandfather was chief – they told us about the creation in six days. But we were sure it must have taken longer than that.'

There was a lot of difficulty over this question, continued the chief, nodding his head. His grandfather solved the problem by calling an assembly of the ten tribes of the Lemba.

'I have never heard this,' muttered the councillor.

'It was long ago. It has never been done since. I now decide that we shall have a meeting of the tribes to decide which secrets can be put into our history, and which secrets must be left out. But I also decide that you', he pointed at Tagaruze, 'cannot be the translator at that meeting, or at any meeting where secrets are revealed. We will have our own translator, one who is a circumcised, initiated Lemba. And you must do your job – guard the Englishman.'

Everyone laughed except Tagaruze. He had become deeply interested in the Lemba and had already formed decided views. So much so that often, I noticed, he only translated what he wanted me to hear. In addition, in his spare time, he was preparing himself for a Cambridge 'O' level in Religious Studies, and any discussion of Jews fascinated him. Again the chief banged his knobkerrie on the floor. His older wife, an evil-looking woman with a perpetual scowl, appeared and was told to fetch the chief's messenger. He would instruct him to inform the tribes that the meeting – the first for 100 years – would be held in two weeks' time.

As we prepared to leave, Chief Mposi said, 'There have been many changes in the world. Once we were the most powerful nation in Africa. We were the richest people. We had gold, we had cities. If we had a meeting like this, we were dressed in white cotton robes. The other tribes used to call us "the gods who wear clothes". We dressed in white when the *wasenzhi* were naked. In the past we were not like this,' he continued, pointing at the rags and tatters in which he and his companions were clad. 'But even though the world has changed, we are still Mposi, we are still Lemba, we are still Mwenye. We do not dress like the old Mwenye, but we are still "the gods who wear clothes".'

I asked him to tell me more about the clothes of the Lemba, but neither he nor the other elders knew more than this. The oral tradition has now dried up and we have to rely on earlier accounts.

16

When white settlers first arrived in Vendaland and Mashonaland, the black population wore little more than leather breechclouts. In this respect the Lemba were no different. In 1931, Jacques was told by a Lemba informant that in the nineteenth century the men had worn a duiker skin passed between the legs and tied around the loins: it was called *silovelo* or *mabenga*. Lemba women wore an apron, usually made of buffalo hide, below a long skirt of ox hide or goatskin. 'It is clear', Jacques concluded, 'that a hundred years ago the Lemba wore no clothes peculiar to themselves and distinct from that of the surrounding Bantu population.' The grandson of Jacques's informant, M. N. Mphelo, repeated the same tradition a few years later, adding the information that in cold weather a soft tanned calf's hide was worn as a sort of cloak.

This had not always been the case and was not, indeed, the case a hundred years before Jacques. While Robert Moffat was at the court of the Ndebele chief Mzilikazi in the 1850s, he got to know the Lemba who had come to the royal *kraal* to sell his medical wares and to practise his profession. He and the Lemba who were with him wore 'a good deal of blue check and printed linen'. Similarly, in 1894, the German missionary Schlomann, who was working in the northern Transvaal, wrote:

They used to wear white robes . . . an old Lemba told me that in the past . . . they celebrated a great feast. On this day no one was allowed to prepare food or partake of it. Warriors searched the various villages to ensure that no fires were burning in the cooking-huts. Whoever transgressed the laws of the fast was punished with the greatest severity. When the king called from the capital city, they all hurried there and the meeting-place was soon filled with people. In the middle stood the chief with his entourage dressed in flowing white robes . . .

This tradition is supported by others. In 1937, Van Warmelo, who relied upon elderly Lemba for his information, wrote: 'The men used to wear a long cotton upper garment (*khanzu*) as found along the east coast.' By the 1930s, as we have seen, this custom had completely died out.

Traditionally in the plateau areas of South-East Africa only nobles and their families were allowed to wear cloth. In earlier times the same practice was followed. Peter Garlake, formerly Senior Inspector of the Historical Monuments Commission of Southern Rhodesia and author of *Great Zimbabwe* (London, 1973), writes of the court of the Monomotapa:

Protocol was unostentatious and the Mwene Mutapa [Monomotapa], as befitted a traditional religious figure, dressed simply in cotton cloth grown and woven in his kingdom. His immediate circle, however, displayed the wealth of the kingdom in skirts and cloaks of imported silks and cotton, often embroidered with gold thread and numerous bracelets of fine gold or copper wire. Such luxury set this group far above the general populace who were still completely dependent on subsistence agriculture for their living, had little interest in mining or trade, and could afford to wear no more than small aprons of bark cloth or animal skins.

The fact that the Lemba once wore white cotton garments and considerable amounts of copper jewellery supports their claim that they had been an elite group within African society.

The back-breaking and dangerous tasks of mining and elephant hunting had been undertaken to satisfy the desire of the interior for foreign cloth and beads: gold and ivory were exchanged for them. As well as imported cloth, locally produced material was also available in the interior. But the technique of cloth production was so cumbersome and the cost in human labour so great that it was usually considered worthwhile to mine gold and hunt for ivory in order to be able to obtain in exchange ready-made Indian cotton cloth from the coast. The reason that the Monomotapa preferred to wear the local product might have had more to do with its high cost than with the humility suggested by Garlake. Cloth was thus one of the essential items in the trade between the interior and the Indian Ocean. Writing around 1516, the Portuguese Duarte Barbosa noted:

> The manner of their trade was that they came in little vessels, which they call zambucos, from the kingdoms of Kilwa, Mombasa, and Melinde, bringing much cotton cloth, some white and blue, some of silk, and many grey and purple and yellow beads, which came to the said kingdoms in other larger ships from the great kingdom of Cambaya ... the Moors of Sofala kept this merchandise and sold it afterwards to the heathens of the kingdom of Benomotapa, who came there laden with gold, which they gave in exchange for the said cloth, without weighing, in such quantity that they commonly gain a hundred to one. These Moors also collect a large quantity of ivory which is found about Sofala, which they likewise sell for the kingdom of Cambaya.

The Lemba, who even today have an atavistic tendency to dandyism, must once have looked and dressed very much like the people Vasco da Gama encountered when he discovered the Zambezi, the River of Good Signs, in 1498. The fifth canto of the *Lusiads* of Luis de Camoens (1572) contains a description of these people who were perhaps ancestors of the Lemba:

> They too were Negroes, but we quickly found
> In touch with other folk more civilised.
> While in their speech we caught a different sound
> Some words of Arabic we recognised.
> About their handsome heads they lightly bound
> Turbans of fine white cotton which they prized.
> About their waists (to modesty a due)
> They wrapped a length of cotton tinted blue.

In the past the Lemba no doubt obtained most of the cloth they wore from the coast. But they had probably been producers too. At the beginning of the century there were Lemba in Mashonaland who were weaving wild cotton and the fibrous bark of the baobab tree probably to make small skirts such as the ones worn by Lemba officiating at funerals in Venda at about the same time. Perhaps by then the traditional trade routes to the coast no longer existed; perhaps home-spun cloth had some particular significance, as it may have had for the Monomotapa. We do not know. The decline in the wearing of cotton clothes was perhaps connected with the decline in gold mining during and after the *mfecane*. Style might have had something to do with it too: we know that after the Ndebele invasion, a Ndebele leather skirt was often adopted by the Lemba – and might well have provided valuable social camouflage.

The name of the traditional Lemba cotton garment has

been preserved: *chilemba*. I had first heard it from Selinah
Munuonde, the beautiful Lemba girl in Soweto. The garment
she had worn was a sort of cloak of bright modern design,
but the name is ancient. It is still known on the east coast of
Africa. In Swahili it means turban, or the gift a man gives his
bride to buy fine clothes. The word Lemba probably means,
therefore, those who wear turbans. As the Rain Queen had
put it, 'those whose heads are wrapped in clouds'.

17

A tin bowl half full of tepid, muddy water was waiting in my hut. A little girl arrived carrying a cup of hot water, which she poured into the bowl taking care not to spill a drop. All the water in the *kraal* was carried by the girls from the borehole a mile away. It was only towards the end of my stay when the Ford finally turned up that I was able to help them with this back-breaking task. The little girl was joined by one of her sisters, a handsome full-breasted sixteen year old, who kneeled in front of me and presented me with a towel smelling of carbolic soap. Then she left, giving me a shy smile. It was extraordinary that even when there was water for nothing else, there was always water for ritual washing before and after meals. After washing, the dirty water was used to irrigate the small garden protected by barbed wire, old doors and netting, where Sevias was growing maize cobs and round, white cabbages.

That evening Mama served up the ram for dinner. It was not the great dripping roast I had been looking forward to all day, with guests from other *kraals* and tribal music and dancing. These days meat of any sort was a rare treat and had to be used sparingly. Mama had made a small, fatty stew, an *usavi* of wild herbs and *sadza*. A jug of brownish water stood on the table. I ate with Sevias, Darana and Tagaruze. After our meal we walked over to a small, rocky outcrop beside the village. We smoked cigarettes and looked up at the sky: the band of stars overhead was like a lunar rainbow. On the way we passed the cooking-hut. Glancing inside I saw twenty or so faces smudged with the russet reflection of the fire, in a circle around the pot, eating in silent exaltation. 'They are feeding on the big honour,' said Sevias. 'They rarely eat meat, they thank you.' In fact, the big honour was to feed us all, the whole *kraal* for the next three weeks.

Everyday the councillor came to Sevias's *kraal*. Despite his initial misgivings, the Lemba's cultural heritage had now fired his imagination. While I was working on my book in England, he announced, he would organise the building of a hotel, a museum and a proper road to attract tourists to the area. As he would no longer be a teacher because of the difficulties he had had with the Ministry, he would have the time for it. He would build an emporium, the Black Jews' Bazaar he would call it, where souvenirs and Lemba artefacts could be sold. For my part, I would have to write a guide-book in various European languages which could also be sold. In addition, I would be responsible for the raising of funds for these projects. Rich English Jews, he thought, would be interested. The more he talked, the wilder his schemes became. I felt I was not the only one to be uneasy in his company.

'What do you think of all these plans?' I asked Sevias one evening after Dongijena's departure.

'All men are like *meshunah* trees, crooked and bent. How can any man, in this case, make a straight thing?' He smiled his patient, lopsided smile, but as usual tried to salvage the good from the bad.

'But something good and straight has happened,' he continued. 'We have sat together and talked. If this had been possible in Rhodesia times, there would have been no war.

But there was no contact. They never came here and they still do not come here. They travel to see African animals, and sleep in the bush, but they refuse to visit African people and sleep in their *kraals*. You know, after a hundred years of the white man, the only difference it has made here is that we know the Bible and we have aluminium pots for cooking. They had a world for themselves. We had our world.'

Darana broke in: 'I used to go to the town to sell and to buy. There were special shops for whites and special shops for blacks. We never got to know each other. That is why the war happened. If the whites had come and shared our food and slept in our huts, that would have meant that we were all humans together. But they did not – they treated us like animals. I used to go to the town,' he growled, 'the whites beat me up four times. The fifth time I walked over the border into Mozambique and joined our fighters. I spent seven years in the bush. But now I am back and, with God's help, they'll never beat me again.'

Darana spoke of the war and his past experiences with a sad smile, but without any bitterness. He looked tough and competent.

'You look like a soldier but sound like a priest,' I said. They all laughed at that, but it was so: his voice combined a firmness of tone with a priestly melancholy.

'You know, I never wanted to be a soldier,' said Darana. 'I am a Jew and a Lemba and against violence. We are not black or white. I love white people like I love black people, but white racism forced me to kill. To kill many, many men.'

We were sitting outside looking at the new moon which was rising over the *mushava* tree. The conversation turned away from warfare to witchcraft, to stories of magic and the moon.

'It's beautiful,' I said, nodding at the moon's silver crescent.

Sevias laughed. 'Many years ago,' he told me, 'Rupengo, a great chief, sat in his *kraal* and looked at the new moon. "It's beautiful," he said. "It would make a fine ornament for my chest."'

The following day Rupengo commanded his people to get together and gave them instructions to chop down some of the tallest trees in the forest and construct a high wooden platform. But even from the platform the moon was inaccessible. He gave orders for more trees to be felled and for another platform to be added. The following night they would try again. But ants had eaten through one of the legs of the platform and the wooden tower collapsed, killing many people. Rupengo ordered a new tower to be built. Again it fell down, with great loss of life. This time the people arose and cut down Rupengo, for they saw that he was completely mad. And the moon stayed where it was.

'But,' he continued, 'we Lemba used to catch the moon in a different way. And *we* really caught it.'

In the past, he said, the Lemba had been proud of their ability to see the new moon before it was visible to their *wasenzhi* neighbours. It was one of the many ways in which they showed their superiority. The *wasenzhi* used to say, 'The Lemba can even pull the moon out of the sky.' Just before the time of the new moon a bowl was placed under a tree or in the shade of a hut. And the day before it was seen by anyone else, sometimes two days before, the moon became visible, reflected in the water, usually around noon. It was customary to ensure that the young saw the new moon only this way. When the moon was seen, all the men shaved their heads and fasted for the rest of the day. The following day no work was done and that evening the Lemba would look at the moon and say, 'This is the *wasenzhi* moon, our moon has been seen in the pot.'

Savias's account tallies with earlier Lemba descriptions of this ritual. A number of ethnographers claim that the practice actually works. One of them wrote: 'I would suggest that the obscurity under the thick foliage made it possible to see through the branches the pale crescent invisible in broad daylight, just as stars may be seen at noon from the bottom of a pit.'

'Do you still look for the moon in a bowl of water?' I asked Sevias. He shook his head. The last time he had seen it done was when he was a boy, and he could throw no light on the meaning or origin of the custom except to say that it was important for the Lemba to know exactly when the moon came. A precise knowledge of the moon's cycle is of extreme importance for Muslims and Jews alike.

'And do some people still shave their heads at the new moon?'

'Not in this *kraal*, *Mushavi*, but there are many who still do.'

There was a silence, broken by Darana. 'Would you like to hear some music, *Mushavi*?' he asked. 'You know we Mwenye used to be great musicians. Every chief, every king, had Mwenye musicians. You want music?'

I was more than happy to listen to Lemba music. The tribe's musical abilities had clearly been important both in royal *kraals* and long before at the courts of the great pre-colonial African kingdoms, perhaps at Great Zimbabwe. In Venda, as we have seen, the Lemba 'used to play their musical instruments from morning to sunset ... Wherever you went in Vendaland at that time there was music in the sky.'

The traditional instrument of the Lemba was the so-called bush piano, which was usually played inside a large calabash which acted as a resonator. P. Kirby's authoritative work on

174

the subject of native musical instruments in South Africa notes that instruments of this type

> are rarely met with in South Africa. With one exception they are not characteristic of the people. The exception is the *deze* which is found in Bavendaland, where it is made and played by the Lemba who are iron-workers. It is identical with one type used in Rhodesia and which goes by the same name, although the natives there also give it the generic name *mbila*.

Six or seven musicians played these instruments in unison, often singing in accompaniment. The same instrument was described by the Portuguese missionary, João dos Santos, in 1586:

> The iron rods being shaken and the blows resounding above the hollow of the bowl after the fashion of a Jews' harp they produce altogether a sweet and gentle harmony of accordant sounds. This instrument is much more musical than that made of gourds, but it is not so loud, and is generally played in the king's palace, for it is very soft and makes but little noise.

The court musicians, according to Dos Santos, 'have no other office than to sit at the first room of the king's palace, at the outer door and round his dwelling playing many different musical instruments and singing to them a great variety of songs and discourses in praise of the king.'

The concert in Sevias's *kraal* must have been prearranged, for within a few minutes fifty or sixty people had arrived from the neighbouring *kraals* and were standing around the fire, blankets around their shoulders. To start with they sang songs from the bush war; then, at my request, traditional Lemba songs. The women chanted songs of female initiation; the men songs of circumcision and sacrifice; and together they sang songs of rain and hymns in honour of the ancestors.

From time to time one of the men would blow a long piercing blast on the ram's horn, which the women would accompany with their shrill ululation; and all the time there was the relentless beat of the women's drums. But there was no sign of the *deze*; the only other instrument was a guitar made from two pieces of boxwood and an Esso oilcan.

The last song they sang was the anthem of the African National Congress: 'God bless Africa, its name be uplifted, listen to our prayers, God bless us, its children, come spirit to bless us, its children ... *Woza moya, woza moya, woza moya oyingcwele nkosi sikelel iAfrika.*' This they sang in half-a-dozen African languages.

Mama's beautiful daughter was sitting on one side of me, Darana on the other. His cheeks were wet with tears.

'Ah! These war songs,' he said.

'Were people here involved much in the war?' I asked him.

'Everyone was. Even the cockerels. Even the dogs. When the whites and their troops came, the dogs barked, the cocks crowed and the *shiri ye denga* circled above the *kraals*.' He paused and with a sigh whispered, '*Nkosi sikelel iAfrika.*'

When the girl brought in my washing water the next morning, it was still dark. As usual, she kneeled in front of me, lit a candle and gave me one of her shy smiles and, as usual, I felt gratitude and embarrassment in more or less equal measure. Ever since my first morning in the *kraal* it was always this pretty girl who appeared with my water. Indeed, for some time Mama had been referring to her as 'my girl'. One evening around the fire Sevias had become grave and business-like. The *lobola* – the bride price – was exorbitant, he said. He had four daughters who had to get married. Each one would bring with her 150 Zimbabwe dollars and ten cattle. In the old days you did not give money, you just gave cattle. If you did not have cattle, you could give a hoe. Nowadays the value of the cattle could be expressed as 100 dollars a head, which is to say that the total in monetary terms would be 1,150 dollars. Other things, huts, land, hoes, could be thrown in; even family and tribal secrets.

'Ah!' I said.

'Of course, all is negotiable, *Mushavi.*'

'It sounds very generous,' I muttered.

Sevias looked at me speculatively.

After this conversation I became increasingly aware of the girl's apparent devotion and solicitude. She would bring me water several times a day, despite its critical scarcity, and would often kneel with her head bowed in the doorway of the hut for half an hour at a time for no apparent reason. On other occasions she would sit with her face in profile, her chin raised, and I came to believe that she was proud of her long face and Semitic nose.

A Lemba girl, I was told, at the onset of puberty was traditionally required to sit up to her neck in river water, for two weeks, with a gourd on her head. As a further preliminary of initiation she would be presented with a sharp, conical wooden object decorated with a red tassel, upon which she would be expected to impale herself in the river for a further three days. These prolonged immersions were considered exercises in humility.

This girl's attentiveness might then be explained by an excess of humility, but I also remembered reading a description of the probationary period leading up to marriage during which the bride-to-be was given a clay pot and 'exhorted to bring water to her husband every morning without his ever having to ask for it'. I began to fear complications, but took some comfort from the traditional reluctance of the Lemba to give their daughters to *wasenzhi*. However, with increasing regularity Sevias would tell me that I was an English Lemba and these days, when he called me *Mushavi*, there was a twinkle in his eye – almost, it seemed to me, a paternal twinkle.

The days turned into weeks and the gentle routine of the *kraal* began to numb my sense of time. I would often walk for hours alone on the hills only to find that someone was following me, at a discreet distance, keeping an eye on me as they said. Sevias and Chief Mposi, whom I visited most days, spoke long and often of their Jewishness. They also mentioned their love for Jesus Christ and their mild affection for a more remote ancestor called Muhammad.

'Some old men from other *kraals* say we are Arabs,' Sevias said one day. 'Some say we are Jews. We all say we are Jews here. What do you think, *Mushavi*?'

'You can be a Jew and an Arab at the same time,' I replied. 'Many Jews lived in the Arab world in the past and spoke Arabic and were part of the Arab cultural world.'

This information made Sevias extraordinarily happy and thereafter his and his father's references to various religious traditions became increasingly promiscuous. The Lemba's tendency towards syncretism, their readiness to allow different religious traditions to flow into each other and into their own, made me wonder if the Lemba had always been particularly syncretistic. And at what point, I asked myself, does a religious melting-point create a new faith?

One day the calm of the *kraal* was broken. A kid had disappeared during the night and was feared lost. Sevias sent one of his sons to find it, but by nightfall neither the child nor the kid had returned. Sevias was distraught. We took sticks, walked out into the bush and found them, at the top of a nearby hill, the boy asleep beneath a tree, the kid in his arms.

'Thank you, Lord, the Good Shepherd,' said Sevias. 'Thank you, Abraham, our father.'

And I thought of a line of Yehuda Amichai, the great Jerusalem poet:

> Searches for a kid or for a son were always
> the beginning of a new religion in these hills.

18

Chief Mposi had sent a message asking me to go and see him again. He urgently needed more vitamin pills and brandy. Mama packed us a picnic of *sadza* and ram and Tagaruze, Sevias and I walked across the parched hills to the *kraal*. The chief looked worse than he had ever looked.

'Your presence is a special cure for Chief Mposi,' said Sevias. 'Because you are here, he must look strong.'

'I am strong,' grumbled the chief, 'but I'll be even stronger with some brandy.'

I went to the cooking-hut and made a jugful of brandy and lemon, which the chief drank throughout the morning. He had decided to have a feast in honour of the ancestors, to which all the important Lemba would be invited. Beer was already being brewed and there would be dancing. I was invited too.

'Can I bring something?'

'What would you like to bring?' asked Sevias, smiling.

'I'll bring some whisky,' I suggested.

There was a long discussion in Shona. Eventually Tagaruze declared that Chief Mposi was not the sort of man to make important decisions like this on the spur of the moment. My proposal would be considered by the *kraal* elders and I would be told what kind of gift might be appropriate. To pass the

time I went for a walk in the woods beyond the village. Along
the path I met a very drunk girl incomprehensibly carrying
an enamel chamber-pot on her head.

'How,' she said.

'Hello,' I replied.

'How d'you do?' she continued.

'Fine. How are you?'

'What's that?' She pointed at my camera. 'What's do?'

'Makes pictures.'

'How?'

'I don't know exactly,' I confessed.

'Me beer seven days,' she said lurching back into the wood
in the direction from which she had come. When I got back
to the *kraal*, I mentioned the girl.

'She is a bad girl,' said Sevias. 'She was found with her
hand in the chief's grain bin.'

'She was stealing?'

'No. It means that she planned to steal the chief's seed. To
sleep with the chief. She was insulting the chief's wife! She
was punished and now she is drinking out of shame.'

The matter of my contribution to the party had been
settled. Sevias explained that the chief's wives had been busy
brewing beer. The ingredients were costly. The chief's financial situation was not good. His sheep were gone. He still
had some cows, but because of the drought they had been
taken to a 'resettlement area' – a former white farm. This
cost three dollars a month per head. In short, explained
Sevias, the most useful gift, in all the circumstances, would
be money.

'How much money?' I asked Sevias.

'A lot,' he replied, his expression as innocent as always.

The men clapped their hands and murmured '*Mushavi*'.
Calculating the cost of two bottles of Black Label whisky, I

peeled off a good number of Zimbabwe dollars and presented them to the chief, who cupped his gnarled hands to receive the gift. Again the men clapped in appreciation. His disagreeable oldest wife, a powerfully built woman, observed this transaction and, lumbering forward into the centre of the hut, made an urgent plea for a gift for herself. She was no longer young, she said, but she wanted to look her best for the party. The only beads you could get these days were plastic beads, which lost their colour in no time. If only she could get her hands on some glass or clay beads such as they had in the old days. I thought to myself that if other African villages were like this one, an enterprising Lemba could do a great deal worse than going around the villages selling precisely the same trade goods as his forebears had a hundred years before. In those days a chief's wife would certainly not have been short of beads. If she could not find glass beads, I asked, how could I? The men laughed, but she scowled before she left. Without meaning to I had made an enemy.

Outside the hut the heat, dust and glare were unbearable. By the time we got back to Sevias's *kraal* I was exhausted. I longed for a cold, clean drink. As usual I was handed a tin of warm, thin mud. Even mud was now in short supply. The borehole was practically empty. Sevias had told me that even the *mikute* – trees under which water had always been found in the past – were now dying. If rains did not come immediately, the situation would be desperate.

The ferruginous liquid and withering heat were doing their work. I had been suffering from dysentery for several days and I was not feeling well. The assembly of the Lemba clans would take place the following day and I wondered if I would be well enough to go. Sevias said that Mama would soon make me well. The old lady padded into my hut and stated quite categorically that she knew what was wrong;

Professor Mathiva wearing ceremonial gown

A Soweto Lemba with his Lemba Cultural Association identity Card

Mberengwe at the funeral

Phophi

Above left Lemba woman weaving a beer filter

Above right Lemba potter

Left The Rain Queen

Below Lemba procession in Vendaland

Chief Mposi

A Semitic looking Lemba in Mposi

Author sharing a joke with Sevias

Above & below The party for the Ancestors – with Lemba horn and drum

Dongijena (left) with two Lemba inside the 'old town'

The assembly of the clans

The Hill Ruin at Great Zimbabwe

One of the Zimbabwe soapstone birds

Dumghe Mountain

Father Fatch

Dhow underway to Tumbatu

A conical tower in the Hadramaut

A conical tower at Great Zimbabwe

Qabr Hud

Above The road to Sena

Right The Mukhtar of Sena

Below The Eye Woman of Sena working her magic

indeed, she had known all along that I would get ill. It was all the travelling, from Sevias's *kraal* to Mposi's *kraal*, from Mposi's *kraal* to Sevias's *kraal*. If local people moved around like that they always ate the earth of the *kraals* they visited. 'You must eat the earth of here. Plenty earth.' The water I had been drinking for the last few weeks had not been altogether deficient in earth, I reflected, and I was sure that it was the earth which was responsible for my churning stomach, but to humour Mama I mixed a little soil with a finger of whisky, drank it and climbed into my sleeping-bag.

A few minutes after I had lain down, Sevias hurried in to the hut carrying a large wooden drum. It was a present from Chief Mposi. In return, the chief wanted me to send him a copy of *The Thirteenth Gate*. As I pulled a copy out of my bag, Sevias said, 'A drum for a book. A book for a drum. It makes me remember our Lemba saying: "Once we had a drum because we were a holy people – and once we had a book because we were a wise people." I told you we lost our book. Also, we lost our drum and now we have nothing. In the past, long ago, we followed our drum. It was the drum which brought us from Sena. Maybe it was the drum which brought us from Israel. It was the drum which brought us here. If we could find the drum, if you could find the drum, *Mushavi*, it could take us back. Back where we came from.'

'Are you sure the drum is lost and not hidden?' I asked.

'Where would it be hidden?'

'In Venda, in the mountains. Or here on Dumghe. Perhaps in the cave?'

'I have seen the cave. There is nothing in the cave. But behind the cave there is another cave. Only the chief has seen in that cave. I don't know.' He shrugged. 'Maybe the drum is there. Maybe. If it is there, we should know about it. That drum can take us back to Sena. But even if it takes us nowhere, we must find it: the finding of lost things is more important than anything.'

And later, as I lay in the darkness of the hut, Sevias's words brought to mind the lines of T. S. Eliot: 'There is only the fight to recover what has been lost and found and lost again and again.'

19

The story of the drum known as *ngoma lungundu* is one of the most mysterious aspects of the Lemba's tradition, although these days little memory of it remains. I was convinced that Sevias knew no more about it than he had told me. The other Lemba I questioned were either ignorant or gifted actors. Fortunately early ethnography has preserved a number of Lemba and Venda accounts of this drum, and the Venda of today still cherish the tradition that, when they moved from Central Africa, they were guided by the Lemba who carried the *ngoma* and a wooden basket of magical beads. Van Warmelo described the *ngoma lungundu* as 'the sacred drum which was borne along on their wanderings like the Ark of the Covenant'.

In Bulawayo I had come across a book about the *ngoma* by Harald von Sicard. Based in part upon the notes of the Rev. J. Othenius, the missionary forcibly circumcised by the Lemba, this work, which I read while I was in Mposi, is nothing less than astonishing. Von Sicard believed not only that the Lemba drum resembles the Israelite Ark of the Covenant in some important ways, but also that there is a direct connection between the *ngoma* and the Ark.

According to the book of *Exodus*, the Israelites were commanded by God to make an ark of shittim wood: two cubits and a half shall be the length thereof, and a cubit and a half the breadth thereof, and a cubit and a half the height thereof ... thou shalt cast four rings of gold for it, and put them in the four corners thereof and two rings shall be in the one side of it and two rings in the other side of it. And thou shalt make staves of shittim wood and overlay them with gold. And thou shalt put the staves into the rings by the sides of the ark, that the ark may be borne with them. The staves shall be in the rings of the ark, they shall not be taken from it. And thou shalt put into the ark the testimony which I shall give thee.

In the first book of Kings we read that the testimony was none other than 'the two tables of stone which Moses put there at Horeb'. The Ark, with powers of its own to save the people of Israel from its enemies (e.g. I *Samuel*, 3, 4), was carried by the Israelites into battle and acted as a talisman and a guarantor of victory.

What happened to the Ark is unknown. According to Ethiopian tradition, it was taken to Ethiopia by Menelik, Solomon's son by the Queen of Sheba. Menelik had been sent to Jerusalem to be instructed by his father. When the time came for Menelik to return to Ethiopia, Solomon gave him a retinue made up of the first-born of the notables of his state, headed by Azarias, the son of Zadok the High Priest. Unwilling to be separated from the holy Ark of the Covenant, the exiles resolved to steal it – leaving a replica in its place. The Angel of the Lord appeared unto Azarias and conspired in the theft of the Ark and in the manufacture of the replica ark. On the long journey back to Ethiopia, Menelik's retinue, with its stolen treasure, was guided by the Archangel Michael. The journey was not particularly arduous: according to the Ethiopian chronicle, the *Kebra Negast*, the caravan floated along, wagons, camels and Ark, 'raised above the ground to the height of a cubit'.

The idea that the Ark was taken to Ethiopia also had some currency outside Ethiopia. Abu Salih the Armenian, writing in the thirteenth century, expressed the general belief of his time:

> The Abyssinians possess also the Ark of the Covenant, in which are the two tables of stone, inscribed by the finger of God with the commandments which he ordained the children of Israel. The Ark of the Covenant is placed upon the altar; it is as high as the knee of a man, and it is overlaid with gold . . . the Ark is attended by a large number of Israelites descended from the family of the prophet David who are white and red in complexion, with red hair.

What can be taken as historical fact, without doubt, is that the notion of the Ark, the legend of the Ark, was implanted in Ethiopia in very early times, probably during the first few centuries of the Christian era.

Von Sicard pointed to a number of striking similarities between the Ark and the Lemba *ngoma*. An ancient *ngoma* found in a cave near the Limpopo was of similar size to the Ark: 1.4 feet high and 2.5 feet in circumference; it also had four handles at each corner. According to oral traditions still maintained in Vendaland, the *ngoma* was carried before the people on poles which were inserted through the handles and certain sacred objects were customarily carried inside the drum, which, like the Ark, had an intense sanctity of its own and could barely be distinguished from Mwali himself. As the Ark had a priestly caste to tend it – the Levites – so the *ngoma* had the priestly caste of the Lemba. The *ngoma*, like the Ark, was carried into battle and led the people on their wanderings throughout Africa; it was too holy to be placed on the ground, so at the end of a day's march it was hung from a tree or a special platform was constructed for it. Von Sicard maintained that the *ngoma* tradition can be connected with the Ethiopian traditions of the Ark and that the *ngoma*, as well as the many apparently Judaising customs of the Lemba, derive from the Falashas, Ethiopian Jews, who at some time in the past fled their native land and found a haven in the Zimbabwe area.

Von Sicard concluded his book with the words:

> There is good reason to suppose that the Hamitoid people of Rhodesia brought with them the Jewish Lemba who were blacksmiths and builders and it was through this that Old Testament traditions entered Rhodesia. Among these traditions the *ngoma ungundu* occupied a special place. The belief in God of the Lemba has been preserved along with that part of Mwari [Mwali] worship which emphasises God's sacredness and uniqueness . . .

The idea of the Falashas marching through Africa carrying their ark or their drum before them is a stirring one. Could it be that one of the few documented glimpses that we have of African life almost a thousand years ago could be referring to this event? In the twelfth century Al-Idrisi, the Arab geographer, wrote a few words about El Banyes, the last region inhabited by the negro Zanj, abutting Sofala and not far, therefore, from the town of Sena on the Zambezi. 'The inhabitants of El Banyes', wrote Idrisi, 'worship a drum called *Arrahim*, as big as *Albaba* covered with skin on one side only and attached to a length of cord with which one beats the drum – it makes a terrible noise which can be heard about three miles away.'

The name *Arrahim* is a curious one. It is not a Bantu word. It is phonetically identical with the Arabic *Al-Rahim* (pronounced Arrahim) which means The Merciful One – a common designation for God. For a drum to be worshipped and called by one of the names of Allah would have been deeply offensive to a Muslim. Yet Al-Idrisi passed over it without comment. The word *Albaba* is unknown.

Al-Idrisi relied on travellers and various other oral sources for much of his information. Could it be that in view of the fact that L and R are interchangeable in many languages – and particularly in Bantu languages – what he heard was actually *Errohim*, a Bantuised form of *Elohim*, the Hebrew name for God? In any event, it is an odd name and one which may be of Semitic origin. Certainly the passage cannot be ignored in the context of von Sicard's grand theory.

The idea that the Lemba are descended from groups of Falashas was one that I had first heard from the Lemba themselves, but it is an idea which has come to them fairly recently. None of the early ethnographers reported Lemba claims of Falasha ancestry. Indeed, it is most unlikely that the Lemba had ever heard of the Falashas, or of Ethiopia for that matter. Solomon Sadiki, the Lemba elder I met in Soweto, visited Ethiopia in the 1950s and met Falashas: he may have been responsible for giving the idea some currency at least in Soweto. The vast publicity attending the Israeli rescue of the Black Jews of Ethiopia from the refugee camps of the Sudan in 1984 is likely to have suggested the idea to many more.

Certainly there are many points of similarity between the Lemba and the Falashas. Like the Lemba the Falashas were great stone builders: indeed, they played a considerable role in the construction of the royal capital of Gondar. Both groups were metal-workers and were economically useful. They both had a reputation as workers of magic. Both groups were outstanding potters. Like the Lemba the Falashas, as well as Ethiopian Christians, placed great emphasis on the moon. Hilltops uncontaminated by outsiders were as important for the Falashas as they were for the Lemba and were used, for instance, during their annual pilgrimage festival, the *sigd*. Both groups were endogamous. They had similar slaughtering rites and food taboos. Their customs of burial and ritual purity are not dissimilar. Points in common have been found between Lemba and Falasha musical traditions. These similarities have led more than one writer to conclude that there may be some connection between them.

Had a group of Falashas somehow made their way down through Africa centuries before and left an imprint so deep that it can still be perceived today? As I read von Sicard's *magnum opus*, I found the possibility intriguing. But equally I sensed that this could not be the whole answer: it was perhaps not credible that anything so improbable was at the root of the mystery.

20

The assembly had been called for eight in the morning. By the time I got to Mposi's village, I was tense with anticipation but otherwise in adequate health. Mama's remedy had not made things any worse.

A few delegates were already sitting in the shade of a great *mumveve* tree in the middle of the chief's *kraal*. As usual, the men were wearing tattered western suits and hats, carried knobkerries and were barefoot. The chief's messenger arrived: he had walked for three hours that morning and had encountered a number of elderly delegates on the way. Everything was going according to plan. He went off to find some chairs and a table. The messenger had a number of roles, explained Tagaruze: 'He is the chief's bodyguard, he makes sure that the chief's bye-laws are abided to, and he organises everything the chief does.'

The councillor was there, marshalling the men into a neat circle, explaining the importance of the assembly and the wealth that would accrue from it. Some of them were missing a day of work from the Government's 'Food for Work' programme, but Dongijena assured them that they would be paid their two dollars anyway as they had attended the meeting.

Over the next few hours the rest of the representatives arrived. For the most part they were elderly and ragged and had come a very long way. By midday all the tribes were represented and, in some cases, doubly so. The last man to pick his way down from the hills above the *kraal* was the spectacularly filthy figure of an old man. 'Klopas!' they all shouted, smiling at each other. Klopas was wearing something which may once have been a dark brown suit. Like the others he was barefoot. One trouser leg was tied at the bottom by a leather thong, the other by a piece of thick rubber. The seat of his trousers was gaping wide, the sleeves of his jacket had been slit and now consisted of three strips of material connected only above the elbow, the lining of the jacket flowed around him in vertical tatters. Under the jacket were the grubby remnants of a shirt and on his head a pith helmet which had seen better days. He was over seventy years old, his face was covered in white bristles and a crust of pustules, and he had a rather grotesque drooping lip. Klopas had walked about twenty miles and was in boisterous spirits. He had dropped in on a beer party in a neighbouring village, which had gone on until the early hours of the morning, and had drunk as much as he was allowed to. He belched and bellowed for beer to be brought. Conscious of the gravity of the occasion the others regarded him askance. He was silenced only when the messenger threatened him with a stick. But the peculiarities of this odd man were borne by the villagers in much the same way as unfortunate deficiencies of a son or a daughter.

When all was ready, the messenger fetched the chief. He hobbled slowly from his hut, not raising his eyes from the ground. He sat down next to me and quietly explained what it was I wanted from them. Sevias then rose and read Mathiva's letter, first in English and then in Shona. The chief pulled himself to his feet and asked the oldest representatives of the ten tribes to identify themselves by their clan. One by one they shouted out the clan name: Sadiki, Hamisi, Mahdi, Tovakare, Hadji, Sharifu, Hasani, Bakari, Duma, Seremane. One man was told to stand because he looked most like what a Lemba was supposed to look like. It was the emerald-eyed man I had met under the *meshunah* tree – the guardian of Dumghe.

They were invited to speak. To start with, the grizzled heads of the men bent close together as they whispered among themselves. Then the voices grew sharper and for two hours the arguments went back and forth. There was an impressive formality about the discussion. There were two main camps: conservatives who wanted to keep the traditional secrets and *status quo* and liberals who wanted change. The liberals contended that as the other tribes, the Ndebele and the Shona, had had histories written about them, the Lemba too should have a book. The conservatives said that the Lemba had always been a separate people and had never made a point of following the example of these other tribes: why should they do so now? The liberals, led by Dongijena, argued that publicity about the Lemba past would bring untold prosperity to the tribe. The conservatives argued that in the recent past the Lemba had been poor and had not suffered unduly. The conservatives, relying on a certain moral superiority and sound historical argument, were beaten every time.

In the end it was agreed that a book should be written about the history of the Lemba. Noisily, and with many interruptions, they gave their different versions of this history. They certainly had come from Sena, but there was disagreement over its location: some thought Israel or Arabia, some thought Egypt or Ethiopia. They had crossed Pusela, and there was general agreement that this was the Great Sea. They were certainly Israelites and there was a sharp distinction to be made between themselves and non-Lemba

Africans – the *wasenzhi*. It was true that their first leaders had been white Jews and it was under their leadership that they had left Egypt/Israel/Ethiopia/Arabia. But these matters were not secrets.

The conservatives insisted that if secrets were to be told, a vote should be taken. This was agreed. But first the chief demanded that any uninitiated, uncircumcised Lemba should withdraw. One younger man, sent by his father who was too ill to come, left the group and, looking shamefaced, walked across to the *kraal*. Tagaruze went with him. A Lemba now came forward to interpret for me. There were fourteen men left.

'What right does this meeting have to make any decision?' growled Klopas.

The chief repeated his account of the assembly called in his grandfather's time to discuss the Creation; the older men murmured assent. It was in the tradition.

'But even so, our very secret words cannot be told,' said Klopas, belching.

'Anything can be decided,' said the chief.

'Who will be responsible for the financial aspects of the history, if it is written?' asked the councillor. The councillor would, it was agreed.

Finally, it was put to the vote: should the secrets be told? Five of the fourteen men were against the revelation of secrets. The chief and the councillor abstained. Even so, there was a majority of two. The day was carried.

The chief was pleased. It was important, he said, for the religion of the Lemba to be known and understood. But were there still practitioners of the religion? I asked.

'Many have become Christian, it is true,' he replied. 'But with a couple of exceptions all the men here today are not Christian, they believe in the Lemba way.'

The chief wanted to conclude the meeting there and then, but I begged him to allow me to ask a few questions. With ill-grace, he agreed.

'Can you tell me anything about *ngoma lungundu*?' I asked, looking at Chief Mposi.

He shook his head and said nothing. No one else spoke or even looked at me.

'Who was Baramina?' I continued.

Mathiva had mentioned Baramina as a Lemba ancestor in Sena. Similarly, a Lemba initiation leader called Nhongo had told von Sicard that the first Lemba to arrive in Vuhindi was Baramina; he had been followed by others. Vuhindi was supposed to be an area of the Zambezi estuary. Later, they left Vuhindi and went to Sena. Here they increased and started worshipping Baramina as a god. According to this Nhongo, it was in Sena that Baramina had given the tribe their tribal customs: he was the great one, the great departed ancestor. Nhongo had claimed that when the names of all the departed ancestors were recited on feast days, and during initiation ceremonies, Baramina was the last to be cited.

The practice of reciting the names of the departed ancestors had been mentioned by Junod in 1908:

The Lemba, that curious tribe settled amongst the Thongas and Vendas of Spelonken which has certain Semitic customs, are much more respectful towards their ancestor-gods [than other tribes T.V.P.]. They have prayer meetings at which the old men of many families gather together; one of them, he who knows the ancestors best, leads the others in prayer, 'quoting all their mountains', viz., all the sacred hills where the ancestors have been buried, and at the end of each sentence they all answer: 'hundjiii' . . . When the prayer is finished, they each raise an arm and say: 'Amen!'

While reading in Bolze's library I had come across a passage in David Livingstone's *Travels* which gave me a moment of scholarly pleasure: the discovery of a key which opened a door which permitted a view of a hoped-for vista (and which, as I was later to realise, fitted the locks of other doors which gave on to quite unexpected vistas). Livingstone wrote:

> The village of Senna stands on the right bank of the Zambesi ... the soil is fertile; but the village, being in a state of ruin, and having several pools of stagnant water, is very unhealthy. The bottom rock is the akose of Brogniart or granite grit and several conical hills of trap have burst through it. One standing about half a mile west of the village is called Baramuana.

I wondered if this dramatic sounding hill of Baramuana close to Sena had anything to do with the Lemba's Baramina. Had this been Baramina's sacred hill? It seemed altogether likely, but I still did not know as much as I wanted to know about Baramina. So again I asked the question: 'Who is Baramina?'

Klopas leapt to his feet, brandishing his knobkerrie. If I knew about Baramina, he said, I must be a circumcised Lemba. There was no other explanation. I told him that I had heard about Baramina from Mathiva. Klopas was unconvinced. Pausing only to shoot a baleful glance in my direction, he started hissing something to his neighbours.

'Who was Baramina?' repeated the chief, pointing to an elder who thus far had said nothing.

'Baramina was the father of the tribe in Sena,' he replied.

'Who came first, Saidi or Baramina?'

'Saidi led us from Sena across Pusela to Africa. Baramina was the father of the tribe in Africa. He died in Sena. Baramina brought the Jewish religion to Africa. He took the religion from Saidi.'

Now I knew that the identification of Saidi was difficult. It certainly suggests, as C. Bullock has noted, an Arab influence:

It is possible [he wrote] that the WaRemba had Arabian forefathers. It may be that they were the 'Moors' whom the Portuguese chroniclers found living near Sofala, and we know that a man of another tribe once addressed a MuRemba as *Mulungu*, which signifies a superior Being, and once had that implication in one of our own designation. But if they have something in the nature of a distinguished ancestry, and if among them we can find considerable divergences from Mashona culture, it would seem that they salved the pricks of conscience and pride of race by calling all women outcasts, and so condoning that miscegenation which may have reduced them to what they are now – a Bantu tribe not greatly outstanding among other tribes of that race. They still swear by Sayid, but they know not who he was – nor do they care, for Africa has enfolded them in her smooth black arms.

Van Warmelo went a few steps further. Knowing the outline of the Sena epic and the Lemba custom of referring back to Saidi, he wrote:

A tradition about early origins has lately come to light. According to this, the ancestors of the Lemba came from a huge town somewhere across the seas, where dwelt many craftsmen in metalwork, pottery, textiles and ship-building. They came to this country to trade their goods, especially for gold. They began leaving some of their men behind with unsold cargo and thus established posts. They moved further and further inland and became well known to the natives, but did not mix with them as they deemed themselves superior. Then one day came shattering news: the city had been taken by the enemy, they could never go back home. So they began taking native wives, chiefly Rozwi,

Karanga, Zezuru, and Govera. By this time they were already organised in the clans as we know them today.

Now, starting from the other end, it is well known that in the year 696 the two princes of Oman, Sulaiman and Said were attacked by the forces of the Khalif 'Abd al-Malik ibn Marwan of Damascus, and forced to flee to the land of Zanj (East Africa). There we also find the tradition of the coming of the Arabs who settled along the coast, and the name of their chief, who was Haji Said.

The problem is that there are a number of unreliable traditions which attempt to give a precise historical framework for the arrival of the Arabs on the east coast of Africa. One such claims that the first colonisers were sent by Harun al-Rashid. The story of Suleiman and Said is of similarly dubious authenticity. It became more or less current in books about East Africa after 1871 with the publication of the Rev. G. P. Badgers's translation of the *History of the Imams and Seyyids of Oman* by Salil ibn Raziq. Ibn Raziq, who died in 1873, got the story from Sirhan ibn Said ibn Sirhan's *Annals of Oman* written in 1720, but there is no record of the story before that. The Portuguese historian João de Barros, writing in the sixteenth century, tells of the arrival of heretical Muslims, who 'from their entrance moved down the coast like a slow plague' and then moved into the interior. He called them '*Emozaidij*', which may be an attempt to formulate the Arabic *umma zaydiyya* (the Zaidi nation). This has been taken to refer to followers of the Shi'ite pretender Said ibn Ali, who was killed in 739. Although de Barros was probably dependent upon contemporary oral accounts for this tradition, which is not mentioned elsewhere, there may none the less be some truth in it. According to the distinguished archaeologist Neville Chittick, the story 'may incorporate memory of the arrival, in the eighth or ninth century, of some Zaidis on the Banadir coast, from which they were later displaced by orthodox immigrants, becoming largely absorbed in the interior by the pagan inhabitants'. The Lemba ancestor Saidi is referred to by most of the ethnographers who have described the tribe, and he may conceivably have some connection with de Barros's '*Emozaidij*'. There is no proof either way. Said, however, is a common Arab name and the presence of this name in the Lemba tradition is strongly suggestive of Arab influence.

Baramina, too, may derive from a Semitic language, although not obviously from Arabic. *Bar* in Hebrew and Aramaic means 'son'; *emunah* in Hebrew means 'faith'. 'Son of the faith' would be an unusual but not impossible designation for a Jewish leader.

In mounting excitement I continued with my questions: 'And what are the secret words used in the slaughtering and circumcision ceremonies?'

If these words were the Hebrew formulae in some form, it would clearly weigh very heavily. Notwithstanding evident traces of Muslim and Arab influence, the Lemba would arguably be what they claimed to be – descendants in some historical sense of an ancient group of Jewish exiles. At the very least an ancient Jewish influence would be suggested.

The answer to this vital question was to be provided by the unexpected agency of Klopas. No doubt to punish him for his earlier truculence the chief had ordered the purulent old man to reply. Slowly rising to his feet, his eyes bulging with fear, he said, 'When we cut the beast we say "*Bismillahi*", when we initiate the boys we say "*Allahu Akbar*".' He farted audibly and sat down.

The two most sacred formulae of the Lemba were Arabic phrases – 'In the Name of Allah' and 'Allah is Great'. This was unequivocal. It now seemed to me that the Lemba, despite their protestations to the contrary, had originally been Muslims – perhaps Shi'ites – who for almost five hundred years had preserved intact these expressions of faith. While I pondered the implications of this revelation, the chief rose to his feet, murmured '*Mushavi, Mushavi*,' to his guests and hobbled back to the *kraal*. There was not a breath of wind, it was hot, and the elders had had nothing to drink since their arrival. Now, led by a subdued Klopas, we strode towards the village, the day's business concluded.

'I think that what Klopas told us shows that originally you must have been Muslims,' I said to Sevias as we reached the shade of the chief's hut.

'I do not think so, *Mushavi*,' he said with his gentle smile. 'We are certainly Jews. There are other things for you to discover. You will see . . .'

21

At the meeting the elders had agreed that I could visit Dumghe, the Mountain of the Good Men. It had never been permitted before, but now, it was thought, the circumstances were different. Sevias, Darana, Dongijena and, at his own insistence, Klopas were to accompany me. Tagaruze could come as far as the escarpment and would wait for us there. In fact, he confided to me, nothing would have persuaded him to set foot on the mountain.

The Lemba have a long association with the mountain. The most dramatic event on Dumghe to have come down to us took place in the first half of the nineteenth century. One day the children of a Lemba notable, Mpapuri, were out tending cattle when they saw a wild pig. They killed it and ate it. News of this came to the elders and it was decided that the children should be put to death for breaking the tribal taboo. Before the sentence could be carried out, Mpapuri fled with his family to Wedza, where he formed an alliance with the Dumbuseya tribe by marrying the daughter of their chief. Together they decided to conquer Dumghe and the land it controlled.

Observed from the north, Dumghe is a flat-topped mountain which slopes up gradually from the plateau. From the south it is a mighty wall of rock. Mpapuri, therefore, attacked from the north.

The night was white with moonlight, so the Lemba subsequently claimed. It was the night Chinyoka, a Lemba diviner, had decided to identify a sorcerer whose spells appeared to be killing one of the chief's wives. Chinyoka had a great audience. Silently the Lemba watched the sacrifice being prepared. The throat of the sheep was slit with a knife; the windpipe was pulled out and cut off, the gullet was tied. No impurity could be allowed to mix with the blood. Everything had been done according to the laws of slaughter: there had been no mishap. Chinyoka started to dance, the catskin around his waist streaming out as he whirled in the firelight. It was at this moment that Mpapuri and the Dumbuseya attacked. Half the Lemba were stabbed to death. The remnant, along with their Chief Mposi, fled down the deep ravines on the south side of the mountain and escaped.

Mpapuri took over the lands and cattle of the defeated Lemba. According to tradition, those Lemba who survived fled south across the Limpopo and settled for a while in Vendaland. Finally they decided to seek redress from Mzilikazi, the Great One, the all-powerful pot-bellied king who had led the Ndebele from Natal to Matabeleland in the 1820s and 1830s and who had turned his impis into one of the most formidable military machines Africa has ever seen. The king of this Black Sparta had contempt for the pacific Lemba but, at the same time, he knew of their prowess as medicine men and sorcerers and, indeed, kept a Lemba doctor in his royal *kraal*. He therefore decided to help them.

A group of Mzilikazi's elite troops were sent under the leadership of Ganduzani to fight alongside the Lemba. But how could a surprise attack on Dumghe be successful when the Dumbuseya knew the Lemba? asked Ganduzani. It was decided that the Lemba would conceal themselves around the base of Dumghe while the Ndebele, the overlords of the earth, marched openly towards the mountain. A few miles from Dumghe Ganduzani sent Mpapuri a message: the King's Mouth was visiting, he said, beer should be prepared. Fearing the might of Mzilikazi, Mpapuri greeted the King's Mouth cordially. Ganduzani instructed Mpapuri to call together his warriors. Mzilikazi, he told him, wanted a new head-dress made of the feathers of the Gwala-Gwala bird – the Mzilikazi Roller, so-called because Mzilikazi had the exclusive use of its purple feathers. Mzilikazi, said Ganduzani, would accept the feathers as tribute. Mpapuri agreed. Great gourds of maize beer were brought out. The warriors would drink that night and the next day would hunt the precious birds. The following morning Ganduzani announced that he and his impis would wait at the summit of Dumghe while the Dumbuseya went hunting, but then he cried out, 'Your men don't need spears to kill birds. Anyway, it is against the law for men to carry arms in front of the King's Mouth.'

When they had laid down their spears and taken up their throwing sticks, the Ndebele struck. Mpapuri and his warriors were hacked to death.

The King's Mouth fired his gun, the signal for the Lemba in the ravines to attack the fleeing Dumbuseya. The Lemba's task was made easier by their use of magic. They had sprinkled the hillside with their famous herbs and potions. When the fleeing Dumbuseya crossed them, their testicles inflated alarmingly. Some died on the spot. The remainder were killed like sheep. It was the last time the Lemba were dislodged from Dumghe.

We left Sevias's *kraal* just before daybreak and followed a path across the hills. The track marked the seasonal migration of people and livestock from the valleys to the higher ground. The antiquity of the land and his tribe gave Sevias great pleasure. This path had been here since ancient times, since the time of the Lemba's first arrival here and beyond, said Sevias, since the time of Great Zimbabwe. In places rocks had been so smoothed and polished by the passage of countless feet and hooves that they shone. There was normally grass up here even in times of drought. And as we got higher there was a green tinge to the land, although the grass had been cropped so close by goats and sheep that it was only just visible. After an hour or so we came across a crowd of Lemba men, women and children removing boulders and trees and cutting a neat, straight verge across the hillside. This 'Food for Work' project would bring a dirt road to some of the remoter villages. They seemed to have heard about me because they threw down their tools and shouted out 'English *Mushavi*' in greeting as I passed. On all sides rocky outcrops pierced the turf topped with gigantic balancing boulders created over the millennia by the erosion of wind. It was a warm rather than a blistering day. There was a pleasant breeze.

'The ancestors are pleased with the visit,' said Sevias; 'they want us to have a cool walk on our mountain.'

We could see Dumghe now: a long, dark mass, forested at one end, the central part great granite cliffs and the top scrub. But soon the weather changed. As we came closer to the mountain, the wind picked up and the sky became overcast. But there would be no rain, they predicted; it was too cold and the wind was too strong. The signs were not good, they said. The mountain would be dangerous in this wind. In addition, the fierce weather might bring out the animals sacred to the mountain.

'What animals?' I asked.

'The lion,' hissed Klopas.

'Is there a lion?'

'Yes. There is a white lion,' he said.

'No one would harm this sacred lion,' murmured Sevias piously.

We left Tagaruze and started climbing the wooded escarpment. From time to time the men turned from the track to collect twigs and berries. 'What is good is good,' said Sevias, 'what is good on the mountain is good twice over. This is a parasite,' he said, showing me a twig he had broken off a livid green bush, 'it is good for nosebleed.' another peeled off a piece of bark with a strong scent of lemon and held it close to my nose: this was good for women. Klopas, having heard of my recent indisposition, gave me a leaf to chew which was good for the stomach.

As we reached the flat top of the escarpment, I noticed pieces of cut stone scattered haphazardly over the thin crust of turf. The Lemba used to live here, long ago, they said. There were rectangular stones, remains of walls. The few trees up here were dead, the turf was crisp and brown. A branch snapped underfoot and sent its report into the silence of the mountain. The men stopped and looked around in fear. Klopas pointed up at the grey sky. Again the wide-winged 'bird of heaven' was circling above us. 'It is keeping guard and watching out for enemies,' said Sevias.

'There is a lion around,' muttered the councillor uneasily.

'I can certainly smell lion,' declared Klopas, taking off his pith helmet and sniffing the air. I was sure that any lion within a ten-mile radius could equally have smelled Klopas, who was highly redolent in the strong wind.

As we approached the summit, we followed a narrow track which led along the top of the cliff. There was a sheer drop of hundreds of feet. At some time in the past a section of the mountain had separated from the main mass and now formed two great granite slabs set at a sharp angle to the mountain.

The deep defile thus created was invisible from the valley – and it was at the base of the defile that the Lemba holy-of-holies was situated: a cave where the circumcision rites were carried out and which had provided the Lemba with a hiding-place and shelter from enemies in the past. This was only visited normally during the initiation period. We stopped behind a boulder balanced on the edge of the cliff. The wind was howling around us now: it was blowing so hard it would have been suicide to go too close to the edge.

'How do we get to the cave?' I asked.

'There is a path down the cliff,' said Sevias, 'but it is too windy today. In any case the cave is too sacred.'

'The ancestors are angry,' muttered Klopas. The rest were silent. I said I wanted to see the cave, but without saying anything they refused to go any further.

The men sat for a while smoking in the shelter of the boulder. My mind returned to Klopas's revelation at the assembly of the elders that *Bismillahi* and *Allahu Akbar* were the benedictions used for ritual purposes. With a burst of inspiration I asked, 'Do all the Lemba use the same secret words for ceremonies?'

'No,' said Sevias, smiling.

'The words I was told, *Bismillahi* and *Allahu Akbar* – are these words used by everyone?'

'No. These are words we have learned from the Hamadis. Those who have made their initiation with the Hamadis and have been circumcised by the Hamadis, they started to use these Hamadi words. The Hamadis are the ones who say we are Arabs. Now we usually use the Hamadi words.'

'Who are the Hamadis?'

'They are Chawas from Malawi, they work in the mines. Some Hamadis are Indians in the towns. They are Muslims. They come here and teach.'

'Are there no Lemba circumcisors and initiators?'

'Not here, *Mushavi*,' said Sevias, 'but there is one famous man in Tedzembwe. A circumcision leader who does things as we used to do them before the Hamadis came.'

'Were all of you here initiated by Hamadis?'

The wind was moaning in the great granite crevice below us. Lightning streaked across the sky, followed by a distant rumble. 'We call it the needle which stitches heaven and earth together,' said Sevias. 'It is the *shiri ye denga* which bring lightning.' But neither Sevias nor the others answered my question. Again Klopas sniffed the air. Then, jerking his hand up towards the central part of the hill, he shouted, 'Look! Lion! The white lion!' Startled, we followed his gaze and it was true that up there, somewhat obscured by bushes and the poor light, something white was moving from side to side. But it did not suggest a lion to me, or to Sevias. 'It's the chief,' he said, and led the way, half running up the hill. Chief Mposi was sitting wraith-like on the summit wearing the white shirt I had given him. He was still waving when we got there. His evident frailty and the improbability that he had managed to walk all the way lent weight to the impression that his appearance here was some sort of transcendental manifestation.

'Walk with me,' he commanded in a somewhat distant fashion motioning the others away. 'There are some things which are not known to all and, before telling you, I wanted to talk to the ancestors.' He paused to catch his breath and glanced at the group of men who were talking together in the shelter of a rock. We walked down a barely marked path on the wooded side of the hill. For a while he said nothing. Once or twice he took a breath and opened his mouth as if he were about to say something. It was only when we were off Dumghe that haltingly he started to speak. 'I went up there to speak to the ancestors,' he murmured. 'And now I can tell you this. Once we followed Saidi, a friend of Muhammad. He was not so important as Baramina. When we left Sena we came to this country and lived in Great Zimbabwe. But before that Moses was our father – and it was his son King Solomon who built Zimbabwe. King Solomon, the son of Moses, is our father, too.'

I was moved both by the courage of the chief and by his dramatic revelation, but he would say no more in the presence of the others. On the way back from the Hill of the Good Men Sevias wanted to show me what he called the 'old town'. We crossed the valley floor, climbed up the hill towards the most outlying of the ring of Lemba villages and started trudging up a narrow path towards a peak which dominated the confluence of two valleys. As we approached the summit, the men started to point, with some excitement, at pieces of cut stone which were scattered around the path. We rounded a great boulder and the source of these stones became visible. On three sides the top of the hill was protected by high stone walls connecting three giant boulders. The stone blocks were of similar shapes and sizes and followed regular courses. On two sides there was a sheer drop to the valley below. The strategic importance of this site was clear: this had been a stronghold which would have been difficult for any enemy to take and which dominated the two valleys leading into the Lemba heartlands. The place had never been excavated and, according to Chief Mposi, had never in his lifetime been visited by a white man. This was confirmed later when I discovered that the Zimbabwe Department of Antiquities, which keeps a detailed record of all ancient stone structures in the country, was ignorant of this one.

'It was here,' said Sevias, 'that we used to sacrifice and

perform the circumcision. It was a holy place. In the time of the Chief Mezere, in the time of the Ndebele wars, we abandoned the town and moved over to Dumghe.'

The men were walking around the site in a proprietorial way, pausing to pick up a stone here or kick away a fallen branch. As I watched them, it occurred to me that this site could well represent a direct link between the Lemba and the stone-building traditions of the Great Zimbabwe civilisation.

'I think this is an important place,' I said.

'Very important,' said the councillor. 'We will bring the tourists here when we've made the museum and the shop. It will make us all rich. But it's being ruined. The boys from the village come and play here. The walls used to be much higher than this. Look,' and he pointed at a more recent structure built in the centre of what they said was the old sacrifice area: it was a mini-fort built by the Lemba children of stones taken from the walls.

'You see, *Mushavi*,' said Sevias, 'it is in the tradition. They are just keeping up the tradition.'

As we walked back, the men talked of the 'old town' and of the sacrifices which had been performed there. They also spoke of the great chief's house which had stood at one corner, overlooking the valley. And now that the chief had permitted it, they spoke of the great Solomon, the father of the tribe of Seremane, which means Solomon, the mighty king, the father of the 'white men who came from Sena'.

22

Traditions built around the biblical story of King Solomon have very often been invoked to explain Africa's past. Solomon, the ruler of Israel in the tenth century BC, acquired a remarkable reputation for both wisdom and wealth. As his fame grew, 'all the earth sought Solomon to hear his wisdom – and they brought every man his present, vessels of silver, and vessels of gold, and garments, and armour and spices, horses and mules...' In addition to such tribute, Solomon's wealth was based on trading ventures which he undertook with Hiram, the King of Phoenicia:

And King Solomon made a navy of ships ... and then they came to Ophir and fetched from thence gold, four hundred and twenty talents, and brought it to King Solomon ... and the navy also brought in from Ophir great plenty of almug trees, and precious stones. And the King made of the almug trees pillars of the house of the Lord, and for the King's house ... and all King Solomon's drinking vessels were of gold ... silver was nothing accounted of in the days of Solomon. For the King had at sea a navy of Tarshish with the navy of Hiram; once in every three years came the navy of Tarshish, bringing gold and silver, ivory and apes, and peacocks. So King Solomon exceeded all the kings of the earth for riches and wisdom.

The King's most illustrious visitor was the Queen of Sheba, who

came to Jerusalem with a very great train, with camels that bore spices, and very much gold and precious stones; and when she was come to Solomon, she communed with him of all that was in her heart. And she said to the King: 'It was a true report that I heard in mine own land of thy acts and thy wisdom. Howbeit, I believed not the words until I came and mine eyes had seen it; and behold the half was not told me; thy wisdom and prosperity exceedeth the fame which I heard.

And she gave the King an hundred and twenty talents of gold, and of spices very great store, and precious stones; there came no more such abundance of spices as these which the Queen of Sheba gave to King Solomon.

And Solomon gave unto the Queen of Sheba all her desire, whatsoever she asked, beside that which Solomon gave her of his royal bounty. So she turned and went to her own country, she and her servants.

These texts were to provide the basis for religious and national traditions in many parts of the world. Within Africa the best-known version of the Solomon and Sheba story is the Ethiopian one, which maintains that the first Emperor of Ethiopia, Menelik, was none other than Solomon and Sheba's son. According to Ethiopian tradition, the Queen returned to Sheba with her son and looked after him for some years before sending him back to Jerusalem to be instructed by his father. In due course he was crowned Emperor of Ethiopia in the temple which Solomon had built in Jerusalem.

The idea that it was Africa where Solomon had acquired his gold and other valuable items was mooted by Cosmas

Indicopleustes, the Egyptian merchant turned monk who in 547 wrote the *Christian Topography*, which includes a description of a journey the author undertook in AD 525.

> This very fact [he wrote] you will find mentioned in the Book of Kings, where it is recorded that the Queen of Sheba, that is, of the Homerite country, whom afterwards our Lord in the Gospels calls the Queen of the South, brought to Solomon spices from this very Barbaria (Somalia) together with bars of ebony, and apes and gold from Ethiopia ... We can see again from the words of the Lord that he calls these places the ends of the earth, saying: The Queen of the South shall rise up in judgment with this generation and shall condemn it, for she came from the ends of the earth to hear the wisdom of Solomon, Matthew, XII, 42. For the Homerites are not far distant from Barbaria, as the sea which lies between them can be crossed in a couple of days, and then beyond Barbaria is the ocean, which is there called Zingion. The country known as that of Sasu is itself near the ocean, just as the ocean is near the frankincense country, in which there are many gold mines.

In the Muslim world the Solomon and Sheba legend was no less important than in Christendom. Muslim tradition gave the Queen the name of Bilqis and associated her with the ruins of the pre-Islamic temple of Marib in the Yemen, which, it was believed, was built for her by Solomon with the aid of the *jinn*, the sprites or goblins of the Arabian tales. Solomon himself became a gigantic figure in Muslim belief. Along with Nimrod, Nebuchadnezzar and Alexander the Great, he was regarded as one of the four great rulers of the world. He was the prototype of Muhammad. His knowledge, it was said, was deeper than the Jordan valley, justice and wisdom were engraved on his forehead. His exploits were endlessly embroidered throughout the Muslim world: legions of *jinn* were constantly at his bidding; they fought in his armies, dived to the bottom of the deepest seas for the choicest of pearls and, in Browning's words, were ready 'to pile him a palace straight, to pleasure the princess he loved'.

Legends often travel in search of facts, to which they can attach themselves. It could be that the legend of Solomon and Sheba had reached South-East Africa before the arrival of the Arabs, perhaps from Ethiopia. We have no means of knowing. In any event, it would have been natural for the Arabs to use their own beliefs and heroes to explain the complexities of the land in which they found themselves. One way or the other King Solomon and his army of *jinn* were made responsible for the gold mines and stone structures of the Zimbabwe civilisation.

These notions coincided with the ideas which Vasco da Gama brought with him when he rounded the Cape in 1499. Already, as the Borgia map of 1452 shows, Ophir – the biblical gold land – was considered by some to be at the extremity of Africa. Once this was discovered, the Portuguese were confirmed in their view by the Arabs they encountered there. Thomas Lopez, who visited the east coast in 1502, wrote that 'the Moorish merchants told us that in Sofala there is a wonderfully rich mine to which, as they find in their books, King Solomon used to send every three years to draw an infinite quantity of gold'. Three years later Edward Pachero Pereira wrote to King Manuel of Portugal: 'Your captains have discovered and occupied the great mine which some believe to be Ophir, and is now called Sofala.'

In 1552, João de Barros, basing himself in part on the

Arabic *Chronicles of Kilwa*, wrote his famous *Da Asia*, which includes an account of the mines and ruins in the interior beyond Sofala

> ... and these mines are the most ancient known in the country, and they are all in the plain, in the midst of which there is a square fortress, of masonry within and without, built of stones of marvellous size, and there appears to be no mortar joining them ... The natives of the country call all these edifices symbaoe ... when and by whom these edifices were raised ... there is no record, but they say they are the work of the devil, for in comparison with their power and knowledge it does not seem possible to them that they should be the work of man.

It is probable that the suggestion that the ruins were the work of the devil was a reference to the *jinn* of Solomon and came from an Arab source. In any event, an account written in 1609 by João dos Santos makes the matter clear. He wrote:

> The natives of these lands, especially some aged Moors, assert that they have a tradition from their ancestors that these houses were anciently a factory of the Queen of Sheba, and from this place a great quantity of gold was brought to her, it being conveyed down the rivers of Cuama to the Indian Ocean ... Others say that these are the ruins of the factory of Solomon, where he had his factors who procured a great quantity of gold from these lands ... I state that the mountain of Fura or Afura may be the region of Ophir, whence gold was brought to Jerusalem, whereby some credit might be given to the statement that these houses were the factory of Solomon.

The earliest Arab reference to Solomon's role in the interior of South-East Africa and the earliest description of the greatest of the Zimbabwe buildings – Great Zimbabwe – is perhaps to be found in a fourteenth-century section of the Arab romance, the *Sirah Antarah*, which purports to describe the mythical hero Antarah ibn Shaddad's conquest of an African stone-built city – the Fortress of Monoliths. The discovery of this reference to Great Zimbabwe was made by a colleague of mine at the School of Oriental and African Studies, Professor Harry Norris. He was watching a television programme about Great Zimbabwe one evening when he realised that this must be the Fortress of Monoliths, part of the capital of King Humam, conquered by Antarah on his way to meet the Negus, the supreme ruler of all Africa. His identification of the kingdom is based on the Arabic text which is so graphic 'that it can only be explained satisfactorily by reference to a real city visited by Arab merchants'. This is the description given by the *Sirah*:

> This King Humam (or Hammam) was a man of great courage. He was stubborn and resolute in battle. He used to raid tribes and capture women. He used to attack horseman and footsoldier equally. He had a city which was built of white stone. There was no other like it in that land. By report it was attributed to *jinn* builders who had raised it for our Lord Solomon, King David's son, peace be upon him. Near to that city was a hill which (rose up) like a pyramid. It was covered with vegetation and impressively sown with every kind of tree and bush. In the middle of that hill stood an upright 'sword' over which the bird constantly hovered. None could pass that 'sword' save him who was clad in white raiment.

From the rest of the *Sirah* it can be deduced that the city of King Humam was probably situated in East Africa: the relationship of the city and the neighbouring hill 'like a pyramid' is remarkably suggestive of the topography of Great Zimbabwe. The bird hovering over an upright sword suggests the famous Zimbabwe birds on their columns. This passage not only provides what is probably the first description we have of Great Zimbabwe, but also demonstrates the relative antiquity of the notion that the city had been built by 'Lord Solomon, King David's son'.

23

The Solomonic ideas of dos Santos and other Portuguese geographers, derived in part from Muslim sources, were repeated by European geographers for the next two hundred years. They quickly became so widely accepted that in *Paradise Lost* Milton, repeating the accepted opinion of his time, could write of 'Sofala thought Ophir'.

The intellectual context of these ideas forms part of the world-view of our European forebears and has an almost uncanny bearing on Europe's more recent colonial past. From the time of the Muslim conquest of Egypt in 641, Africa and the Indian Ocean were effectively removed from the European sphere. Even in classical times East Africa had been isolated from Greek, Roman and Egyptian influence by barriers of mountains and marshes. Muslims in time acquired a great deal of geographical knowledge about certain parts of Africa and the Indian Ocean, but Europeans had almost none: the Dark Continent was not even an outline on the map, the interior was utterly unknown. For mediaeval Europe the Bible and classical texts were the sole sources of information and consequently it was these texts which created the basis for European thinking on Africa.

In the *Odyssey* Homer had claimed that there were two Ethiopias, one in the east and one in the west, at opposite ends of the earth. This polarised Africa was in time taken to represent the 'admirable Ethiopia' of the Nubian Meroitic civilisation on the one hand, and the barbarous regions of sub-Sahara on the other. For Herodotus the men of Meroe were 'the tallest and most handsome in the world', whereas the sub-Saharan negro population were 'dog-faced creatures and beasts without heads'. This division helped to generate the idea that at the extremes of Africa were both a terrestrial hell and, beyond the Mountains of the Moon described by Diogenes, a terrestrial paradise.

There was some biblical support for this notion. The Nile was often taken to be the Gihon, one of the four rivers of Paradise, described in *Genesis* as the river 'which flows around the whole land of Cush, where there is gold, and the gold of that land is good'. It followed, then, that somewhere beyond the Nile lay an earthly paradise. Many fifteenth-century maps include the river Gihon, '*qui descendit de montibus paradisi*', and paradise itself is often presented, as it is on the Munich portolan of 1502, as a walled mountain-top town in East Africa. This terrestrial paradise underwent a number of transformations and was viewed variously as the fabled empire of Prester John, the biblical gold land of Havilah, or as Solomon's Ophir.

Mediaeval Jews had a similar idea, which might spring from the same sources. Parallel to the notion of a remote Christian empire which might eventually come to the assist-ance of a Christendom threatened by the encroachments of Islam, was the Jewish idea that somewhere in Africa a Jewish kingdom, Sambatyon, harboured the lost tribes of Israel. Vividly described by the ninth-century traveller and writer, Eldad ha-Dani, in his *Sepher Eldad*, the idea of Sambatyon, surrounded by its miraculous river which spewed stones rather than water, nourished Jewish hope during the long night of the Middle Ages.

As against the African paradise there was always the other Ethiopia – the successor to the terrestrial hell: the Africa of cannibalism and the slave trade, of unbearable heat and decimating disease, of foetid swamp and jungle – the white man's grave, the heart of darkness, what D. H. Lawrence called 'the continent of dark negation'. In modern western fiction Joseph Conrad, Graham Greene and Bruce Chatwin represent the one tendency, Rider Haggard, John Buchan and the Happy Valley literature, the other.

This ambiguous view of Africa achieved splendid iconographic form in the famous Hereford *Mappa Mundi* probably drawn by Richard de Bello in 1289. The map presents a symbolic world with Jerusalem at the centre, paradise at the top, and damned souls being dismissed from the seat of judgment to join the bestial figures which are heading towards a crescent-shaped Africa which borders the edge of a flat world. Africa is divided roughly by an elongated Atlas range: on one side there are many historical references to biblical and classical stories and to pious depictions of the lives of the saints; on the other side are monsters: some with ocular irregularities like the four-eyed Maritime Ethiopians, or the Blemyes with eyes in their bosoms, or the one-eyed panther-eating king of Ethiopia; then there were hermaphrodites, snake-eating troglodytes, humanoid creatures with mouths so small they were obliged to suck their food through a straw. In short, the known side of Africa was an extension of Christendom, the unknown the epitome of barbarism. In time it would be de-mystified by the imposition upon it of Christian and European ideas.

King John II of Portugal nurtured the pious hope that Prester John's Christian empire, the long hoped-for ally against the infidel world of Islam, would be discovered somewhere on this unknown side of the continent. The arrival in Venice in 1403 of an embassy from Prester John had excited speculation about this fabulous monarch, whose robes were woven by salamanders and washed in fire and who was descended from Melchior, Caspar and Balthazar. For a while, Christian Ethiopia fascinated the Portuguese and absorbed these hopes and expectations. A black civilised Christian kingdom was almost exactly what they had hoped to find. But a number of events, particularly the expulsion of Portuguese Jesuits from Ethiopia in the early seventeenth century, led to Portuguese interests being transferred to the so-called empire of the Monomotapa, about which they knew little but which they took to be Ophir.

A certain confusion between the Monomotapa and Prester John began to be apparent: a vivid example of this is the fanciful description of the turreted gold and ivory capital of the Monomotapa in Vincent le Blanc's *Les voyages fameux de Vincent le Blanc* (Paris, 1648), which drew heavily on earlier accounts of Prester John's supposedly magnificent palace and citadel. One can also see here the influence of the mediaeval idea that somewhere in Africa was to be found a terrestrial paradise. This notion was first attached to the Prester John myth and later to the territory of the Monomotapa or Ophir.

The hope that a biblical land existed in Africa had other somewhat practical consequences. The Cape Dutch had sent a number of expeditions cross-country from the Cape in search of the mines and temples of Solomon. Even after the Great Trek the Boers firmly believed that just to the north of their newly founded republic lay Ophir and they mounted numerous treks in search of it.

But exceeding even their hope of reaching Ophir was their desire to reach the *Beloofteland* – the Promised Land. Writing of the 1860s Thomas Baines noted that:

The heaps of stones collected by the kaffir women when they clear a field for cultivation, and which remain long after that field has reverted to its primitive condition as part of the wilderness, were supposed (by the Dutch Boers) to be monuments piled up by the Children of Israel ... and when the Jerusalem trekkers or pilgrims came to the Maghaliquain and found it flowing north, they at once christened it the Nile and fondly hoped it would lead them down into Egypt, where they could easily reach the Beloofteland.

The Boer hunters who were among the first Europeans to be seen in parts of Matabeleland, Mashonaland and Venda were thoroughly imbued with these ideas. It can almost be said that if they had not found an apparently Semitic tribe to the north of the Transvaal, they would have had to invent one. Certainly most of the early Boer travellers and explorers were convinced that the area had strong Semitic and biblical associations. Such ideas, fed into Afrikaaner religious symbolisms, were to serve the Boers' gauntly secular purposes for generations.

Thomas Baines, who had gone out to the Cape Colony as an artist in 1842, and joined the Livingstone Zambezi expedition of 1855, was no stranger to these ideas. In his *Gold Regions of South Eastern Africa*, he wrote:

The seaboard or Coast Region was known under the name it still bears of 'Sofala' which signifies in Arabic a plain or low country. Sabia lies more inland behind Sofala, and is supposed by some authorities including Josephus, and no less a personage than the author of the Koran, to be the ancient kingdom of the love-sick Queen, who visited Solomon when in all his glory ... Several ruins of ancient buildings are found still in this region which is drained by a river disemboguing on the east coast, still called Sabia ... The memory of the Queen of Sheba is still preserved among the Arabs of Sofala ...

In 1862, two German missionaries, the Rev. Alexander Merensky and Albert Nachtigal, set off from the Transvaal to find Ophir. Merensky was convinced that 'in the country Northeast and East of Mosilkatze the ancient Ophir of Solomon is to be found'. Although their mission failed, speculation about the whereabouts of Ophir continued. In 1869, H. M. Walmsley published a novel, *The Ruined Cities of Zululand*, in which a missionary, evidently modelled on Merensky, burning with desire to find Ophir, declared: 'There lie the gold fields of Solomon somewhere in the neighbourhood, the ruined cities of the mighty Egyptians, the ancient gold-diggers, crumbled into dust.'

A little later the European imagination was to be stirred even more vigorously by Rider Haggard's *King Solomon's Mines*. Rider Haggard's hero, Allan Quartermain, found his way to the legendary mines by way of a sixteenth-century Portuguese letter and map.

'I, Jose da Silvestra, [ran the letter] who am now dying of hunger in the little cave where no snow is, on the north side of the nipple of the southernmost of the mountains I have named Sheba's Breasts, write this in the year 1590 with a cleft bone upon a remnant of my raiment, my blood being the ink. With my own eyes have I seen the countless diamonds stored in Solomon's treasure chamber behind the White Death ... Let him who comes follow the map, and climb the snow of Sheba's left breast until he reaches the nipple, on the north side of which is the great road Solomon made, from whence three days' journey to the king's palace ... Pray for my soul. Farewell.

The discovery of Great Zimbabwe by the German explorer Karl Mauch in 1871, and Mauch's firmly held conviction that the ruins had been erected by the Queen of Sheba and were in fact a copy of Solomon's temple in Jerusalem, gave

rise to a spate of books about Solomon's Ophir. Great
Zimbabwe soon became a symbol of the potential wealth of
the new Ophir, whose goldfields in the past were commonly
believed to have produced no less than twenty-one million
ounces of gold. In a conversation recorded in the introduction
to *After Ophir* (1872), Captain August Lindley expressed the
gold fever of the time:

> 'Mauch has declared that his gold discoveries surpass the gold
> fields of either California or Australia, and others corroborate
> him. Now old boy, I vote that we wait for the next mail, and
> then supposing that the statements are still credited and receive
> fresh confirmation, be off at once.'
>
> 'Carried *nem con*,' cried Roger, 'then hey for Ophir and its
> nuggets!'

Time and again writers of the period came back to the
fabulous wealth of ancient Ophir. In *The Eldorado of the
Ancients* (1902), Carl Peters, the founder of German East
Africa, who was forced to resign from the German Imperial
Service accused of cruelty to the local population and who
retired to British South Africa to study the ruins at Great
Zimbabwe, wrote:

> It stands to reason that an Eldorado from which a single expedition
> lasting three years returned to Jerusalem with a mass of gold
> weighing 420 talents . . . must be indicated today by unassailable
> archaeological remains . . . so large a quantity of gold could not
> have been obtained without extensive mining operations, and of
> these there must be distinct traces remaining somewhere . . .

And indeed, there were ancient workings throughout the
Rhodesia area.

However, very little gold was found in the new Ophir. It
had been mined out. In his usual mocking way, Hilaire Belloc

observed: 'Far land of Ophir, Mined for Gold By Lordly Solomon of old, Who sailing northward to Perim, Took all the gold away with him.'

The desire of the British to exploit Solomon's Ophir led to the Rudd–Rhodes Concession of 1888. In return for a pension of £100 a month, 1,000 Martini Henry rifles, 10,000 rounds of ammunition and a steamboat on the Zambezi, Lobengula, the Ndebele king of Matabeleland and Mashonaland, ceded 'the complete and exclusive charge over all metals and minerals situated in his kingdom'. Two years later Mashonaland was occupied by the forces of Cecil Rhodes's British South Africa Company and 'Ophir' had become part of the British Empire. As E. P. Mathers, a contemporary observer, put it,

> Today, then, the Englishman is in the land of Ophir – opening the treasure-house of antiquity ... At least before many years are out, we may expect to see the image of Queen Victoria stamped on the gold with which King Solomon overlaid his ivory throne, and wreathed the cedar pillars of his temple.

The legends of Solomon and Sheba played a decisive role in determining the way Europeans viewed South-East Africa. As we shall see, the same legends were to affect the way Europeans viewed not only the land and its history but also its people – and particularly the Lemba.

And where did the Lemba's Solomon come from? Was theirs a mangled reference to some long-dead ancestor, perhaps the Suleiman who, along with Said, is said to have led his people from Oman to East Africa? Or was the Solomon story which had been used to explain the Zimbabwe ruins one which the Lemba had adopted centuries ago to explain their own mysterious past? Or was this Solomon a vestige of some Judaic past only dimly remembered?

24

It was the day of Chief Mposi's party for the ancestors and already everyone in the *kraal* was preparing for it. Drums were being treated with beeswax and tested for tautness and resonance, the pitch being raised, I noticed, by holding the open end over a fire to tighten the leather top. The rising sun revealed a clear blue sky: there was no suggestion of the rain for which the villagers had been longing.

'No sign of rain,' I said to Sevias.

'Not yet, *Mushavi*,' he said. 'The rain will come after the party. But only if the ancestors are pleased with it.'

The only description I had seen of a Lemba ancestor party was an account written by one missionary in 1931:

The Lemba do not believe that the spirits come back spontaneously to trouble the living. They must be called up by means of certain ceremonies which take place at more or less regular intervals, and in which all the women also take part. These ceremonies would seem to be of a religious character. The women dance alone inside a hut, while the men remain outside, participating in the proceedings by singing and making music. The women often spend four to five days in this way, dancing without interruption and without taking any food, until they finally get into a state of hysterical frenzy, leap as high as the roof of the hut or break through the walls and run away.

In the middle of the afternoon we took the by-now familiar path to Mposi's *kraal*. The party was to bring rain, Sevias said, as we walked through the parched land; it was for the ancestors, it was for the possession of good things, and it was for power over evil forces and enemies of all kinds. Sevias told me that I was the first white man in his lifetime ever to have been invited to such a party among the Lemba. I would be surprised by what I saw, he said. In fact, he was surprised that I was being allowed to attend at all. Not everyone was in favour of it.

We crossed the dry river-bed and climbed the hill which looked down over Mposi's *kraal*. The land was drier than ever. The view had changed from even a few weeks earlier: the patchwork of fields had now turned into an uninterrupted expanse of grey dust. The land seemed to have stretched beyond the horizon and into the beaten metal mirror of the sky.

The guests were arriving in the *kraal* from all directions. Groups sat under trees on the hills around the village waiting for things to start. They were dressed in the second-hand western clothes which are imported to Africa – as aid – in great bales, mainly from the United States, and then bought up by unscrupulous traders to be sold in markets throughout the continent. But some of the women had created a local style by winding coloured scarves around their heads and some of the men had slung white cotton sheets over their shoulders, creating the effect of the Ethiopian *shamma*. They called these sheets *chilemba*, but they had nothing in common with the colourful garment Selinah Munuonde had worn in Soweto. These were undoubtedly closer to the traditional *chilemba*.

A group of high-spirited villagers were standing outside the chief's reception hut, waiting for the party to begin. This could only happen when the chief arrived. His wives were carrying in earthenware pots of freshly brewed beer and placing them in a row in the centre of the hut. All of a sudden the crowd fell silent. The chief was approaching, hobbling on a knobkerrie, his eyes fixed on the ground. He went straight into the hut and, with an irritable movement of his stick, invited his guests to follow him.

It was dark and cool inside. We sat down on the baked clay bench which ran around the hut. The chief's health was no better and he gave the impression of being preoccupied. He stared at the mud floor, resting his head on the knop of his stick. With a sudden movement he bawled at his wives to serve beer.

'It's sitting there and is no good to anyone.'

'I'm serving it,' snapped his oldest wife.

'Too late,' he growled.

He caught my eye and smiled a watery smile. The other guests were not so favoured. He glowered around him and then fixed his gaze, as before, on the floor. There was an uncomfortable silence which lasted for several minutes. The beer pot was passed from hand to hand, from right to left, with no unseemly show of haste, like a decanter of Madeira after a dons' dinner. When Klopas's turn came, he took a long, noisy swig and looked around like a child, expecting a reproach; someone snickered, but still no one spoke.

The silence was broken by the chief calling out the names of his four wives. They answered in turn, knelt side by side in front of him, and started to clap. As the wives lit candles, the other women began ululating and whistling. The party had started.

A long antelope horn – reminiscent of the *shofar* of the Yemenite Jews – was thrust through the opening into the hut and a triumphant blast silenced the shrill sound of the women. The hornblower was a tall, muscular man wearing a skirt made of strips of black fur. He had a band of leopard skin around his forehead and *magagada* rattles, dried marrows filled with seeds, were attached to his ankles with bark fibre thongs. He was the witchdoctor, said Tagaruze, the leader of the ceremony, a man of the tribe of Sadiki.

Stamping his feet on the ground to make the *magagada* rattle, he blew a second time on the horn. Following the rhythm established by the *magagada*, four elderly women who were sitting together on the clay bench started pounding on wooden, hide-covered drums. Their hands moved so fast that they seemed to hover, trembling, over the drums. The hornblower stood in front of the drummers stamping his feet in a counter-rhythm. The rest of the guests were clustered behind him, propelled into the juddering movements of the dance by the furious rhythms, yet barely moving, lost in concentration. Sadiki stood at the epicentre of this storm of sound, directing its pace, controlling its pulse. The drummers looked far too frail to be able to produce such a sound and yet they were to drum for hours without a pause. They were calling the ancestors with their music.

The beer started to circulate faster. Some of the men were drunk. The chief's oldest wife, the one who had asked me to get her some glass beads, was apparently possessed by the spirit of the ancestors. Staring from side to side she fell to the ground weeping. Glaring around her in a wild and unfocused way, she got to her feet, pulled her dress up past her fat-marbled buttocks and over her head. As she danced naked in front of the drummers, the pulse quickened again. The hornblower, sweat rolling down his chest, took a head-dress of black eagle feathers and put it on the naked woman's head – to show respect to the ancestors. She danced on, casting great shadows on the candle-lit walls. Then, clutching her head-dress, she fell sobbing to her knees, this time in front of her husband, the chief. Taking the head-dress in her hands, she placed it tenderly on the old man's bowed head. Then, crossing the hut, she sat on the part of the bench reserved for those who had been possessed. The men had removed their jackets and, with sheets draped over their shoulders, they returned to the dance. By now all their inhibitions had fled. Bleary-eyed, they raised their arms above their heads in supplication. The atmosphere was charged. I confess that I, too, was beginning to feel drunk and possessed. Outside it was turning dark. The party would go on right through the night because the ancestors were among us, whispered Tagaruze. There were good signs. A great blessing would follow.

An hour or so later the chief's first wife took the floor again. She danced alone, covered in sweat, her eyes swivelling out of control. Then a younger and prettier woman pulled off her dress and joined her, moving her body in a sexy, ironic way. She shouted '*vurungu Mushavi*' – 'white *Mushavi*' – at me and smiled, running her hands over her breasts and down her sinuous body. She beckoned me to dance. I was happy to – for a long time I had been longing to dance. Amid shouts of ribald encouragement from the men, drunk and elated, I stumbled to my feet. I wanted to dance, I wanted to rip my shirt off and be like everyone else. Perhaps soon they would start reciting the names of the ancestors or liturgical formulae. If I blended in, perhaps they would forget I was there. This was surely good anthropological practice. As I unbuttoned my shirt, the chief's wife said something to me in Shona, but Tagaruze, who could have translated her words for me, was out of earshot. Shrugging, I started to dance, turning my smiling face towards the thatched roof. I had not understood what the chief's wife said and I did not see her cross the space separating us, but the Esperanto of a fist driven into the side of my face was comprehensible. I fell to the ground and for a few seconds lost consciousness.

In fact, I had not quite fallen to the ground; I had fallen on Klopas who was lying prostrate on the floor exhaling violent eructations and acrid farts on the edge of the circle of dancers. It was some time before I could move. I lay there in a stupor until Tagaruze, helped by some of the men, pulled me outside. Time to leave, he said. They did not want us to stay. We had to go. My head hurt, I was still drunk, and I was put out: what had I done to deserve such an attack? Rebelliously I muttered to Tagaruze that I did not want to leave. I certainly did not want to leave without saying good-bye. The following morning I meant to continue my journey north, but I would not go without saying farewell to the chief. He was still in the hut, the feather head-dress on his head, shuffling his feet backwards and forwards in a slow, deliberate dance. Tagaruze went back into the hut, took his elbow and steered him out into the cool of the night. Sevias was standing by his side as I murmured my thanks to both of them and a rather terse apology to the chief for having upset his wife.

'You have not upset the chief's wife, *Mushavi*,' said Sevias. 'You have not upset anybody. You really uplifted us and made us think about our past. This blow was a welcome from the ancestors. Perhaps also it was a little warning. Just a little warning – because if they did not want you here at all, they would not have given you a little, light blow like that, they would have torn you into pieces. Now you must go because the ancestors are coming among us.'

Hours before, the chief had removed his shirt. Sweat beaded his thin chest and his old man's shoulders were dwarfed by the mass of feathers on his head. His limbs still twitched to the sound of the drums: he looked drugged and half-dead. He took my hand in his and whispered in my ear:

'The ancestors have come from Israel: they have come from Sena. They are here with us. Good-bye, *Mushavi.* Perhaps we shall see each other in Sena.'

With these cryptic words ringing in my ears I left Mposi's *kraal* for the last time. It was only about eleven o'clock, it was a cool, still night and it was good to be out of the stifling atmosphere of the chief's hut. Neither Tagaruze nor I wanted to sleep. The rhythm of the drums, still audible from the *kraal,* by some curious metamorphosis had become a few lines from Kipling: 'something hidden' went the drums, 'go and find it. Go and look behind the ranges, something lost behind the ranges, lost and waiting for you. Go!' Impulsively I suggested we go to Dumghe. Beyond the ranges of Dumghe there were things to find, particularly the cave, and there would never be a better opportunity than this. The man known as the guardian of Dumghe was at the party. Anyone not at the party was asleep. To my surprise Tagaruze agreed.

We took the path across the hills which we had taken before, but this time we gave the villages a wide berth. Exhausted from our walk, we arrived at the foot of Dumghe and paused near the *meshunah* tree under the wall of rock behind which the Lemba cave was said to be hidden. I took out a torch from my jacket pocket and flashed it around. There was no one to be seen. Tagaruze as usual had his revolver stuck in his belt. We walked to the wooded end of the hill and slowly started climbing the path to the summit. There was no movement on the hill: looking over the valley I saw no sign of life.

'The ancestors must be here. It is not good,' said Tagaruze, his face stiff with fear. 'Let's go back.'

'The ancestors can't be everywhere,' I said. 'They're all having a good time at the party.'

Tagaruze gave me a wan smile. The effects of the *chibuku* were wearing off now. As we reached the summit I was excited more than afraid. If my instinct was right, and increasingly I was convinced that it was, the *ngoma lungundu* must be in the cave. This was after all the Lemba holy-of-holies. Maybe there were other things, perhaps some vital clue which would lead to the solution of the mystery of the Lemba; perhaps even their lost book. But to find the *ngoma*, the drum which Lemba tradition still venerated and which these strange people had followed through Africa, would be remarkable: Al-Idrisi's drum, perhaps, 'Arrahim, as big as *Albaba* . . .' I dimly remembered some lines of the South African poet, Guy Butler, who had written about *ngoma lungundu*:

The great king, Mwali, like the drum, was never seen,
    no one saw the king or the drum except the old high priest,
    he, Dzoma-la-Dzimu, he, the mouthpiece of God.
The king's dwelling and the drum's dwelling were guarded by
        plaited fences,
    where snakes with a head at each end kept slithering watch;
    also by twelve lions, watchdogs of the king:
    quiet, quiet they were, only rousing to roar
    in praise of their lord when the drum beat,
    drum of the dead, *ngoma lungundu*.

There had been something in Chief Mposi's face when I had asked about the drum at the meeting of the elders which had suggested to me that the drum was not lost. I had my camera over my shoulder and would be able to photograph it. I decided to use the close-up mode: it would make a marvellous cover for the book I hoped to write. At that moment the path fell away under my feet and it was only Tagaruze's swiftness in grabbing my arm that prevented me from disappearing over the edge. Loose stones fell over the cliff in a tidy avalanche. A flat, neat echo sounded below us. We paused and looked down into the ravine. Now I could just make out the path which led down the cliff opposite the great wall of rock. It was steep. But there was no wind tonight, unlike the day of the official visit. With considerable caution, pausing from time to time to rest and to flash the torch around, we edged our way down. Once there was a crack of dead branches; once the sound of a large bird and of rushing air, then silence. I wondered if it were the 'bird of heaven' – the protector of Dumghe. Then the path stopped. There was a great round boulder in front of us. To one side the ground fell away into darkness, on the other there was a gap. I flashed my torch into it and saw the outline of the mouth of a cave. This, I thought, must be the Lemba holy-of-holies. Between the boulder and the cliff-face there was a mound of loose scree. I placed my desert-booted foot into it, holding the torch with one hand and resting the other against the side of the boulder. As I shone the torch further into the void of the cave, I heard a sort of rasping sound, a cough or a snarl, and then a louder sound, a snort, perhaps, which became a deafening roar as it bounced off the surrounding rock-faces. My hand gripped the torch in terror. The gun, I thought, shoot it, whatever it is. But Tagaruze had the gun, and he had disappeared. I turned, scrambled up the narrow track after him and fled through the wooded slopes of Dumghe. Within seconds, we arrived panting at the *meshunah* tree. We sat down and I offered the policeman a cigarette.

'What the hell was that?'

'It must have been a Lemba ancestor in the body of a leopard or a lion. Everybody knows their ancestors prowl around this mountain. That was a terrible, big mistake.' After a few minutes his police training took over and he added, 'Or it might have been Morgan.'

You do not hear rain falling on powdery earth or on a thatched roof. It was the cold rather than the rain which woke me and before dawn I pulled on some clothes and went out into the *kraal*. It was pouring down with rain. Sevias, Tagaruze and Darana were already up. The Ford had finally been delivered to the *kraal* and they were sitting in it trying to keep warm. The two Lemba seemed unaware of our nocturnal visit to the cave. As we talked in the car, the men agreed that the party had been an uncommon success and that without doubt the ancestors would bless the villages in the coming year. I was amazed. No rain, not even a modest fall of rain, not even the mist-like rain they call *guti*, had fallen for months, some said for years. And already in the early morning, within minutes of the end of the ancestors' party, there had been enough rain to turn the *kraal* into a mire and put water in the borehole. The chief, if he's well enough, must be out of his mind with joy, I thought.

As the sun was rising, Klopas arrived and squeezed his unfragrant self into the back seat. I apologised for having fallen on him during the party. He gazed at me in a fairly benevolent way and admitted that he had not been aware of it. Because of his great age, he said, it was true that he had taken a nap in the middle of the party and I might have fallen on him then, he did not know. But afterwards he had rallied and had carried on drinking as long as there was anything to drink. Now he had come to say good-bye.

I went back to my hut to pack and to put aside a few things which could serve as farewell presents. Mama's eligible daughter seemed sad that I was going, but was glad to be given my sunglasses. To Mama, the provider of picnics, I gave my red spotted handkerchief; to Klopas, the drunkard, a metal hipflask full of rum; to Sevias, the sage, a rather good notebook; to Darana, the fighter, a penknife; and to my bodyguard Tagaruze, the detective, a plastic watch with a number of function buttons. I have never given presents which caused as much pleasure. With an onset of uncharacteristic gaiety Klopas waved his flask around his head explaining how useful it would be for his journeys in the event that his zest should ever temporarily fail him. The others showered me with thanks and showed off their gifts to other members of the *kraal*. 'I shall be a very big man at HQ,' said Tagaruze, fastening the watch to his wrist.

But had I obtained all the information I needed? asked Sevias. If there were further questions and mysteries, I could stay or I could come back. His daughter would be in the *kraal* for some time to come, he added, looking at me meaningfully.

I told him that I would return one day, but that I was still confused. There were indeed mysteries which needed solving. For one thing, I said, it was difficult to understand why, on the one hand, their traditions maintained that they were Jews while, on the other, so much pointed at a Muslim origin.

'We're not Muslims,' shouted Klopas, and stalked off in the direction of Dumghe, explaining wildly that now the rains had come he was going to have a bath. The others joined in a chorus of protest.

'We learned the Muslim things from the Hamadis,' said Sevias. 'We lost our path and followed theirs. But there are some Lemba who have not lost their path. There is one Lemba called Zinowanda who lives over the mountains in Tedzembwe and who is an initiator and circumcisor. He does not follow the Hamadis; he keeps to the Lemba path. You must find Zinowanda in Tedzembwe. And you must find a

Muslim called Mr Ali; he is a rich man with many shops and a car. We have bought many things from this Ali in his shops in Masvingu. You can find him easily. He will tell you how the Muslims came to the Lemba. And to know where the Lemba came from you must find Sena. Go next to Great Zimbabwe. Then Harare. And then I don't know.'

Promising to return, I drove off to find Dongijena. He was in the bar behind the bottle shop. It was ten o'clock in the morning and as usual the bar was full. The young men were starting on their day of *chibuku*; the village whore, dressed up today like a Sunday School teacher from the American Deep South, was slumped alone in her corner. A crowd gathered around Dongijena were haranguing an Indian-looking official from the Ministry of Education. Neither the councillor's protests nor his friends' assurances, nor even his remarkably youthful appearance, could counter the over-whelming evidence of the document which the official was holding up for all to see, which showed that Dongijena was now sixty years old and therefore eligible for a richly deserved but obligatory retirement. Dongijena said that it was a forgery; that it was discrimination against Jews, against black Jews. The official said that they were not Jews; Muslims maybe, but not Jews. Tagaruze, who had received orders to stay on in the village until further notice, threw himself into the fray. He was quite sure that they were Jews, Israelites in fact. When I left, a few minutes later, they were still arguing.

PART THREE

Great Zimbabwe

25

The road to Tedzembwe passed through a series of valleys and wooded mountain ranges. The rain which had fallen the previous night seemed to have benefited only the area around Mposi's villages. Within a few miles the mud tracks were dry and hard. I saw few villages. Not far from one of them an extremely short, bespectacled man flagged me down with an imperious wave of his knobkerrie. He was wearing a black suit, shiny with use, which looked as if, long ago, it might have belonged to an English schoolboy. He had no shirt, vest or shoes. He appeared to speak no word of English. 'I' I pointed at my chest, 'Tedzembwe.' He nodded, prodded his own bare chest and repeated. 'Tedzembwe, Tedzembwe.' I was relieved to have found a guide.

The map I had was not up to much and road signs in those rural areas were few and far between. My passenger pointed through the open window at a distant mountain range: 'Tedzembwe,' he said once more. We drove for a couple of hours. He did not speak, but whistled between his teeth, beating time with his stick on the floor. Every now and then he tapped the dashboard with his knobkerrie to indicate a left or right turn. Once, when I took a wrong turning, he gave me a sharp tap on the knee. Eventually the mud track petered out and we drove on through well-cropped meadows studded with great grey stones. The going became rougher.

239

He indicated that I should turn into the hill and drive straight up the mountain. Often the car grazed exposed rock or the gradient was too steep and the wheels spun in the loose soil, raising clouds of dust, before losing its grip and slipping back down the hill. Finally we reached a small *kraal*. My guide tapped on the steering wheel and announced, in English, 'I'll be all right here.' With a deft movement he opened the door, stepped out and, without a word of thanks or adieu, skipped across the shingle to one of the huts. 'Where's Tedzembwe?' I shouted. He pointed at a mountain range more or less in the direction from which we had come and yelled back, 'Tedzembwe's there – and we are here. Very good.' And, with something akin to a salute, the little man disappeared into a hut.

I drove back the way I had come and a couple of hours later found myself in Tedzembwe, a predominantly Lemba village some thirty miles south-east of Masvingo. The village boasted one general store cum bottle shop in front of which, under a great leafy tree, were three discrete groups of men: one was drinking *chibuku*, another had been drinking *chibuku* and was now asleep, and a more promising group was playing *tsoro* – an African game not wholly unlike draughts. Neither of the conscious groups displayed the slightest interest in my arrival or in my presence. I produced Mathiva's letter. They had never heard of him. Showing them my last copy of *The Thirteenth Gate* with its much admired photographs of the Lemba in South Africa, I proclaimed myself its author. No flicker of interest animated their faces. I mentioned Chief Mposi. They shrugged and carried on with their *chibuku* and *tsoro*. I had one card left. The day after the assembly of the Lemba clans at Mposi, one of the elders had told me that the Lemba could best be regarded as a sort of secret society: as such, they had a password which they used to identify themselves to other Lemba. Two fingers, pressed together, are raised to shoulder height and the secret word 'tabi' is uttered. I lifted my fingers and growled, '*Tabi.*' A gratifying silence fell upon the group.

'What do you want?' said one of them.

'I want to speak to Zinowanda. It is an urgent matter. It has to do with the history of the Mwenye.'

'You come at bad time, baas,' drawled an old man.

'Zinowanda not here. He's in jail. He stole seven cows from a neighbour and drove them over to Mberengwe where he had to pay *lobola*. Come back in two years. He may be out then.' The men laughed, but remained watchful.

Which jail was he in? No one knew. How could I find him? No one could say. I said that I needed to talk to him about the circumcision rites and the words used.

'These are big secrets,' said one of the *tsoro* players.

'Do you say *Allahu Akbar* and *Bismillahi* when you slaughter and circumcise?'

'No,' said the old man, 'these are the Hamadi words. We use Mwenye language, not Hamadi.' But these were secrets, which, they insisted, they would never share. I drank a few beers, tried to understand the principles of *tsoro*, and then went to sleep under my mosquito net on the shop veranda.

At first light I drove off. Zinowanda, the great repository of genuine Lemba tradition, had escaped me. Perhaps I would have better luck with Mr Ali.

Masvingo, formerly Fort Victoria, is a white Rhodesian town with wide streets and Wild West arcaded wooden walkways. There is a pervasive sense of rural America. Once in a while you see young 'Rhodies' roar by on motorbikes, cowboy boots on their feet, stetsons jammed on their heads. Their parked pick-ups exude the tinny jangle of American country music. The little restaurants serve hamburgers and fried chicken. The Rhodies here gave the impression of still being a force to be reckoned with. And, indeed, in Zimbabwe, they still control the industry and the greater part of the commercial farming. However, it is the Indians who control small-town commerce.

When the British occupied Matabeleland and Mashonaland, the entire population was black African, roughly split between Shona groups in the east and the Ndebele in the west. The plateau occupied by present-day Zimbabwe was completely sealed off from Muslim influence. The British soon changed that: thousands of indentured labourers were imported, mainly from India's North-West Frontier, to build the Victoria Falls bridge over the Zambezi and other imperial projects. Many of them stayed on. Now there are communities of Indians in all Zimbabwe's main towns.

Sevias had been right. Mr Ali was not very difficult to find. In fact, a number of shop-fronts carried his name. An Indian shop-girl in one of them guided me to the flagship establishment – a large emporium on the main commercial street. 'Ali Will Dress You!' gaudily coloured notices proclaimed; 'Suits for Gents and Ladies! Where Masvingo Shops!'

Ali, a short, bearded man with greasy, shoulder-length hair, was standing behind a wooden counter piled high with men's acrylic suits, cheap dresses, jeans and bales of cloth. He gave me a suspicious look. When I mentioned the Lemba, he relaxed. Shouting at his black assistant to get me a Coke, he took me into a small, untidy office behind the shop.

'Very interesting tribe, those Lemba!' he exclaimed in a remarkably high-pitched voice. 'It all happened about thirty years ago. A certain Mr Khan came in here one day and told my dad to his very considerable astonishment that he had found a tribe with very pronounced Islamic characteristics.' As he enumerated these characteristics he wagged his head in that peculiarly Indian way which is half affirmation, half begging to be believed: 'They used to kosher their animals; they would never share their food with other tribes; they had these Muslim names. You see, they were having traces of Islam. They had no Arabic then, except for these names, but they had these traditions I was telling you about. This was back in 1955 or 1956. One man very involved was Barna Hassan, an African, a Chawa from Malawi, who had married a very nice Lemba lady. It was Hassan who told Mr Khan about them. So then we started going to their villages on Saturday afternoons – we were staying one night and coming back the next day – and we converted quite a bit. When we went, they knew nothing of Islam, no Arabic, not a word of Islam, no Arabic at all, except some of their names. Then we sent some very educated Muslims from Malawi, Chawa people, to go and teach them. We used to call the Lemba village at Mashawasha Islamabad – there was so much missionary activity going on at that time. The Libyans found out something about it and sent some money and we built mosques in Mashawasha, Gutu and Chinyika. Then Indian Muslims from Salisbury – Harare now – came at the weekends and slept for two or three nights with the Lemba. Fifty or sixty of them used to come and preach and convert Lemba all weekend. Very wonderful people, the Lemba,' he said. 'In fact, all the Africans here are very wonderful. The whites used to kill them, put them in prison, beat them, and now, what do they say, "God bless them," they say, "We forgive them!" They forgive them! I am taking my hat off to them!'

At that moment Ali leapt to his feet wagging his head and shouted, 'You must go to Chinyika. There is a meeting today in Chinyika Mosque. You can meet the Lemba *Imam* and you can meet many, many Muslims from Harare and all over. My employee can take you. He is knowing the Lemba.'

He ordered his black assistant to accompany me and to show me the way to Chinyika. Before going, I bought some glass beads which were arranged in a bowl on the polished wooden counter and asked him to post them for me to Chief Mposi for the attention of his senior wife. I gave him rather more money than was necessary and, in return, he gave me a book – *Islam in Zimbabwe* by E. C. Mandivenga, now a lecturer at the University of Zimbabwe – which confirmed, with some differences of detail, what Ali himself had told me. Mandivenga wrote:

In 1961, an Asian Muslim stopped at a Lemba *kraal* to ask for water. Responding to questions from his host the Muslim stated that he did not eat the flesh of swine and he was circumcised. The local Lemba . . . were surprised to find a person outside their tribe who observed such customs. The historic encounter . . . was reported firstly to the Masvingo Islamic Society and thereafter to the Harare Muslim community, who began taking an interest in assisting the Lemba towards understanding the Islamic faith. What ensued was that a small number of Muslims from all over Zimbabwe travelled to Buhera to teach the Islamic faith and customs to the Lemba people. The outcome of these efforts is that at least 200 Lemba were reintroduced to the religion of their forefathers . . . Prior to this they had what may be designated vestigial Islam. It was decided to send three Lemba men at a time to the Muslim Society in Masvingo where the *Imam* would teach them Arabic expressions and salutations . . . A . . . branch of the Lemba was contacted by the Islamic Society in 1974 in the Gutu district. Sheikh Adam was on a . . . visit to Masvingo. An old Shona-speaking man, who claimed he had been instructed in a dream to find an Arab, came to town. He had felt compelled to visit Masvingo. The old man (Abu Bakr Hamandishe) was directed to Sheikh Adam ... who explained to him Islamic customs and beliefs. The similarity between Islamic and Lemba customs apparently impressed the old man, for he invited the Sheikh to come to address his people in the Gutu district. The historic meeting was arranged and 300 to 400 Lemba assembled at Chinyika to hear Sheikh Adam. The Sheikh reports that he wondered what to say, so he simply told the enthusiastic gathering who he was and what his religious beliefs were. And when he had informed them that he did not eat the flesh of pigs and that only his people may slaughter the animals whose meat he eats, the crowd clapped their hands as a gesture of approval. Before the meeting ended the Sheikh was already being openly treated as a fellow Muslim. He was profoundly moved.

Chinyika is a small village forty kilometres east of Gutu. The land is flatter than around the Mposi villages and there was more evidence of European farming. In addition to the mosque, the village boasted a whitewashed church with a Dutch steeple. The mosque was a long, white building, badly in need of a lick of paint, with a corrugated asbestos roof. It was set in a large plot of scrubland filled with debris. Attempts had once been made to create a formal Islamic garden: there were the remains of a hedge bordering the rough path leading to the mosque, but the only plants to have survived the drought were three red flowering cacti.

Behind the mosque a concrete block with facilities for ritual ablutions had been built, but nothing worked. Spare parts for the pump had proved impossible to find and, in any case, the borehole was empty. The *Imam* of Chinyika, a tall, lean Lemba called Ali Mutazu, lived in one end of the mosque. We went into his house, which was a large room sub-divided by a screen. The floor was concrete; everything else was makeshift. The *Imam* was washing his hands at the sink from a plastic jerry can. His wife and children were making a racket behind the screen. Seeing us, the *Imam* yelled at his family to be quiet, turned towards us and bowed.

'*Salamu aleikum*,' he said.

'*Aleikum salam*,' I replied.

'You are a Lemba, I believe,' I started.

'I am a Muslim, yes.'

'Are there many Lemba here?'

'Here we are a few only. But over the mountains in Buhera there are so many Lemba,' he shook his head in the gesture of wonderment the Lemba reserve for discussions of their tribe's number.

'Do many Lemba come to the mosque?'

'Sometimes a few come on Friday. But they like it really when we go to their villages. It is far for them to come. They live far, far, far away.'

'But I thought this was a Lemba village.'

He nodded thoughtfully and agreed that it was really a Lemba village.

'Were you always a Muslim?' I continued.

'Before the Islamic preachers came to us we lived, really, a system of living which was related to Islam. We used to wear topees' – he pointed at the white skullcap on his head – 'and the old men always knew the first *sura* of the Quran.'

'Is that really so?' I asked. 'I have just come from near Mberengwe and never once did I see anyone wearing a topee and never once did I meet an old man who knew the Quran.'

'Oh! Yes. I know one old man. He is eighty years old. He learned *Sura* One from his father. His father learned *Sura* One from his father; his father from his father; his father from his father: his father from his father . . .'

I interrupted him gently.

'Can I see this old man?'

'Perhaps later. I must pray now,' and, collecting a number of rusty tins open at one end, he went off to perform his ablutions.

I sat and waited for him to return. Behind the screen, the children were wailing again. A hen sitting in a blue plastic bowl laid an egg. The *Imam*'s wife peeped around the screen and disappeared. Pinned on to the screen I noticed a few glossy photographs of the Kaaba in Mecca, an Islamic calendar and a large map of the Islamic Republic of Iran. A few minutes later, the *Imam* returned, clanking his tins together.

'Islam is great,' he said, grinning. 'It is *really* great in Zimbabwe, in South Africa, Zambia, Malawi – everywhere *really* great! Soon they can control even the whole world! You stay here. I must go to pray in mosque now.'

A minute or two later, out of curiosity, I followed him towards the mosque end of the structure, a camera, as usual, slung over my shoulder, zipped inside its leather pouch. But long before I approached the door of the mosque an elderly Indian had rushed towards me imploring me to 'consider our holy religion. No pictures please. But do come in.'

The *Imam* was not actually praying: he was sitting cross-legged along with a dozen Indians around a Persian rug. Heaped in front of them was a mouthwatering feast: fried chicken, kofta, lamb curry, pilau rice, puris, mangoes. The *Imam* himself was eating a meatball. No *sadza* and *usavi* for him, I thought. The Indians pressed me to eat my fill and, while I ate, they told me about their mission. Their group was from Harare. They had just arrived (the food had been prepared the previous day by their wives and mothers) and they were intending to spend forty days in the wilderness, as they put it with unconscious irony, working among the

Lemba, introducing them to the Islamic faith. Now they were keen to get into the mission field and to visit one of the outlying Lemba villages.

'There is no blessing in hurrying,' explained the elderly Indian as he prepared himself for a siesta.

However, the young men insisted on leaving the mosque and, at the *Imam*'s suggestion, we piled into a minibus and set off to find the old Lemba man who had learned the first *sura* of the Quran from his father. The old man, it turned out, was none other than Abu Bakr Hamandishe, the very one who, according to Mandivenga's account in *Islam in Zimbabwe*, had been 'instructed in a dream to find an Arab' and who had met and been influenced by Sheikh Adam.

It was late afternoon when we arrived at Abu Bakr's *kraal*. The old man was sitting on a stool in front of his hut. He remained seated and the Muslim missionaries sat on the ground, somewhat in awe, at his feet. He clapped his hands together in the local African way and said '*Salamu aleikum*.' I started to ask him questions. Abu Bakr thought that he was about seventy-five years old; what he knew for certain was that he had acquired a registration certificate in 1921 and by that time he was already 'a big boy'. He had been born in this village and his parents and grandparents before him. I asked him if it was true that he had known some Arabic before he met Sheikh Adam.

'No,' he said; 'no one knew any Arabic before the Indians came. What I knew was this, which is a kind of Hiberu. The other prayers were like Shona.' And slowly he recited these lines:

> Fara fara wa-fatiah
> wa-meira hind agabara
> burumburu baramina amina.

He paused and looked around at his sallow-faced audience of urban Indians dressed for the mission field. Then he continued:

'Our forefathers came from Sena. They came from the north. They came from Hundji. When we slaughter our animals, we look north; when we bury our dead, they point north. The Jews were the first people we knew. Our forefathers were Muslims and Israelites. And we are Jews too. They circumcise like us and they cut . . .' – he paused again and looked at the young Indians who were observing him gloomily – 'and the moon, we saw the moon before the others. And when we saw it in the water, we thanked our ancestors for the secrets they had given us. The secrets of the Jews.'

During the drive back to the mosque Ali the *Imam* was not in the best of moods.

'You were not absolutely right about the first *sura* of the Quran,' I said.

'I was right.'

'"Fara fara wa-fatiah" is not from the Quran.'

'It is! It is!' he said. Then he jerked his chin up and said, 'No, maybe you right. Maybe it is not Arabic. Not good enough Arabic. Not Quran Arabic. But I want to know for what you came. I want to know for what you went to see Abu Bakr. I am suspicious!'

'Why are you suspicious?'

'I do not think you are a Muslim,' he began with a pious scowl. 'You think the Lemba peoples not Muslims also.'

As we drove back to Chinyika, the *Imam* sulked and the young missionaries were subdued. If the Lemba had been Israelites, one of them said, that meant they were Jews and it was well known that the Jews were the enemies of Islam. Converting lapsed Muslims was one thing; taking the truth to the enemy was another. I did not join in. I gazed out at the scarlet sun which hovered and then sank behind the blue outline of distant hills. The *Imam* was partly right: I was not convinced that the Lemba had been Muslims in the full sense of the word. I was not sure what they had been. It was a complicated question and at this point in my journey it was still open. But now there was a further question, a fascinating one, which I would have to address: were the Lemba, as they claim, the builders or co-builders of Great Zimbabwe – the greatest civilisation of sub-Saharan Africa?

26

As we have seen, the European usually credited with the discovery of Great Zimbabwe was Karl Mauch. Financed by Jonas Bergtheil, a Jewish philanthropist, he spent seven years, from 1865 to 1872, in almost continuous travel in little-known parts of Africa. His desire to be an African explorer had come to him young. One day, gazing at the enigmatic gaps on his father's map of Africa, he decided that his destiny was to unlock the hidden secrets of the Dark Continent. His father was a carpenter called Joseph.

In 1871, Mauch decided to explore the completely unknown territory to the north of the Limpopo. Before setting out he spent a month in the northern Transvaal with João Albasini (the arch-scoundrel, Mauch called him). Despite a great deal of local suspicion and resentment brought about by Albasini's slave-trading activities, Mauch was finally able to persuade some native bearers and a guide to accompany him. To allay their fears he paid them their wages in advance, in cloth, six yards of blue salempore a man.

On 30 July, the morning of his departure, he wrote in his diary: 'In the sight of the reunited Fatherland, standing in the forefront of all the nations, and with the image of the Kaiser, crowned with victory before me, may now the most valuable and important, the hitherto most mysterious part of Africa be tackled – the ancient Monomotapa or Ophir.'

On 5 September, he arrived at the ruins of Great Zimbabwe, guided there by Adam Render, an unscrupulous American elephant hunter, gone native, who had discovered the ruins some time before. After his examination of the site, during which he found an undamaged wooden lintel (subsequently shown to have been made from an African hard wood called *Spirostachys Africana*), Mauch wrote:

> It can be taken as a fact that the wood which we obtained is in fact cedar-wood and from this that it cannot come from anywhere else but from the Lebanon. Furthermore only the Phoenicians could have brought it here; further, Solomon used a lot of cedar-wood for the building of the temple and of his palaces: further – including here the visit of the Queen of Sheba and considering Zimbabe or Zimbaoe or Simbaoe written in Arabic (of Hebrew I understand nothing) one gets as a result that the great woman who built the *rondeau* could have been none other than the Queen of Sheba ... Today I dare to close this account with:
>
> The Queen of Sheba is the Queen of Simbaoe;
> Psalm 72:10: The Sheba mentioned there is Simbaoe;
> Matthew 2:11: Of the three Kings the one was from here, the others from Arabia and India.
> The ruins are copies of Solomon's temple and palace.

Mauch's conversations with the local people were sufficient to persuade him that

> the festivals of the Jews of Solomon's time were imitated until about thirty to forty years ago when the Matabele from the west and the Zulu from the east invaded the country ... If I add everything together I cannot doubt any longer that Bebereke (the

local chief) must be a descendant of the high priestly officer that Solomon sent out with the Queen of Sheba who, with her whole retinue, had converted to Judaism.

Whether these conclusions were in any way affected by a desire to please his Jewish benefactor it is impossible to say.

During his travels Mauch also came across the Lemba, whose customs he described. He noted that they were physically and culturally distinct from their neighbours. They reminded him of the 'Israelitish types'. His is the first detailed description we have of the Lemba.

Adam Render was convinced that Mauch would make a fortune out of Great Zimbabwe and, well in advance, he claimed half the profits for himself. But although the discovery was to receive world-wide attention, Mauch himself was to gain nothing from it. From Great Zimbabwe he made his way to Sena on the Zambezi and from there to Germany, where, having failed to secure employment in a university for lack of formal academic qualifications, he found a job in a cement works near Ulm. At the age of thirty-eight he fell to his death from the window of his small garret.

The ruins of Great Zimbabwe lie on a plateau 4,000–5,000 feet above sea level. Because of its elevation, the entire area is free of tsetse fly and normally provides an ideal habitat for man and cattle. The hills to the north of the ruins are gold-bearing, and the plains a few miles to the south are open grassland admirably suited for the breeding of cattle. Gold and cattle are thought to have been the chief sources of the wealth of Great Zimbabwe.

The walls of Great Zimbabwe were built of slabs of rock from the surrounding hills. Horizontal courses, without mortar, were laid out to form walls about twice as high as they were thick. The outer stones were carefully chosen to create a smooth surface, but the area between was filled with irregularly shaped slabs. Inside the complexes of stone walls originally stood dwelling huts built of *daga* – the most common African building material – a fine gravel bound together by clay.

The masonry work at Great Zimbabwe can be divided into three styles. The most sophisticated walls were constructed of carefully selected slabs, which were laid out in long and very regular courses. The outside of the wall was knapped to create a smooth and near vertical surface. Each course was very slightly set back to give the wall an inward slope, and the walls were often set in foundation trenches. The other building styles exhibited less regular coursing, less carefully chosen stone blocks, poor bonding, no knapping and no foundation trenches. Archaeological work has shown that the more poorly coursed walls were earlier than the regularly coursed and knapped walls, whereas the worst walls of all – no more than loose piles of stones – were the most recent.

The site is dominated by a 300-foot granite ridge on the north side which is studded with huge, rounded boulders. This is the site of the Hill Ruin or the Acropolis, a complex of formidable walls and ramparts built between the boulders.

In the valley beneath the Hill Ruin is the most impressive of all the Great Zimbabwe ruins – a building known to the local people in the nineteenth century as *Mumbahuru*, the Great Woman's House, and in English variously as the Temple, the Circular Ruin, the Great Enclosure or the Elliptical Building. This structure is by far the largest pre-colonial building in sub-Saharan Africa. The walls are seventeen feet thick and, at the highest point, thirty-two feet high; 182,000 cubic feet of stone in the form of 900,000 stone blocks were used in their construction. The outer wall of the Elliptical Building is over 800 feet long; some 200 feet of the wall, in the south-east area, are decorated with the chevron pattern which some early travellers may have taken to be an inscription. Inside the south-western part of the wall stands a conical tower in front of which is a raised stone platform.

'Zimbabwe' is a Shona word, which is usually understood as being a contraction of '*dzimba dza mabwe*' – 'houses of stone'. But there are other interpretations: Peter Garlake prefers the derivation '*dzimba woye*' – 'venerated houses', while Thomas Huffman takes its derivation from '*dzimbahwe*', which means 'home, court or grave of a chief'. As sixteenth-century Portuguese documents and most later maps usually rendered the word as '*zimbaoe*', or 'simbaoe', Garlake's explanation seems more likely. In 1552, João de Barros explained the term as follows:

> The natives of the country call these edifices, Symbaoe, which according to their language signifies court, for every place where the Benomotapa may be is so called; and they say that being royal property all the king's other dwellings have this name. It is guarded by a nobleman, who has charge of it after the manner of a chief alcaide, and they call this officer Symbacayo, as we should say Keeper of the Symbaoe . . .

Great Zimbabwe was the capital of a centralised state and the apex of what is generally termed the Great Zimbabwe civilisation. The term 'civilisation' has not always been accepted with respect to this culture. In the nineteenth century, Victorian anthropology divided the history of human development into three phases: savagery, barbarism and civilisation. Savagery – in effect man living in his natural habitat as a hunter-gatherer – was supplanted by the barbarism of primitive farming communities, which in turn was replaced by civilisation. Civilisation was usually understood to be inextricably linked with the invention or possession of a system of writing. But today one could argue that writing is not the only criterion of civilisation. Other equally valid criteria include the notion of dwelling in cities, the creation of a hierarchical society and the construction of monumental architecture.

The structures which made up the stone parts of Great Zimbabwe have no parallels elsewhere in Africa. Radiocarbon dating shows that the city flourished between 1240 and 1450. At its peak, in the middle of the fourteenth century, the town housed some eighteen thousand inhabitants and was about three miles in diameter. It was thus the largest prehistoric conurbation in Southern or Central Africa and controlled a state which was bounded by the Kalahari Desert in the southwest and the Zambezi River in the north, and which included most of present-day Zimbabwe as well as parts of the northern Transvaal, Mozambique and Botswana. Unlike some other southern African societies, the social organisation of Great Zimbabwe was based on a firm distinction between the ordinary people and the ruling class, whose legitimacy is thought to have derived from the notion of sacred kingship.

Throughout the area there were numerous lesser Zimbabwe buildings, such as the ones I had seen around the Lemba villages. In most cases these were the dwelling-places of some elite group. Excavations have shown that one of this group's characteristics was that they only ate beef whereas the common people in the surrounding mud huts ate sheep, goats and whatever wild animals fell to their spears. There is reason to suppose that this elite, like the elite at Great Zimbabwe itself, practised animal sacrifice.

Before the rise of Great Zimbabwe, the Zimbabwe civilisation had its capital at Mapungubwe, which lies approximately at the point at which present-day Zimbabwe, South Africa and Botswana meet. For reasons which are still unclear, Mapungubwe was abandoned a few years after the rise of Great Zimbabwe.

In or around 1450, Great Zimbabwe too was abandoned, again for reasons which are far from certain. The original kingdom was split into two: in the south-west, a state developed ruled by the Torwa dynasty with its capital at Khami, near present-day Bulawayo; in the north-east, the kingdom of the Monomotapa or Mwene Mutapa rose up with its capital at Fura, near present-day Mount Darwin. Both these states and, to an extent, the societies which immediately succeeded them form part of the 'Zimbabwe civilisation'.

Although the kingdom of the Monomotapa became the better known to Europeans, it was the Torwa state which was the more powerful. Khami had a population of between 7,000 and 12,000 people and controlled a territory not much smaller than that of the Great Zimbabwe state. The state of the Monomotapa covered only 31,000 square kilometres, while its capital at Fura could not have housed more than 4,000 people. The process of fragmentation was to continue. By the middle of the eighteenth century, the King of Portugal could complain: 'That vast empire [of the Monomotapa] is in such decay that no one has dominion over it, because everyone has power there.' The last Zimbabwe-like state – that of the Rozwi – was controlled by the powerful Changamire dynasty. Its capital at Dhlo Dhlo was only one-third the size of Khami. However, the Changamire state declined during the *mfecane* and, by the time the British arrived towards the end of the nineteenth century, there was little trace of the rich civilisation which had once flourished on the Zimbabwe high plateau.

Karl Mauch's conviction that the Zimbabwe ruins were of very ancient Semitic origin was to hold sway for the next forty years, particularly in Rhodesia. Cecil Rhodes himself was in no doubt as to the antiquity and the origin of the ruins:

> You will find that Zimbabwe is an old Phoenician residence and everything points to Sofula being the place from which Hiram fetched his gold; the word 'peacocks' in the Bible may be read as parrots and among the stone ornaments from Zimbabye are green parrots, the common kind of that district, for the rest you have gold and ivory, also the fact that Zimbabye is built of hewn stone without mortar.

From the beginning of white settlement in Rhodesia, Great Zimbabwe became a means of justifying the presence of Rhodes's colonists. As Garlake put it, 'Great Zimbabwe . . . quickly became a symbol of the essential rightness and justice of colonisation and gave the subservience of the Shona an age-old precedent if not biblical sanction.' Until independence, the cover of the Rhodesian journal *NADA* showed a Nordic St George defending the ramparts of Great Zimbabwe against a dragon, its flank inscribed with the word 'barbarism'.

A further factor which was enlisted to justify the colonists' presence in Rhodesia was the supposed similarity between the ancient Phoenician civilisation and the British Empire. The Hon. Alexander Wilmot, a contemporary writer, wrote:

> What the great British Empire is to the nineteenth century, Phoenicia was to distant ages, when Solomon's temple was built at Jerusalem, and Hiram, King of Tyre, sent out expeditions to

the distant shores of India, Arabia and south-eastern Africa. The principal carrying trade of the world was performed by the Phoenicians. No state of antiquity understood the art of successful colonisation so well and none was more fortunate in the choice of those whom she used both for mining and commercial purposes. Her manufactures were the most excellent and the most valued in these times and her trade both by land and sea had no rival . . .

In other words, both Great Britain and Phoenicia were small maritime nations whose citizens had colonised a great deal of the world. As the blacks had been controlled in the distant past by the Phoenicians, so they would be controlled now by the British: it was part of the natural order of things. Cecil Rhodes himself perceived the arrival in the area of his British South Africa Company as 'the second civilising influence'. It thus became politically expedient to reinforce the notion that there had been a first civilising influence and that it had been that of the Phoenicians.

As there was no actual proof of this hypothesis, Theodore Bent, an antiquarian with an intimate knowledge of the Middle East and a particular academic interest in the Phoenicians, was asked to undertake the excavation of the Great Zimbabwe site. This was considered of sufficient importance that it was put in train only a few months after the British occupation of Mashonaland in September 1890.

Initially Bent viewed with suspicion the idea that the ruins might be connected with the Phoenicians, King Solomon and the Queen of Sheba. Installed at his camp site at Great Zimbabwe he recorded: '. . . the names of King Solomon and the Queen of Sheba were on everybody's lips and have become so distasteful to us that we never expect to hear them again without an involuntary shudder.'

Everything that Bent uncovered in the Elliptical Building appeared to him to be 'native'. But in the Eastern Enclosure on the Hill Ruin – tackled because he thought it might be free of 'kaffir desecration' – in addition to native objects such as axes, spearheads and pottery sherds a number of carved soapstone objects came to light. These included four of the famous Zimbabwe birds on top of columns, monoliths inscribed with geometric patterns, decorated dishes and carved cylinders. These were thought to be completely unique to Great Zimbabwe: nothing like them had ever been found elsewhere in Africa. Consequently Bent tended to concentrate on these objects: the soapstone birds, he thought, had something in common with Assyrian and Egyptian stelae; some of the patterns on the cylinders and monoliths seemed to somewhat resemble Phoenician motifs.

He then compared the overall architecture of the ruin – particularly the Elliptical Building – with the well-known temple of Marib in southern Arabia, while the conical tower was compared with a vaguely similar structure depicted on a Phoenician coin from Byblos. His conclusions, which were not very precise, broadly indicated that the ruins were the work of some early Semitic civilisation from the Arabian Peninsula.

Something of white attitudes to the site can be gleaned from *The Rhodesians*, a contemporary book by Gertrude Page:

> The Valley of the Ruins no longer lies alone and unheeded in the sunlight; and no longer do the hills look down upon rich plains left solely to the idle pleasure of a careless black people. The forerunners of today's great civilising army have marched into the valley and beside the ancient walls there is now a police camp of the British South Africa Police, presided over by two robust

young troopers. . . . Laughter and gay music and devil-may-care colonists awaking echoes that have been more silent to civilisation for how many thousand years? Says one of the troopers: 'That's a rum theory of his about the corpses in the temple being buried deeper than anyone has yet dug and hung with valuable ornaments. Wouldn't it be a jolly lark to dig down for one and have a look at it?' He gave a low half-hearted chuckle over his gruesome suggestion and lazily getting to his feet Moore gave a corresponding chuckle and remarked: 'Begorra lad! If we could get a few out one at a time on moonlight nights and fill up the bloomin' holes again, we shouldn't want any blasted machinery for our gold mine except a pick-axe and a shovel.'

In the spirit of this passage, the 1890s saw the wholesale pillaging of Zimbabwe civilisation sites by a company – Rhodesia Ancient Ruins Ltd – permitted by the British South Africa Company 'to explore and work for treasure'. An enormous amount of gold jewellery and grave furniture overlaid with gold was discovered. It was smelted down and sold. The notes kept by one of the treasure hunters were given to an impecunious local journalist, Richard Nicklin Hall, who turned them into a book which had a modest financial success and which established him as the authority on the subject of the ruins. In 1902, he was appointed Curator of Great Zimbabwe. Much influenced by Augustus Keane, the Emeritus Professor of Hindustani in the University of London who had written *The Gold of Ophir, Whence Brought and by Whom* (1901), Hall went on to write a further book, *Great Zimbabwe*, which appeared in 1905. Keane wrote the introduction to this volume, where he elaborated his theories about Zimbabwe's past.

The biblical Havilah, 'the whole land of Havilah where there is gold', he believed to be the 'mineralised region between the Zambezi and the Limpopo' and that 'the ancient gold workings of this region were first opened and the associated monuments erected by the South Arabian Himyarites, followed in the time of Solomon by the Jews and Phoenicians'. These Semitic treasure seekers reached Havilah by way of Tarshish, which Keane believed to be in the vicinity of Sofala. Their off-shore base was Madagascar, where there were Semitic colonies. The gold was transported to Tarshish and shipped to Ophir, which was a great Himyaritic emporium in southern Arabia. In *The Gold of Ophir* Keane had written at length about the ancient links between Palestine and Madagascar which had existed 'certainly as early as the time of Solomon and possibly even during the reign of his father David'. In his introduction to Hall's book Keane mentions further research on the subject by Alfred Grandidier, 'by far the greatest living authority on all things Malagasy who calls my attention to the evidence supplied in his monumental work *Histoire Physique, Naturelle et Politique de Madagascar* (1901) of intercourse between the Jews and the natives of Madagascar and neighbouring islands even in pre-Solomonic days'. Documents are quoted to show that the Comoros, stepping-stones between Madagascar and Rhodesia, were peopled in the reign of Solomon 'by Arabs or rather by Idumaean Jews from the Red Sea' and that the people of the great island preserve many Israelitish rites, usages and traditions, cherish the memory of Adam, Abraham, Lot, Moses, Gideon, but have no knowledge of any of the prophets after the time of David, 'which seems to show that the Jewish immigrants left their home at a very remote date, since if the exodus had been recent they could not have forgotten the great names posterior to David'. Thus, concludes Keane, 'My statements regarding the long-standing relations of the northern Semites with the peoples of Madagascar and South Africa as far as Sofala are thus fully supported by the greatest authority on the subject.'

It was in a similar spirit that Hall, the erstwhile journalist, tackled both the writing of his new book and his custodianship of Great Zimbabwe. Calling his base camp at Zimbabwe 'Havilah', he set himself the task of clearing 'the filth and decadence of the kaffir occupation' to reveal the original levels of Semitic occupation. In this he failed, and in the process he destroyed most of the archaeological deposits within the walls of sub-Saharan Africa's most important archaeological site. Despite Hall's conviction, shared, it must be said, by almost everyone else at the time, that Great Zimbabwe was the work of an ancient Semitic people, it became apparent to him that 'evidence of ... long and successive periods of [Karanga] occupation of these ruins are not only most obvious to all explorers and are confirmed by finds and conditions generally, but are a matter of actual history as well as of tradition among local natives...' He was prepared to concede in addition that some natives 'will affirm the ancestors of their tribe built them. Some tribes make definite claims to have built them.' But he brushed these claims aside. The Victorian idea which served splendidly the interests of white racial supremacy – viz., that evolution is linear – prevented Hall from seeing what was before his eyes. Incapable of believing that people who live in grass huts could once have been stone builders, he was tied in, notwithstanding the evidence to the contrary, to his Idumean hypothesis that the ruins had been constructed by an ancient Semitic people.

Hall tried to derive further proof of the hypothesis by finding living traces of the original inhabitants in the manners and customs of the people dwelling around the ruins. There had already been speculation along these lines. Andrew

Anderson, who has already been cited, made a connection between the Queen of Sheba and the original builders of the ruins and the Lemba: 'These old diggings', he wrote, 'may have been worked by the Queen of Sheba's people and subsequently by a white race ... from the ruins still standing I think they may have been the same under the name of Abba Lomba.' In 1893, a German missionary, C. Beuster, took this somewhat further when he perceived what he took to be traces of ancient Near-Eastern Baal worship in the religious practices of the Lemba living near Great Zimbabwe. This notion was given much wider currency by Dr Carl Peters. In *The Eldorado of the Ancients,* he wrote: 'All over this district we shall find many ruins of an ancient gold-mining era, and remnants of the Punic Baal-Ashera worship partly in existence to this present day ... This river', he wrote of the Zambezi, 'was apparently a highway for the most ancient Semitic migrations to South Africa. These Semites came from South Arabia and worshipped Baal and Ashtaroth. These we can regard as established facts.' Elsewhere he described meetings with natives in the vicinity of Inja-ka-Fura, which he identified with the biblical Ophir:

How *absolutely* Jewish is the type of this people! They have faces cut exactly like those of ancient Jews who live around Aden. Also, the way they wear their hair, the curls behind the ears, and the beard drawn out in single curls, gives them the appearance of Aden – or of Polish – Jews of the good old type. This is very different from the *general* Semitic type, as we often find it amongst Bantu tribes, which owes its origin to an admixture of Arabian blood. *Here* we had real, unalloyed Jewish physiognomies before us.

Hall took one of the Karanga-speaking tribes – the Lemba, in fact – as being typical of the inhabitants of the plateau:

Among the Jewish customs of the Makalanga the following may be noticed: (1) Monotheism and no worship of idols; (2) worship of, and sacrifices to, ancestors – a practice condemned by the Prophets; (3) rite of circumcision; (4) despising the uncircumcised; the taunt of non-circumcision is commonly used between disputants; (5) purification and shaving of the head; (6) transferring impurity or infection from individuals to some animal, which in some instances is slain and in others purposely lost on the veld; (7) reception by women of parties returning from hunting or war, as in the case of Jephthah; (8) feasts of new moons and invocations to new moons; (9) feasts of full moons; (10) offerings of first fruits; (11) defilement by touching the dead; (12) defilement of eating flesh containing blood; (13) abhorrence of swine as unclean; (14) sprinkling the worshippers with blood; (15) places of refuge for criminals or people believed but not found guilty of offending tribal custom; (16) observance of Sabbath, either every five or seven days; (17) marriage only among themselves, but cannot marry into the same tribe; (18) casting of lots; (19) sacrifices of oxen in times of trouble, such as drought; (20) practice of espousal before marriage; (21) brother succeeds to brother in office and property; (22) brother takes to wife, the wives of his deceased elder brother, and raising offspring, they rank in office as if they were the children of the deceased; (23) a daughter does not inherit property or position except on the death of all her brothers; (24) rigid morality with regard to all fleshly sins, adultery and fornication being punished with death and outlawry.

Additional parallelisms with Jewish customs could be stated, and all these peculiar practices, together with the lighter skin and the Jewish appearance of the Makalanga, distinctly point to the ancient impress of the Idumean Jews, which can also be traced on the present peoples of Madagascar and of the coasts of Mozambique and Sofala. Many of these customs are now falling

into desuetude on the advance of white civilisation. The
Molembo [Lemba] tribe of Makalanga is noted for the preser-
vation and observance of these Jewish practices, which are in
character distinctly pre-Koranic in origin.

I have quoted this passage in full because it is of importance
for our understanding of the Lemba. It is not certain that the
Lemba possessed all the Semitic characteristics ascribed to
them by Hall. The passage is important for other reasons.
Hall had been a man of considerable influence in Rhodesia
before his ignominious dismissal from Great Zimbabwe in
1904 for what, quite rightly, was described as 'reckless
blundering'. His and others' public identification of the
Lemba as the descendants of the Jewish builders of Great
Zimbabwe cannot fail to have left some mark on the Lemba
themselves, both via the accounts carried back to the tribe by
Hall's Lemba informants and through the intermediary of
interested European missionaries, teachers and administrators. After all, an observed system inevitably interacts with
its observers. It is possible that some of the seeds of the
Lemba's identification with Jewry originate here.

Of equal importance is the fact that Hall's reference to the
Lemba helped to relegate them to complete obscurity as far
as the history of southern Africa is concerned. Henceforward,
their association with Great Zimbabwe would be linked with
the Idumean hypothesis and the self-serving historical vision
of the early white colonists. Any attempt to see links between
Central Africa and the Semitic world would be viewed as an
effort to denigrate African culture and to bring respectability
to old racial prejudices.

Almost accidentally Hall did, however, provide us with
fairly convincing evidence that some Lemba had inhabited
Great Zimbabwe at some time in the past. On the Hill Ruin

– what Hall called the Acropolis – he found 'about fifty Makalanga graves . . . and the remains in a score of instances were removed. Practically all were in a sitting position, only three having been buried lengthways.' As we have seen, the Lemba were the only tribe in the area to bury their dead lengthways. We do not know the date of these graves; but even if they were relatively recent, they show that some Lemba had maintained a link with the ruins they say they helped to build.

It was not long after Hall's 'reckless blundering' that serious archaeological work began to be undertaken at Great Zimbabwe. In 1905, David Randall-MacIver, a student of Flinders Petrie, the father of modern archaeology, was invited to conduct a dig at Great Zimbabwe. On the basis of the objects that had been found there he concluded that, when it was built, Great Zimbabwe 'belonged to tribes whose arts and manufactures were indistinguishable from those of the modern Makalanga'. Foreign, datable objects found by Hall persuaded him that the buildings had been constructed in the mediaeval period. Hall's denial that these objects had been at a level which would associate them with the builders of Great Zimbabwe left the dating of the ruins open. A fierce controversy erupted, partly fuelled by Hall's publication of yet another book on Great Zimbabwe, *Prehistoric Rhodesia*, a refutation of Randall-MacIver's *Mediaeval Rhodesia*. The arguments became increasingly racist in tone, Hall maintaining that 'the decadence of the native [is] a process which has been in operation for many centuries [and] is admitted by all authorities', brought about by 'a sudden arrest of intelligence and mental development [which] befalls every member of the Bantu at the age of puberty'.

In 1929, further excavations by a distinguished British archaeologist, Gertrude Caton-Thompson, confirmed Randall-MacIver's conclusion. Caton-Thompson ended her book with the words:

> Examination of all the existing evidence, gathered from every quarter, still can produce not one single item that is not in accordance with the claim of Bantu origin and medieval date. The interest in Zimbabwe and the allied ruins should, on this account, to all educated people, be enhanced a hundredfold; it enriches, not impoverishes, our wonderment at their remarkable achievement: it cannot detract from their inherent majesty: for the mystery of Zimbabwe is the mystery which lies in the still pulsating heart of native Africa.

After the Second World War, the discovery of extraneous, datable objects – such as Chinese porcelain – plus the invention of radiocarbon dating helped to pinpoint the dates of the Great Zimbabwe site. In the minds of contemporary experts such as Peter Garlake and Thomas Huffman, there is no doubt at all that the ruins are both mediaeval and indigenous.

But the controversy has not died away. There are many whites in Zimbabwe and South Africa who cling to the idea that the ruins were the work of some ancient Semitic people and maintain a proprietorial interest in them. At the same time, a number of different African tribes claim that their ancestors built the Zimbabwe cities. For white and black alike, Zimbabwe has become a symbol. Until independence the conical tower at Great Zimbabwe was depicted on the Rhodesian pound note, while a slightly modified Zimbabwe bird formed part of the arms of Southern Rhodesia. Since the beginning of majority rule the same bird has become the symbol of the success of the black liberation movement and, in 1980, the new Government named the state Zimbabwe after the site, and the culture it represents.

27

'The velvety darkness of a southern night with its sense of rich, luscious breathing intensity lay over that romantic spot in Southern Rhodesia where the grey walls of the Zimbabwe ruins with sublime, imperturbable indifference continue to baffle the ingenuity and ravish the curiosity of all who would read their story. Scientists, archaeologists, tourists come and go, but the stern old walls guarded by the sentinel hills give back no answer to eager questioning, eager delving, eager surmise . . .'

I had bought this pre-First World War imperial romance, *The Rhodesians* by Gertrude Page, in a second-hand bookshop in Bulawayo. Now, late at night, on the veranda of the Great Zimbabwe Hotel, with Page's book on my knee, a cold beer at my elbow, and the immediate prospect of a shower and clean sheets, I contemplated the distant outline of the sentinel hills with some satisfaction and looked forward to my ingenuity and curiosity being baffled and ravished in equal measure the following day.

Great Zimbabwe is much visited, by black Zimbabweans for the most part, for these days there are not many foreign tourists in the country. Now black Mercedes cars bring the new potentates of Zimbabwe – the new masters of the ruins – to gaze at their weathered walls: they wear white suits, straw hats, black shirts, and they take proprietorial pride in this place which was built, as they believe, by their forebears. But the Rhodies, the local whites, who frequent the rather luxurious Great Zimbabwe Hotel for sales conferences and the like, do not move much further than the pool or the bar. Great Zimbabwe belongs to them no more. They have had to find other ways to legitimise their presence.

When I first visited the ruins, no one was there and the only sounds were of shrill birdsong. In the early morning light the Hill Enclosure, built on great humps of rock, seemed like a massive Roman fortification, bigger than it actually was, as the walls and the rocks on which they stood were both painted an identical dawn pink. From this angle the towers and monoliths atop the walls looked like precise, squared-off battlements; the further enclosures, their walls flowing into the contours of the natural granite, were barely visible. Between the hill and the Elliptical Building – or the House of the Great Woman – is a series of low, stone enclosures of baffling complexity, stunted drystone cones and alcoves, passages and mounds of stone which give no idea of the original purpose of the place. And cycads growing through the stone rubble give an air of desolation to what must once have been a bustling town. Within the enclosures *daga* huts used to shelter the inhabitants. But what created the civilisation? And what did its inhabitants do? And why did they leave?

As I was walking around the site I came across Dr Dave Collett, a deeply tanned, bearded man, Zambian by birth, English by extraction. A Cambridge-trained archaeologist, he was a site director at Great Zimbabwe. He confirmed that the dating of the ruins was no longer a problem and that refinements in radiocarbon technique meant that the walls could be placed rather precisely between 1250 and 1450. The improvements in the building style which are apparent to anyone came about gradually: the new techniques, he believes, were learned by experience. But what, I asked, gave rise to this culture in the first place?

'Ah!' he replied. 'That is more controversial. Some people see this as the centre of a rather simple state which grew out of a cattle economy. But that really is nonsense because gold, ivory and all sorts of imported items came into it. The wealth, the great wealth, which created this place came from both cattle and trade: from the concentration of great herds in relatively few hands, and from trade with the coast and with the Indian Ocean basin. There has been something of a debate over this. Some Africanists think that a number of factors – divine kingship, long-distance trade, military considerations and cattle – all played a role in creating this culture and that to concentrate on any one factor to the exclusion of the rest is to miss the point. But the fact is that the real prime mover here was the long-distance trade with the coast. All of the other factors existed elsewhere. It was the coastal trade which really created everything.'

In Johannesburg, I had met Thomas Huffman, who had given me a number of his articles to read. One of them dealt with the mysterious and sudden abandonment of the Great Zimbabwe site:

> An ecological explanation has been suggested for the decline of Great Zimbabwe, which is virtually indisputable. The constant demand for firewood over several decades and the gradual exhaustion of the soil must have made it increasingly difficult to live there without a more efficient agricultural system ... The African strategy of abandoning the land once it is exhausted is well known ...

'So that's how the culture came into being,' I said. 'But how did it end? I have heard the argument that the population grew too big for the supportive capacity of the surrounding land and that finally the land became over-grazed and useless.'

'No, that's a colonial myth,' snorted Collett. 'A mytheme. Ecological degradation is the buzz-word. The fact is that no town anywhere in the world can feed itself. Food was always brought in here from a wide area. The surrounding country-side was therefore not particularly relevant. The myth implies, you see, that blacks are essentially incapable of doing anything right. Even if they start something off well they'll soon give up, the work will soon deteriorate. The idea that blacks can't do things properly, can't keep the effort up, all that gave white colonial society the justification for perpetual domination. What are the real reasons for its decline? You know, I'm really not sure! What do we have to go on? The Arabs don't mention it, nor do the Portuguese, and African oral traditions are contradictory. There is one tradition which has it that the king of Great Zimbabwe decided to up sticks and move to a salt-producing area nearer the sea because he got fed up with eating salt made from goat dung. I know that Huffman takes that as being some kind of metaphor or social rationalisation for abandoning the land because it was no longer productive. But I don't know. In this part of the world the past is another country. Practically unknowable.'

'The Lemba, the people I have been studying, say that they are Jews, that they played some role in building the city, and that they left for essentially religious reasons. They believe that they offended Mwali by eating taboo animals – mice, in fact – and that thereafter it was impossible for them and indeed for anyone else to live here.'

'As good a reason as any,' said Collett with a shrug. 'I don't know if the Lemba played any role here. I don't know anything about the Lemba. Most of the tribes, especially these days, claim to have had something to do with Great Zimbabwe. It's become a tribal status symbol. The Venda have perhaps the best claim. But you know, you can impose what you like upon this site. It's like blotting-paper. It will absorb anything you throw at it. One thing I do know. It was not King Solomon who built it; it was not the Phoenicians; it was not the Sabeans; it was not the Arabs. It was black people, local people who lived here in mediaeval times, not in the mists of antiquity. This is African, wholly African and nothing but African.'

By this time we had reached the splendid Elliptical Building in the valley and were standing in the shade of the conical tower.

'But is it not a little absurd to suggest that there was no outside influence?' I asked. 'What society or culture has been absolutely isolated from all others? The very orientation of this place is towards the East as if to symbolise some sort of connection with the coast. This tower, for instance, looks as if it might be a sort of reflection of a Muslim minaret. I believe Gertrude Caton-Thompson thought so too.'

'Well, I don't see it and Garlake didn't see it, and Garlake was an expert on east coast Muslim architecture. It's obviously symbolic. It has no practical function.'

'It's as practical as a minaret. But anyway, how would you explain the tower?'

'Tom Huffman thinks that the tower and all the other little towers all over the place were phallic and denoted male areas: the vertical slit alcoves you find on both sides of some openings denote female areas. Tom's a great archaeologist, the best African archaeologist around, but I don't buy all that. It's too crude, don't you think? I think that the slits denote ritual areas and the towers are symbolic grain bins – symbolic of wealth, well-being, control. Very African. But if you think that this tower represents somehow a minaret or something Islamic, wouldn't that in any case suggest that the Lemba were Muslims, not Jews, assuming they had anything at all to do with the place?

'I'm beginning to think that by the time they got here – that is, the high plateau – they were probably a mixture of various things. Semitic, in some sense, perhaps with some Jewish and certainly some Muslim influence, migrants who brought with them religious ideas, relatively advanced technology and architectural ideas they had picked up on the way. If you had seen splendid minarets on the coast, and you wanted to build something striking here, you could well copy the form without necessarily being a Muslim. Another possibility is that the tower may have something to do with circumcision. I've read somewhere that small stone towers shaped like this were used for circumcision rites not very far from here and in relatively recent times. If circumcision was essentially a coastal idea, what could be more natural than to use a coastal symbol to express it?'

'If it's to do with circumcision, it's phallic. That's Huffman's argument,' growled Collett. 'Anyway, what kind of evidence can you come up with to link the Lemba with Great Zimbabwe? No, hang on! Let's go back and have a beer and talk about this. I don't often get the chance to talk shop.'

Over a couple of Castles at the hotel bar, I put forward the argument that the Lemba may have contributed to Great Zimbabwe: that to this day there are concentrations of Lemba around Great Zimbabwe; that there is clear evidence that some Lemba had lived at the site in the past; that the Lemba's traditions on the subject are strong and consistent; that like the Great Zimbabwe elite, the Lemba did not eat game and practised animal sacrifice; that the Lemba's material culture resembles artefacts found at Great Zimbabwe; that such artefacts have been found close to areas connected with religious ritual; that the Lemba had played an important role at the Venda court which might reflect a role they once had here; that the Venda were thought by many, including Huffman, to have been the builders of Great Zimbabwe; that the Lemba seem to have been involved in the cult of Mwali in the Matopos Hills thought by many to have been the successor cult to the religious dispensation of Great Zimbabwe; that their trading, mining and metalworking prowess reflect the skills of the Great Zimbabwe civilisation; that they had been involved in the same kind of trade which had contributed to the wealth of this civilisation; and that the Lemba might therefore represent a link between this civilisation and the coast.

'No! No! No!' exclaimed Collett. 'What you're saymg is that blacks are not capable of building without outside assistance. That's what practically every white man in Rhodesia believed. I can't accept that,' and he got up to go.

'Come on, sit down,' I said. 'That's not the point. I am not saying that black people did not or could not build in stone or could not do anything else. From what I understand stone building occurred throughout vast areas of southern Africa. All I am saying is that the Great Zimbabwe civilisation should be understood in the context of coastal culture, of mediaeval Indian Ocean culture. I am putting forward the idea that the Lemba – black people themselves, let's not forget – were carriers not only of the normal trade goods – Indian cloth, Chinese porcelain, Persian beads– but also of some ideas – religious, social and no doubt architectural – and that they played some role and exerted some influence here. All civilisations and cultures are influenced by others.'

'No. The architectural modes are *sui generis* here.'

'I don't see that. Look, there are walls and towers and steps and doorways built in stone. How can you categorically say that the idea of building a flight of steps did not come from elsewhere? Not every culture has to invent the wheel.'

'But what proof do you have of the Lemba's stone-building tradition?'

I told him about the stone walls I had seen opposite Dumghe on the hill the Lemba called the 'old town'.

'That we can check out,' he said. 'All stone constructions throughout Zimbabwe are marked on the Ancient Monuments Survey.'

We walked to a site hut where he asked me to pin-point the ruins on an ordinance survey map. It was not difficult: Dumghe was clearly marked, as was the hill opposite it. Collett checked the map-reading against a file index. After a few minutes he said, 'It's not marked. I'm afraid your Lemba site doesn't exist.' I assured him that it did and somewhat reluctantly he decided to come with me to have a look at the hill.

Two bone-shaking hours later Collett drove his Land-Rover up to the village adjoining the 'old town'. After a cursory walk around he said, 'Yes. You're right. It's interesting. There are a number of sites like this, but if Lemba traditions about this place can be made to stick, it could prove to be important. You might be right. There may be something in the Lemba's claim.'

Back at the Great Zimbabwe Hotel Collett gave me a book written by Ken Mufuka, his colleague and assistant, a black Zimbabwean archaeologist. 'I don't say this book is the last word on Great Zimbabwe,' he said, 'but I've just remembered something Ken wrote that might interest you.' He indicated the passage I should read. From the preamble it was clear that Mufuka believed that the Venda were the 'legendary Dzimbahwe stonemasons', as he put it, but,

> The second tribe associated with the Dzimbahwe culture are the WaRemba (Lemba). The WaRemba can definitely trace their history to the Mwene-mutapa (Monomotapa). Today they live among the BaVenda and are known for their custom of removing blood from a dead carcase. They were the adventurers of southern Africa; they travelled widely between the east coast and Dzimbahwe. They lived by their wits; they were merchants and seemed to have settled down only after the demise of the Dzimbahwe confederation. They were known particularly for their skill in stretching copper wire into fine bracelets. A few of these bracelets are now in the Great Zimbabwe museum and show the unmatched skills they had acquired. The Mwene-mutapas ... allowed these VaMwenyi to ply their trade. They became so powerful that they resented competition from the Portuguese and were accused of all sorts of crimes by their competitors. At Zimbabwe, the copperwares and goldwares speak for their abilities ... Future research on Great Zimbabwe should move to the BaVenda and WaRemba rather than concentrate on the monument itself.

'That's pretty much what I'm saying,' I said. 'Are you saying he's a racist as well?'

'Well, that's true,' he said, grinning. 'Nobody has ever called Ken Mufuka a racist!'

I was later to discover that the Lemba's connection with Great Zimbabwe had been considered by at least one other archaeologist. Roger Summers, an Englishman who went out to Rhodesia in 1947 to become Keeper of Antiquities in Bulawayo, spent years researching the Great Zimbabwe civilisation. In *Zimbabwe: A Rhodesian Mystery*, he wrote of the Lemba:

Recently these people have claimed that their forefathers built Zimbabwe and, when due allowance is made for group pride, their claim is one which deserves attention on grounds of technical ability. This claim has never been recognised, for its validity is hard to judge on account of the difficulty of studying their many scattered groups, yet we ought not to lightly dismiss it, since the building of Zimbabwe presented many technical problems which they are more likely to have been able to solve than their Venda, Karanga, Rozwi, Duma or other Shona neighbours. On the other hand, Zimbabwe building problems were administrative as well as technical and one wonders just how well the Lemba would have measured up to matters of organisation in which nowadays they seem so unskilled . . . it may be that the Lemba provided the technical skill, while the Rozwi provided the administrative drive. The Lemba had undoubted connections with the Arabs and they may well have inherited some of the secrets of masonry although . . . unfortunately the fundamental ones were forgotten.

However, most modern books about Great Zimbabwe do not mention the Lemba. The reasons for this are not hard to find. Over the last seventy years or so the historical context around Great Zimbabwe has been revised. The notion that the ruins were built by an ancient Semitic people has been discredited. Richard Nicklin Hall and others explicitly identified the Lemba as the descendants of these ancient Semitic people. This has tended to disqualify them from serious attention. The historical context of Great Zimbabwe has been revised; the historical context of the Lemba has not. Hall was right to connect the Lemba with Great Zimbabwe, but for the wrong reasons.

*

Just before I left Zimbabwe, I arranged to have tea with Ian Smith, the former Prime Minister of Rhodesia. His substantial 1930s brick house, in a prosperous Harare suburb, was surrounded by lawns and flowerbeds, and protected by a wall; but the front gate was open, there were no dogs or guards in sight, and the front door was ajar. I pressed the bell and Smith's familiar figure came to the door, a tea-towel over his arm. He showed me into a very English drawing-room: a small, cheap electric fire stood in front of the fireplace, there were Wedgwood and willow-pattern plates on the wall, and a beige fitted carpet on the floor. Tea and biscuits were already laid out.

I asked him to what extent the Great Zimbabwe controversy had been a political issue. Settling himself in an armchair, he stared through the open window, his manner judicious and a little reproachful.

'The Great Zimbabwe business. Well, it was not a controversial issue, it was of interest, that's all. I remember the time when some rather radical people started talking about it being built by local black people. Prior to that I think all thinking people thought otherwise. But because there was this interest, you see, I used to listen to people with the relevant expertise. What d'you call experts in a place like Great Zimbabwe?'

'Archaeologists?' I suggested.

'Yes, that's the one. And I used to ask them, "What do you think?", and the general conclusion was that it was built by an ancient Semitic race and that the ruins were safe-houses for slaves and gold. Then this new theory came out, about twenty years ago, that it was a black tribe from hereabouts. Always a minority opinion, that. Problem was, if the locals had those kinds of engineering and scientific skills, why was there no sign of it when the whites got here, when Rhodes got here? They all lived in pole and *daga* huts, you see, as they still do. So if they did build Great Zimbabwe, why did they change all of a sudden, and why did they change back? How did they get the expertise?' His voice had risen, but it dropped and, in an equable tone, shrugging his shoulders, he continued, 'Well, it was a fascinating business, whoever built the ruins.'

I asked Smith if there had ever been any attempt to encourage research along specific lines at Great Zimbabwe. There seemed to have been a revival of interest in the Phoenician origins of Zimbabwe in the late 1960s and Gayre of Gayre, an obviously racist writer, was rumoured to have been encouraged to do research in support of such theories, which resulted in a book published in Salisbury in 1973.

'Yes, the name Gayre of Gayre strikes a vague bell, but this is the first I have heard of encouraging research in any particular area. Ridiculous story! Are you suggesting I would have been party to falsifying the record?' He looked at me as if I had violated some important canon of decency. 'I despise people who twist the truth,' he continued. 'Part of my character. Contrary to my own preaching! Maybe there were some cranks who perpetrated that sort of thing. But it would not have been in keeping with government policy. For once and for all, there was no racial connotation to the conflict. We were in control as a result of elections based on franchise qualifications. Merit, not race. In time the blacks would have caught up and we wanted a meritocracy. Not one man one vote. Madness! Always wrong – anywhere in the world. And you think the present situation is fair? The whites produce ninety per cent of the surplus food, and ninety per cent of the GNP. And they should be disenfranchised? Ridiculous, completely ridiculous.'

Again Smith's voice had risen and now he got to his feet to

indicate that the interview was over. I was surprised when he offered to drive me back to my hotel. In the car he went over the subject of Great Zimbabwe again.

'Viewed objectively,' he said, 'there can be no doubt at all where the balance of probability lay for Great Zimbabwe. I know the capacity of our local people. One way or the other, it was outsiders who built it and who then disappeared.' He gave me a wry, rather boyish grin and said, 'Just as it was outsiders who built all this.' All this was Harare: a city of gardens and suburbs, of golf clubs and residential blocks with names like Shamrock Court, Alexander Court, Nelson Court: courts of a lost cause now. He gestured through the window and asked, 'And in a hundred years from now without us around, what do you think will be left?'

At the Can Can Bar at Meikles Hotel, a solitary drinker looked up as I walked in.

'Nname's Rhodes,' he said, sticking his hand out. 'Nnot Cecil. Ha, ha. Can't let a white man drink alone. What's your poison?'

I accepted a gin and sat down alongside him at the bar. Rhodes had a bad stutter and, it seemed, a bad son about whom he wanted to talk. The boy had been trained by the Rhodesian Special Services as a 'counter-terrorist'. His speciality was climbing down rope ladders and throwing grenades through suspects' windows. He had become a psychopathic killer.

'Then,' said Rhodes, 'he gave it all up. Became a minister in the Church of God. Black Church. Making amends, he says. Good luck to him!'

Downing his gin, Rhodes insisted on taking me over to his club, the City Club, which had its premises on the first floor of a nearby hotel.

There was a tiger skin on the wall and a moth-eaten buffalo head above the bar. The club boasted a membership of 200 men, all white, three of whom had congregated at the bar for an early evening drink.

'Anyone can join, anyone at all, as long as he's put up by a member – 'course, you only put up your own,' the speaker tapped the side of his nose.

'One for the major?'

'Pinks all round!'

'Going to Malawi and Tanzania?'

'Trouble with Malawi is it's over-populated. Can't go a hundred yards down the road from Blantyre to Lilongwe without banging into a bunch of blacks; about eight million of 'em. More than we've got!'

'Great Zimbabwe? No mystery there, old boy. Phoenicians built it. King Solomon and all that. Every last bloody stone of it. We know for a blind fact it wasn't this lot. But you can't say that. Not since 1980. Since 1980, we've had culture with a capital K rammed down our throat. And culture in this neck of the woods means only one thing, Great bloody Zimbabwe!'

The Meikles Hotel overlooks a lovely square, like a London square but full of lavender blue jacaranda trees and thousands of querulous little birds. Whatever scholarship has decided or would decide about Great Zimbabwe, I thought, as I packed for the morning, the controversy would continue.

PART FOUR

In Search of Sena

28

There are a lot of poor people in Malawi. It is a hard country with hard poverty. You can see it in the people's clothes, in their cataracts, in the way they eye your bag, your watch, your packet of cigarettes. According to a government handbook I had read on the 'plane, the per capita income here was around 150 kwatchas a year – less than $100 – and Malawi's only 'industrial' manufactured export was iron hoe heads, one of the traditional manufactures of the Lemba more than a hundred years before. I had mentioned something along these lines to the nervy Israeli doctor in the seat next to mine.

'I don't find this strange, or funny, as you say. But nothing is very funny in Malawi. And if there was, we wouldn't know about it. The whites have put black Malawi in quarantine. They never see Africans if they can help it. If they do, they never touch them. Certainly never shake hands. They're terrified. They keep away from them.'

'What on earth for?'

'Because of AIDS. It's the only thing people here talk about.'

'It's the same in London.'

'Maybe, but here it's serious. Believe me. I'm here on what we call *shelihut*. I've been sent by the Israeli Government – part of our famous Africa policy to make friends and influence people. We've been doing a survey of Malawi children under twelve over the last six months. Fifty per cent were sero-positive. Even before AIDS took a hold here there were only three countries in the world which had a higher infant mortality rate than Malawi: Borkina Faso, Yemen and Afghanistan. Now with AIDS the mortality rate for infants must be incredible. But the Government does all it can to conceal the statistics. One of the excuses they use is that even today the majority of kids here die of malaria and that therefore they want to tackle malaria before they go on to fancy stuff like AIDS. Of course, it's crazy. I think that AIDS can destroy Africa. Believe me. They are making a big mistake. And so are you, if you permit me. I know this country well. And if there was anything remotely resembling a Jewish or half-Jewish, or Muslim-Jewish or half-Muslim tribe here I'd know about it. Believe me. And in any case, let me tell you, in Israel we need lost African Jewish tribes like we need a hole in the head, as we say in Yiddish. Bringing the Falashas to Israel was a big mistake. Believe me. Cost us a packet.'

He went back to checking pages of figures on a computer print-out, his forehead knit in concentration.

With the doctor's words ringing in my ears, I paid special attention to the slumped, sick people lying like half-filled sacks of grain in any patch of shade. The thought that Africa was dying on its feet made my enterprise seem pointless. What on earth was I doing here? My relatively comfortable, self-indulgent journey seemed indecent in the face of this. But on the other hand what could I do for Malawi's AIDS problem? I had already decided to leave Lilongwe immediately and to travel to the southern part of the country. So I stuck to my plan. It was in the south, close to the Zambezi River where I would find the Mwenye, I thought. If, indeed, there were any in Malawi. First, then, I would take a bus south to Zomba, the old colonial capital.

At the bus station dozens of black people were sitting behind small, dusty piles of fruit and vegetables. A few had bales of cloth for sale. One or two had little heaps of sea salt measured out in Kiwi polish tins. The only one doing any business was a boy, sitting straight-backed on the mud, a packet of cigarettes in front of him: he was doing a brisk trade selling the contents one at a time.

My other neighbour on the 'plane had been a Yorkshire-man working for a tractor company in Lilongwe. 'Whatever you do,' he had warned, 'don't take the Zomba road in the afternoon, if you take my meaning, else you'll likely come unstuck.' When I told him that that was exactly what I planned to do, he said, 'Do what you like. But folks round here don't take the afternoon bus.'

Even before I saw the bus I knew that by folks he meant whites and that the bus would be full of black people. And it was. Looking down the bus I saw that there was only one seat left, what looked like a good seat next to a window. I soon discovered why. The bus had a bare metal floor, but below my seat there was no floor at all. There was a rust-eaten hole; below it was a wheel. The bus had hard, upright seats covered in grimy blue vinyl; it rattled and vibrated so much you could not talk or read, and it took the bends at a practised lick. It was blisteringly hot and within seconds I was covered with hot, choking dust from the hole below me. It was five and a half hours to Zomba. 'Gimme sigret,' hissed a yellow-toothed man behind me. I offered my packet and he took four. The men behind him snatched the rest. 'Change dollar?' hissed the man. I gritted my teeth, said nothing and tried to concentrate on the view.

For much of the distance the road followed the border

with Mozambique. On the left-hand side of the road, the Malawi side, the villages were surrounded by cultivated fields. Women chattered around boreholes and in the market squares, where piles of tomatoes, onions and macadamia nuts gave a sense of modest plenty. On the right-hand side, the Mozambique side, there was no one, the derelict huts were deserted, roofless, mud-walled rectangles, which looked like pissoirs. And far in the distance sometimes you could see thin spirals of smoke. From time to time on the Malawi side we passed temporary settlements of refugees from the Mozambique civil war, refugees who only had to cross the road to get home.

At seven thirty to the minute the bus pulled in to the Zomba bus station scattering the adolescent hawkers in its path. I had booked a room in the Zomba government rest-house. The man with yellow teeth who insisted on carrying my bag told me that the rest-house was the dingy building facing the bus station. I gave him a very modest tip and went in. The receptionist looked surprised to see me. He had no reservation in my name, he said. But he did have a room, he had many rooms. He showed me to a bare, grey cell whose naked electric bulb was reflected in the high gloss of the polished concrete floor. Outside the room men were lying dead drunk in the corridor. I locked my bag in the room and went to the bar for a beer and something to eat. 'Not worry about your bag, Bwana,' said the night porter. 'Plenty thief here. Not touch you bag in night. I sit outside you window all night, all night, not sleep, not sleep, watching and guarding you property, Bwana.' He showed me a bow and three iron-tipped arrows. 'Not worry, Bwana,' he repeated. 'No man likes arrow in eye.'

In the bar dozens more men were slumped over their 'greens', the local word for a Heineken. A few were dancing funkily to the music of Peter Tosh and Bob Marley. Reggae music, played at maximum volume, carried on for much of the night. And when the music stopped, the dogs started.

The following morning the night watchman was asleep in front of my door. His diminutive fez had slipped down over his forehead, his bow and arrow were held tightly over his chest. I didn't wake him, but the *muezzin* did a few minutes later.

'*Salamu aleikum*,' I said.

'*Aleikum salam*,' he replied. 'Sorry I sleep.'

The government rest-house, it turned out, was elsewhere. It was a lovely building, a little outside Zomba, which reminded me of a Scottish country house, Presbyterian neo-Gothic, with immaculate lawns and high hedges. The building incorporated the most pleasing use I had ever seen of corrugated iron. Painted the green of corroded copper, it was used for gables, towers and even a small Gothic belfry. The walls were white and the woodwork was painted in a peeling light blue, a colour no doubt favoured by the last British administration. It was only when you lifted your gaze to the palm trees and the lush mountains beyond the hedges that you realised you were in Africa.

I booked into the rest-house and took a taxi to the university. One of President Banda's favourite prestige projects, Chancellor University, lies on a splendid site with panoramic views over the forests and mountains of Zomba. I went straight to the Africana library and chatted for a while with its librarian, Mr W. C. Msika. He had never heard of the Lemba or of the Mwenye, but he allowed me to spend the morning in the library browsing through the holdings. From time to time he arrived with a book which might be expected to make some reference to a small and remote local tribe. After a couple of hours I had found nothing and began to fear that there were no Lemba in Malawi after all. Certainly none of the Lemba in South Africa or Zimbabwe had ever said that there definitely were; they just thought that there probably would be. This could be just another aspect of their exaggerated sense of their tribe's size. Then in the *Handbook of Nyasaland* for 1922 I came across this:

Amwenye (60) have settled in the district within the last twenty years. They came from Sena. The tribe practices certain Mahommedan rites, such as circumcision, the bleeding of animals, and abstention from eating the flesh of any animal of the pig tribe. They are supposed to be descendants of the Arabs found by the Portuguese at Sena when they came here in 1572: some twenty peaceful Arab traders lived in Sena and the Portuguese proceeded to torture and kill most of them on the advice of a priest called Monclaro who accused them of bewitching the horses and cattle, which as a matter of fact were dying of tsetse fly bite. The name is derived from the Portuguese word '*monhe*', Arab, and is supposed to be a corruption of an Indian word, '*bunya*'. The natives apply the same name to the Indian Mahommedan traders. The men of this tribe are workers in iron, copper and brass and the women manufacture cooking pots. In appearance they differ considerably from the purely African tribes.

A little later I came across one other reference to them:

The Mwenye or Rabu (literally 'India' or 'Arab') ... claim descent from the pre-Portuguese Arabs, from whom they have inherited their skill in silver smithing and their dietary laws. Another difference with the neighbouring groups is that they do not allow premarital co-habitation until the husband has paid the full bride-price and built a hut. Some Mwenye are very prosperous traders and cattle-keepers.

Here was the proof I needed. There certainly were Mwenye – presumably Lemba – in Malawi. What is more, they definitely seemed to be connected with the Sena on the Zambezi. All I had to do was find them.

At noon Mr Msika came to tell me that the library was about to close. He suggested that I spend the lunch hour in the Senior Common Room. I wandered through corridors which looked and smelled like university corridors anywhere and eventually found the SCR, where a young English sociologist was drinking a 'green' at the bar and eating an English-looking sausage. I introduced myself.

'Job at SOAS? Lucky man.' He scratched the dandruff on his prematurely balding scalp and gestured through the Common Room window at the lush landscape. 'Of course, Zomba's a pretty enough place, but very samey. More than that, to be honest, it's oppressively tedious. But it was the only job going. Did you know that there's a law here which regulates the width of your trousers at knee and ankle, brought in to combat the moral excesses caused by flared trousers with tight arses. Very Scottish, don't you think, the idea that you can have measurable criteria of decency. It's all got to do with offended Presbyterian sensibilities, particularly in the sixties. You know,' he said, lowering his voice and looking over his shoulder at the empty Common Room, 'Paul Theroux says somewhere that the American Peace Corps introduced oral sex to Malawi. That's an absolute bloody laugh. I don't think the Americans have got anything to teach Africans about sex. Not if the essays I get back from my students are anything to go by. But they did introduce many other things and there used to be a lot of clashes about dress and length of hair between the hippy Peace Corps types and the authorities. All that went against the Scottish Presbyterian grain. Don't forget that the Big Fella is an elder of the Church of Scotland – calls himself a black Scotsman. Livingstone's got a lot to answer for around here I can tell you. But it's funny: Banda's emphasis on old-style morality and authoritarian government has created a bizarre situation. On the one hand you've got matrilineal, promiscuous traditions, on the other this Bible-thumping morality. What happens? Even though people can't say, "Fuck your politics," they can say, "Fuck your morality". And they do. So a sort of hole-in-the-wall promiscuity is produced which breeds prostitution and marginalisation. Sort of thing Theroux seemed to like, of course. Nasty piece of work that man!'

'I admire his work very much.'

'Don't say that around here. *Jungle Lovers*, particularly, is considered to be the most gratuitously insulting book ever written about Malawi. To my mind it's the best example of what Edward Said was talking about in *Orientalism*. I've been here for two years and I just don't recognise Theroux's world at all. Of course, no white with any sense screws African girls any more because of AIDS – but quite apart from that, Theroux's Malawi is up there on Cloud Nine.'

I told Dr S. what I was interested in and he took me over to meet an African colleague of his who had come into the Common Room a few minutes before and was sitting reading an old copy of the *Church Times*. Father Joseph had recently finished a doctoral thesis on new religious movements in Malawi. I asked him if he had ever heard of the Mwenye.

He smiled and said, 'Not only have I heard of them, old man, I am one. At least in part.'

Joseph was from southern Malawi and knew exactly where the Mwenye were to be found. He was helpful, but reluctantly so. As we talked, he gave the impression that he had been soured by his years of research. His teachers had not been very helpful, he said, and his university experiences had given him a gloomy outlook.

'I don't know if it's worth your while going down there. They're very closed and secretive. They won't tell you anything. I'm not even sure that it's a subject. There's nothing much of interest in the Mwenye. Anyway, a lot of the stories they tell don't make sense.' However, he kept lurching into helpfulness, as if his own instincts always overcame, albeit with difficulty, the uncharitable academic behaviour he had learned at his English university. And, sure enough, before I left Zomba he gave me a letter to the Catholic mission in the Shire valley which would enable me to stay there, as well as the telephone number in Blantyre of one of the leading members of the Malawi Mwenye community.

Peter Fatch, a Mwenye lawyer working in Blantyre, was not in his office when I telephoned. He was 'in the valley', in Nchalo. When I telephoned him there, he told me to come and see him whenever I liked. He owned a hotel down there, where I could stay if I wished. It was called the Madongi Motel.

On the way back to the rest-house I walked through Zomba's bazaar. There were arcades full of Indian shops: Hassan's Clothing Centre; Rashid Enterprise; Lulat Co. – Tenders Are Welcome Most. Less prosperous Indians sat at tables on the wooden covered sidewalks; some of them had sewing-machines and dealt in minor repairs, others had a few items of clothes for sale. On the bare ground below the sidewalks Africans were selling strips of rubber cut from inner tubes, USAID grain sacks, mangoes, sticks of cassava and bananas. Behind the ring of shops rose the only building in the commercial centre designed in any way to please the eye: a turquoise-painted mosque surrounded by a parapet topped with tiny delicate towers. 'The Mwenye seem to have been Muslims,' Father Joseph had told me, 'but they tell strange stories which have no recognisable basis in Islam. If you're lucky, you'll hear for yourself.'

The following day, in a rented car, I drove down from the highlands to the Shire valley. It had rained in the night, the first blustery rains of the rainy season. Jacaranda bloom trampled underfoot had turned the muddy streets of Zomba blue. The road from Zomba to the Shire valley is said to be one of the most beautiful in Africa, but I saw little of it. A steamy fog covered everything. There were few cars on the road. Occasionally cattle or women carrying things on their heads loomed into sight before being swallowed up again by the fog. At the police road-blocks I was waved past. Any white man driving to the valley was assumed to be going to one of the giant sugar plantations owned by foreign companies and run for the most part by expatriates. I stopped at a village called Chikwawa and drank a glass of strong, sweet tea. On the wall next to the café was a bright metal plaque advertising Kiwi Polish: 'With Kiwi you'll come out shining,' it said. No one in this village was wearing shoes. I asked the café owner what it was used for down here. 'That's the way you make ebony, Bwana,' he said. 'You rub it into white wood until it becomes ebony.'

The village of Nchalo is just one side of a street. The other side is the boundary fence of the Sucoma Sugar Estate. Between the wretched mud-brick buildings and the road was an open space, sodden from the rain, full of deep ruts and pot-holes. In front of the Madongi Motel two brown, long-haired sows, spattered with blood, were noisily fighting each other. A group of black men on the wooden sidewalk were watching, drinking, doing nothing. Most of the buildings were bars, cheap hotels and brothels. They were there to service the 20,000 men who worked in semi-slavery on the

Lonrho-owned sugar estate. Here unskilled men earned twenty-two kwatcha a month, skilled cane cutters eighty kwatcha. A loaf of bread cost just under one kwatcha and here bread was the staple diet. What money was left over was spent on the Nchalo strip.

In the bar of the Madongi Motel two girls in shiny dresses were dancing wilh each other. One of them told me that Peter Fatch was out: he was slaughtering a cow with other Mwenye, but he would soon be back. At the bar a pugnacious, heavily built man was celebrating his mistress's nineteenth birthday. Sam Noel (B.Com., M.Com. [Delhi]) was drunk, but not too drunk to give me his card and to sing. 'Have a drink. Pick a girl. If you like you can marry,' he bellowed to the tune of the Cat Stevens song which had just been playing. 'You only live once,' he continued. 'If you don't do what you wanna do now, you can't do it when you are dead. Am I right? Listen!' he pointed at my notebook. 'You wanna write? You write about me. I've travelled. Been to Dar, been to India, fought the Portuguese.'

He was interrupted by the arrival of an incredibly distinguished-looking man wearing a blue blazer and cravat. He was tall, black and had the bearing and features of a Portuguese aristocrat. Seating himself at the bar, he greeted me in French and explained that he was Sam's distant cousin. They were both from Mozambique. He, Carlos, had been a fighter pilot on the Portuguese side, whereas Sam had fought with Frelimo. '*Noel a vaincu et moi j'ai perdu et maintenant il est obligé au moins de me prêter dix kwatcha.*' And, with a charming smile, he extracted a note from Sam's bulging wallet and called for a round of drinks. Sam and his girlfriend were drinking scotch, Carlos and I had a beer.

Now one or two of the girls moved closer, dancing provocatively, their arms swinging at their sides, taking tiny steps forwards, then backwards, their eyes fixed on their bare feet.

'Buy me a drink? Buy me a drink?' they murmured.

'You buy a girl a drink', said Sam, 'and she'll do it with you. It's part of the custom.'

I shook my head and smiled. We had a few more beers and the girls lit candles which threw the shadows of their dancing bodies on to the pink walls.

'You want to attend to the needs of Mother Nature?' asked Sam, directing me out back to a square courtyard surrounded by a dozen mud-brick cells. This was where the girls lived. I found a sort of toilet and on the way back looked inside one of the rooms. The 'bed' was a split-cane mat covered with a blue sheet; a few dresses hung on a peg; on a square of towel next to the mat were two pieces of soap, three brightly coloured Afro combs and a small pot of Vaseline jelly. And sitting on the mat eating porridge from an enamel basin was a very young, pretty girl. She stood up, removing her dress as she did so, and sat down again, cross-legged, patting the mat, inviting me to join her.

'This is nice girl,' said Sam, poking his head round the door. 'She's only been here two weeks. Fifteen years old. From a country village. I had her. You can have her too. But now Peter's coming back. He'll be here in a minute.'

Leading the way back across the purulent mire of the yard, Sam went through the door and out on to the wooden walkway which overlooked the endless expanse of sugar-cane and told me what he knew about the Mwenye: 'I belong to a superior tribe. I am a Tonga,' he said, beating his chest. 'We use the word Mwenye as a sarcastic word. I would not be proud to be a Mwenye. They were never into kingdomship and fighting. They were somehow associated with the Arabs and their influence was always through trade. In the valley here they were the pioneers of trade. And even now most Mwenye are up-to-do: you do not find them working on the sugar-cane for seventy-five tambals a day. They have houses like this, girls, make money. In the past it was the same. The Arabs used to bring cloth and beads to Sena in the south and Lake Malawi in the north. And the Mwenye used to take the goods into the interior and come back with ivory, animal skins and slaves, which were shipped to Arabia. Basically they were slave-traders. Ah!' he said, lowering his voice, 'here's Peter.' Fatch had entered the motel from the back and was standing at the bar with a beer in his hand. He was dressed in a blue Safari suit and dark glasses. He did not smile when he saw me but shook my hand, distractedly. 'I got fifteen girls here,' he said. 'They get free accommodation, free food. Last week, they tell me, they make no money and they want me to pay them wages. I can't do that. I'm losing money on it. If you want to stay here, you can have my room. It's a good room, but you'll have to pay fifteen kwatcha a night. You pay the girls what you like. But let the office know what you paid your girl in the morning. You can eat your meals here too,' he waved airily at the notice behind the bar: 'Sandwich with margarine 20, Sandwich without margarine 15.'

'As far as the Mwenye are concerned, I don't know much about them. They're mainly down here in the valley. That's all. I'm sorry, I've got to get back to Blantyre tonight. Business. But tomorrow you can see my dad. Father Fatch. He's very old and knows the history and all that.'

He went off to tell the 'office' that I was spending the night and Sam sidled up to me. 'You didn't tell Fatch what I said about the Mwenye? Slave-traders and that? Fatch is a big man down here. A very big man.'

That night the rain lashed the iron roof of Fatch's brothel.

There were fleas in his bed, there were holes in his mosquito net, and his girls danced and wailed until dawn.

Emporium Hapana Fatch was marginally better than the other buildings on the strip. It was made of concrete, not mud-bricks, and was bigger than its neighbours. Inside, a wooden counter ran the length of the room. On the counter were enamel mugs and plates, sarongs and bales of material, hoe heads, fan belts and packets of seeds from South Africa. At one end of it, in semi-darkness, sat Father Fatch, eating his breakfast, a similar breakfast to the one I had just eaten in his son's brothel: an enamel mug of tea, sliced bread and margarine. On the other side of the room facing Fatch sat two men working at sewing-machines. They glanced warily at their master. Fatch said nothing. The brothel receptionist who was acting as my interpreter explained that Fatch would not speak until he had finished eating.

A slim woman entered the shop, her bare feet caked with mud. She wanted to buy an enamel plate, but did not have the price of three kwatcha. She placed two on the wooden counter in front of Fatch, a finger pressed down on each of the grubby red notes. Fatch went on with his breakfast. Very slowly the woman withdrew her splayed hand, sliding the notes towards her, then she went away.

Fatch belched, got up and led the way, still without speaking, into a back room where there were two beds covered with filthy mosquito nets. In one corner of the room spiders had constructed a dense, black empire. I explained my business to him and showed him Mathiva's letter of introduction. With a curt movement of his hand, he indicated that I should sit on the bed and that the receptionist should translate the contents of the letter. He nodded and looked pleased.

'Thank you for the letter,' he said. 'I did not know there

were Mwenye in other countries. Here we call ourselves Masalifu or Amwenye. All others we call Asenzi. I am a Mwenye. I am eighty years old. My father came here from Mozambique to live under the British. He told me that we came from Egypt by ship to Zanzibar. In Egypt we were the Israelites. Then we went by land to Sena. We kill animals in the Jewish way. We say words when we kill animals. We say no words at circumcision, but we used to. The old men used to do something at the new moon, but I have forgotten what. Before, we did not marry the other tribes. Now we do. We still slaughter, and we still do not eat dirty animals. We used to travel in Africa and make hoes, axes, knives and spears. We used to have many slaves, but no longer.'

Fatch told me that the common names among the Mwenye in the valley are Mahdi, Salifu, Sheha, Fachi, Useini, Ungwali, Hasani, Ntakuweise, Hadjabi, Hajji, Suleimani and Musa. There were three Mwenye clans: Masalifu, Hundukweise and Malela. Clearly there was a great deal in common between these people and the Lemba, but there were striking differences in clan names. I asked Fatch if the word Lemba meant anything to him. It did not.

'Do you know the word Baramina?'

'Yes. That is a Mwenye word, but I have not heard it for many years. I had forgotten it. It means "God bless us". It is a worship word. Saidi and Suleiman were our leaders. We had a book once, long ago, but the Arabs were jealous and destroyed the book.'

'What was the book?'

'Ours was the book of the Mwenye. Theirs was the book of Allah.'

'Is Allah the name of your God?'

'Allah is the name of God for the Muslims here, for the blacks and for the Indians. There were many Muslims and they call their God Allah. We do not call our God Allah. We came from Egypt and the name of our God is different.'

'What is it?'

'Sometimes we call him Musa.'

'And Sena? You said you came from Sena.'

'Yes. All the Mwenye came from Sena.'

'Where is Sena? Do you have any idea?'

Father Fatch looked at me with mild contempt. 'Yes, of course I know where Sena is. It's just close by. Just down the road. It's a town in Mozambique. On the Zambezi.'

Fatch clapped his hands together and a servant came in with two enamel mugs of tea and a bowl to wash our hands. The interview was over. But he said a few other things as I drank my tea. To follow the path of the Mwenye I should go next to Sena and then to Zanzibar. If I wanted to learn more, I should speak to the catechist at the Nchalo Catholic mission. He was an educated Mwenye, said Fatch, and spoke good English.

Raphael Bram Ussein was pleased to talk. In the shade of a gigantic baobab tree in front of his house, he said, 'We come from Arabia: we not eatee piggy, and some animals we not eatee. I do not know why even if I starving I not eatee micee. But ants we do eatee. We come from the Jewish people. We come from Sena. Not far. From Sena.'

The following morning Carlos came to see me at the Madongi Motel. He, too, had something for me. One of his friends with an interest in local history had lent him a sheet of paper on which a Mwenye elder, now deceased, had typed a brief history of his tribe:

History of Our Four Fathers
by Sebastiano N. Fatch

Mwenye came from Egypt by means of a ship called Pangaya along Indian Ocean and landed at Zanzibar. There were seven men in the boat. They stayed at Zanzibar for a number of years. There they met the people called Angola and Amakuwa. Amakuwa people were the Lomwe people. From Zanzibar some of them went to Egypt where they met the Boers. And from Egypt some of them went to South Africa at Kimberley. They were as good as Boers and they were marrying each other to Boers. When they reached at Cape Town they saw that there was not enough land to stay. They setted off and crossed the river called Gololodeya and went to a certain Mountain Zinjanja and settled there. And there are no people who have settled in that place since.

Their skill was to invent the new system of weapons like spears, arrows, knives and hoes, ornaments and many others. People had to use the pieces of hard trees as hoes before, after sharpening them.

While in Egypt they married the Israelites, the daughters of Abraham and Jacob. And then they went to Sena where they married the African ladies. They were taming cattle, goats, doves, chickens and not the pigs and they were not eating any meat that was sussenated by any local person. They used the system of surcumesision. They collected many servants and stayed in Sena for good.

Despite the nonsensical character of much of this, it supported in many respects both the accounts that I had heard from the Mwenye here and the stories of the Lemba. I wondered if Mount Zinjanja referred to Great Zimbabwe. Again there was the emphasis on Sena.

'I wish I could see Sena,' I said to Carlos, handing the paper back to him.

'*Et pourquoi n'y allez-vous pas?*' he replied.

There was civil war going on in Mozambique, for a start, I said, and in any case I had not been able to get a visa.

'*Pas de problème. Je peux vous emmener là. Mais je suis terriblement pauvre.*'

That afternoon, for a gift of US$50 (a substantial sum in Nchalo), Carlos guided me via the deserted roads and steaming farm tracks over the frontier into Mozambique. We saw no people and no sign of activity. After an hour or so he told me to stop the car.

'*Là voilà*,' he said, pointing at a smudge on the horizon. '*Voilà votre Sena.*'

It did not look much. In fact, with the slight mist on the low land I was not sure that I could see it at all.

A little further down the track we stopped again and Carlos spoke to a woman who was sitting, weeping, her head in her hands, by the side of a drainage ditch. There had been fighting not far away. There were problems. If they caught him, they would kill him. Either side would. They wouldn't kill me, but I would make a good hostage. So far this was good sport. Now we should go back.

'*Ça ne vaut pas la peine de mourir pour les Mwenye, mon ami, ni pour voir Sena*,' said Carlos.

So I did not see Sena. Disappointed, I turned the car around and drove back across the border into Malawi. But as I drove, I was sure that the Sena on the Zambezi was at least the latest Sena of the Lemba's saga. The Mwenye of Malawi had confirmed this beyond much doubt. Visiting the town would hardly be likely to add anything to this knowledge, and what Carlos said was undoubtedly true: it was not worth dying just to see Sena.

When we got back to Nchalo the strip was a blaze of colour in the late afternoon light. The girls, in red and orange dresses, were sitting on chairs turned back to front, their chins resting on the wooden backs. Half-way down the half street, just past a pitiful photographic enterprise called the Nchalo Paramount Studio, was a bright daub of yellow announcing 'Cafenol Stops Pain'; further on there was a livid green square for Andrews Liver Salts, and next to it a patch of purple – 'Norolon Treats Malaria'. The only malady suffered by these people which was not advertised in bright colours was poverty. Poverty is dun-coloured, the colour of dust; the colour of mud houses and the litter of corn-cobs, the colour of the home-made cars pushed by little boys, the colour of the rags on their backs.

29

Because of Mozambique's civil war I could not follow the trail of the Lemba eastwards to the coast – to what the mediaeval Arab geographers called the lands of Sofala. Instead from Blantyre, the sleazy commercial capital of Malawi, I took a bus north to Lake Malawi, where I boarded an old British-built ship which long ago had been brought overland in pieces from the Zambezi. The *Ilala*, named after the place where David Livingstone died, would take me to the northern end of the lake. The boat passed Makanjila and Nkhota Kota, old Arab slaving stations from which tens of thousands of black people had been marched in chains to the coast. From Chilumba at the northern end of the lake I bought a lift in a beaten-up Land-Rover to the Malawi frontier post, where I was robbed by the border guards. There are ten long hot miles between the Malawi frontier and the Tanzanian border but no transport. You have to walk. When I arrived, exhausted, at Tanzanian customs, I was robbed again, this time by the police. Late that night I arrived at the railhead town of Mbeya and the following day took the Chinese train for Dar es Salaam, for the coast.

The drab ochre of the bush outside was punctuated from time to time by wild animals – zebra, elephant, impala – by wandering Masai tribesmen in their crimson cloaks, or by the gentle pink of a *samdele* tree.

For the entire twenty-four-hour journey I shared a carriage with Benjamin Mwasaka, a lugubrious black college lecturer, who every few minutes muttered, 'We blacks shall remain suffering, suffering until Jesus comes for the *second* time. Until Jesus comes again.' In an attempt to wean him away from his eschatological preoccupations, I told him about my travels among the Lemba, among the Mwenye.

To my surprise he replied, 'I am disappointed, Bwana, that you should have wasted your time among these people. "Mwenye" is a very political word in Tanzania: it means "lords" or "masters" in Swahili. It is partly because of these Mwenye that we shall remain suffering, suffering until Jesus comes for the *second* time. Until Jesus comes again. These Mwenye were the first people to receive religion in this country. But they used it wrongly to keep the people down. In the past they were treated like gods: they demanded goats, they demanded eggs from the people. And they got them. Like the colonialists,' he added, looking at me with his sad, reproachful eyes. 'The Mwenye wear long, white robes and pretend that they are sheikhs. But be careful: it is an insult to call anyone Mwenye in Tanzania. You see they've lost their reputation and they will never regain it until Jesus comes for the *second* time. Until Jesus comes again. If you want to see them,' he continued, 'there are still some in Bagamoyo. They own the land, the coconut palms, the boats. Everything.'

As we got closer to Dar es Salaam Mwasaka cheered up a bit. Hearing I was a writer, he put his hand on my knee and implored me to tell him how you go about getting a book published. For he too, he revealed, had written a book.

'It's about Time,' he said. 'About how it's a fallacy not having enough time. How people use time as an excuse for not doing what they should be doing.' His voice grew a little shriller. 'It's not exactly a book. Each page has a cartoon with a slogan. And it works like this: each cartoon slowly leads the reader on to the final overwhelming realisation that he has all the time in the world.'

A century ago the little fishing village of Bagamoyo was far more important than Dar es Salaam. It was the springboard for the western exploration of Central Africa. Burton and Speke started out from here; so did Grant and Stanley. Livingstone's embalmed body was brought here en route for England, minus the heart which had been buried in Ilala. Bagamoyo had been the terminus from which generations of slaves brought from the interior had been shipped on to the slave markets of Zanzibar. Here as a matter of routine they were flogged: those that survived the flogging reasonably well were bought; those that did not were killed, along with their children. According to local tradition, the name of this lovely place was originally Bwaga Moyo: set sadness aside. It then became Bagamoyo: heart-rending despair.

For the black porters who brought ivory and cattle from the interior it was the end of their journey. As they marched, they sang of 'the town of palms, Bagamoyo, where women wear their hair long, where you drink palm wine all year long, in the gardens of love, Bagamoyo'.

One of the more prosperous Mwenye of Bagamoyo was Abdullah Saleh Abun, an Arab from the Hadramaut. He had seventeen children: five boys and, he shrugged apologetically, twelve girls. His wife and pale-skinned daughters ran his shop, which sold batteries, cloth, single cigarettes, dried fish and tinned food. It had a sandy floor and smelt of the sea. His other interests included coconut plantations, cows, a butcher's shop and fishing boats. As I explained my business, he was ill at ease: his eyes slid from my breast pocket, where my wallet was, to my disgraceful tennis shoes and sockless ankles.

'Bwana mentioned he was from Ingristan?'

'That's right.'

'Bwana is really from Ingristan?' he repeated, making no effort to keep the incredulity out of his voice.

'Yes. From London.'

'And Bwana is a Muslim?'

'No,' I said, 'a Christian.'

This meant, he said, that I was an infidel.

I agreed that from his point of view this was no doubt the case.

'But you speak Arabic,' he said.

I told him that I had learned Arabic in England.

'It is possible to learn Arabic in Ingristan?'

I told him that it was possible and that I was here to study the history of the Mwenye. But Abdullah was not prepared to say anything on the subject, not even what he understood by the term. Before I left, I asked him if at least I might be permitted to take his photograph.

Moving his finger and thumb together he enquired: 'How much?'

I explained that I was not in the habit of giving money to people unless they really needed it, which he obviously did not.

He brushed this aside and said, 'No! By Allah, no! You want to put my picture in a book in Ingristan? What do you think that my people in Hadramaut would say if they saw a picture of Hajj Abdullah in a book?'

I murmured that I did not think that my publishers were likely to sell many copies of the book in the Hadramaut, but he remained firm. The reader therefore will scrutinise the pages of this book in vain for a photograph of Abdullah Saleh Abun of Bagamoyo.

However, what could he have told me? He was a recently

arrived Hadrami. It was clear that here the term Mwenye referred to social and economic position more than anything: it had little to do with religious or ethnic affiliation. But the fact that Mwenye in Swahili, on the coast, means feudal lord or master was interesting: such a sense accorded admirably with the position the Lemba had once had in the interior, in African society.

The dhows go out at night and return at dawn. Hajj Abdullah listened to my request to go out on one of his dhows with expressions of surprise and pain. But he agreed finally to hire out one of his vessels for a few days and the evening before I set out we spent examining it. It hardly looked a sea-faring vessel: fifteen feet long, twenty inches wide and about four feet deep, its shell was a hollowed-out trunk built up along the sides by planks. The gaps between the hull and the planks were plugged by wads of raw cotton. The one sail was made up of four lengths of stained, patched canvas. It had two crudely made, wooden outriggers.

Hajj Abdullah, mystified by my readiness to entrust myself to his flimsy vessel, wanted to know where I was going.

'I want to go to Sena,' I said.

'Sanaa?' he replied. 'If you want to go to the Yemen, you'll need a bigger dhow than this: Very expensive. This can take you to Pemba, to Zanzibar, to Tumbatu.'

I grinned back at him. I had no real idea of where the Lemba's original Sena had been. I was sure that they had come by sea and that they had made their way down the coast to the Zambezi River. I felt they had come from the north.

Just before midnight the dhow left the sultry, perfumed air of Bagamoyo and glided out to sea. The real dhow, Hajj Abdullah had told me, is the same at the front and at the back: this one had a small flat area near the rudder where the captain, Makame, sat cross-legged gazing out towards the open sea; his mate, Hassan, occupied the corresponding surface behind the prow. I sat on the edge of the hull. Makame looked at me expectantly.

'Go in the direction of Sena,' I said.

There was a slight, lazy wind, just sufficient to fill the sail and propel us seawards. The only sound was the outrigger slooshing through the water. The wind soon dropped, the sail flapped overhead and we drifted in the still night. From time to time a gust of wind pushed the boat through the water with such power and ease that you felt confident that a craft like this could take you to Arabia or India – or Sena.

The sea was an empty expanse. The only thing in sight as morning broke was another dhow, its black silhouette over-exposed by the rising sun. Makame was singing mournful songs at the rudder, Hassan was asleep in the shade of the sail. I kept insisting that we head north and each time Makame grew more melancholy. When I asked him why he said simply that he was travelling away from his family and children and that made him sad.

At five o'clock on the second day we saw land. This was where the Mwenye had first landed, said Makame. This was Tumbatu. Beyond the white ribbon of beach, coconut palms, banana trees and mangoes sheltered grass huts and the black, mildewed ruins of some ancient Muslim building. We beached the dhow on the north coast. If the ancestors of the Lemba had come this way from the north, as I was sure they had, they may have landed here.

I sat on the beach and looked north. Where was the Lemba's original Sena? Was it Sanaa? Was it Zion? Was it nowhere? The beach was littered with the treasures of the Indian Ocean: pink fragments of Indian shells, small black stones like the coffee beans of Mocha, crimson points of coral from the Red Sea. I thought of Mathiva's smooth white stone representing Sena, tossed so carelessly into the Indian Ocean. The sounds of the surf pounding on the beach, the sucking suds of the retreating sea and the plaintive cry of the *kunguru* bird gave me some encouragement, but no clue – like a line from one of Louis MacNeice's poems: 'Birds and a white light in the back of my mind to guide me.'

30

I had been led to the Indian Ocean by a remarkable string of stories, legends and half-forgotten memories. But here off the coast of Zanzibar, the trail had gone cold. Insofar as there were any clues they seemed to point north to South Arabia. Back in Vendaland, Mathiva had frequently spoken of the Yemen. So had others.

Their supposition that Sena might be found somewhere in Arabia made good historical sense. And somehow, here in Tumbatu, Arabia was in the perfumed air. Milton's words captured this sense with uncanny precision: 'past Mozambic, off at sea, north-east winds blow Sabaean odours from the spicy shore of Araby the Blest'.

The Lemba always insisted that they had made their way into the interior of Africa along the banks of the Zambezi. There had been links between this steaming lowlands area and South Arabia for centuries. Dominated by the ancient settlement of Sofala this region, the northern shores of Mozambique, was as far as Arab southern exploration went. In the first century the anonymous author of the *Periplus of the Erythraean Sea* had described how after Zanzibar the 'unexplored Ocean curves around towards the West'. But a thousand years later the Arab historian Abu'l Hassan al-Masudi explained that Sofala and the nearby lands of the mysterious Wakwak people were still the outer limits of the known world. It was here that the Sea of the Zanj came to an end. The areas beyond Sofala were unknown and terrifying: there you would find giant birds which carried off oxen, a deadly variety of lizard equipped with a pair of penises and a double vagina.

When Vasco da Gama's seven intrepid caravels unexpectedly arrived from the south, from beyond the Sea of the Zanj, the Arabs of Sofala must have had a disagreeable surprise. The only way to explain this unwanted incursion was that the Portuguese had smashed their way through the mighty dam which Alexander the Great was said to have built to protect the Sea of the Zanj from the unknown terrors which lay beyond.

Months earlier, at the beginning of my journey, poring over the maps in the Gubbins Library in Johannesburg, I had wondered whether the town of Sena on the Zambezi which the Portuguese had discovered in the early sixteenth century and which I had almost seen with Carlos, had anything to do with the town of Sayuna mentioned by the mediaeval Arab geographers. According to Al-Idrisi, in the tenth century Sayuna was a 'town connected to the land of Sofala and peopled by groups of Indians and Zanj and others'. Another Arab writer, Hassan ibn Said, a thirteenth century philosopher and historian, described Sayuna as the capital of the Kingdom of Sofala where the people worshipped 'idols and stones which they anoint with the fat of large fish. Their principal resources are gold and iron. They wear the skins of panthers.' It has normally been supposed that this fabulous Sayuna of the Arab geographers was indeed the Sena on the Zambezi. But there is no proof other than the obvious similarity of the name. Indeed the descriptions we have of Sayuna suggest rather that the town was on an estuary, not way up the Zambezi. It is no doubt significant that a number of early European maps placed a town called Sena in the vicinity of Sofala at the mouth of a river, perhaps the Sabi. It is this Sena which is more likely to represent the vanished Sayuna of the Arab geographers. It is possible then that at different times two Senas may have flourished in the Sofala region – which provides support for the Lemba tradition that they passed through two different Senas once they arrived on African soil. It is also of interest to recall that the name Sayuna is very similar to the normative Arabic word for Zion and identical to the Judeo-Arabic, the form of Arabic used by Jews.

Some sort of a non-African population was again referred to, this time in the fourteenth century, by Ahmad ibn Majid, the intrepid Arab pilot who showed Vasco da Gama the way from the Sofala region to India. He mentioned that the population around Sofala included 'men of the Egyptian Nile'.

By the time the Portuguese arrived on the scene, Sofala and its immediate hinterland had been more or less incorporated into the Muslim world. There were Muslim city states along the coast and particularly at the mouths of rivers. The settlement at Sena on the Zambezi had also become a fairly important town. The inhabitants of these towns were described by the Portuguese as Moors. According to their reports these Moors often lived alongside the Zanj, but some Zanj had become Moors by adopting their dress and by embracing Islam.

The Islam of these Zanj was fairly nominal. The Portuguese chronicler dos Santos, described the converted Zanj as barbarians who were fond of wine and whose only Islamic practices were circumcision and a certain punctiliousness in the celebration of the arrival of the new moon. By the middle of the sixteenth century we know from Antonio Caiado, who accompanied Dom Gonçalo da Silveira to the court of the Monomotapa, that 'Moorish ngangas were the principal wizards of the country'. The remarkable reputation of the Lemba in the nineteenth century as men of magic and medicine seems to follow in this tradition.

According to Antonio de Saldanha in 1511 there were some ten thousand Moors living in the Sofala hinterland. Twentieth century oral tradition insists that these same areas were inhabited by a 'red skinned' race of traders known as Amwenye Vashava. Ahmad ibn Majid also refers to these people: in the first of his 'itineraries' he mentioned that the area around Sofala belonged to the people of Muna Musavi. Muna Musavi is probably the singular form of Amwenye Vashava. It is these people who were no doubt the ancestors of the Mwenye or the Lemba of today. The name Vashava is preserved in the tribal praise-name *Mushavi* and its meaning can be explained from the Bantu root meaning to trade. Mwenye as we have seen means something like feudal lord or master. Amwenye Vashava means something like 'master traders'. The political power of the Moors of the Sofala region was brought to an abrupt end when a Portuguese expedition under Francisco Barretto made its way up the Zambezi to Sena where they put the local Moors to the sword. 'In Sena', as Mathiva had said, 'they died like flies'. Although the Muslims were to regain ascendancy on the East African coast from Kilwa northwards, the Portuguese remained in control in Mozambique and Muslim traffic up the Zambezi came to an end. Those non-Bantu elements in the Sofala-Sena hinterland never made any attempt as far as we know to contact the strong Muslim communities to the north. Nor did they acquire or re-acquire the Quran. As the Lemba so often maintained – their book was lost.

Oral tradition maintains that when the Karanga tribes first

314

took control of the northern part of what today is Zimbabwe, in the first half of the fourteenth century, the central plateau was found to be occupied by Mwenye. Indeed there is substantial evidence of the presence of Mwenye at the court of the Monomotapa whose very name may mean 'Proud Mwenye'. There are various indications that these Mwenye formed themselves into a political entity. Such a state is hinted at in Portuguese records and somewhat later specifically referred to in a Dutch account of 1721 which spoke of a wealthy nation called the 'Walembers' who were rich in gold, who lived 'on the top of the country of Inthowelle' and who traded with the Portuguese.

Most of the evidence then suggests that the past of the Lemba was connected with the Arab world. Ethiopian or Indian antecedents seemed to be based on far more flimsy evidence. But that being the case the question still remains: where was the original Sena? Somewhere no doubt in the Arabic speaking world. But where? And why did the Lemba come to this remote place in the first place? A clue is perhaps provided by the famous fourteenth century Arab traveller Ibn Battuta who wrote that, 'gold dust is brought to Sofala from Yufi in the country of the Limis'. This was surely the magnet for traders coming to Sofala or Sena. And it is probably the lure of gold which explains the rather cosmopolitan character of the city referred to by Al-Idrisi. Or was it simply that Sayuna was as far as one could go, the end of the world, not so much an Eldorado as a remote and welcome haven from persecution?

PART FIVE

The Third Stone

31

The hour of Solomon is the moment at dusk when the narcotic *qat* has taken its effect leaving its adepts with a sense of omnipotence, full of the wisdom of Solomon. In common with most males in the Yemen I had spent the afternoon chewing *qat*. My host was a diplomat who lived in a beautiful mediaeval house in the old city of Sanaa. His *mafraj* at the top of the house had a view over the whole of the city. I had been taken there by Yusuf and now, reeking of rosewater, we were stepping out into the dimly lit alley.

Muslim tradition has it that the Prophet Muhammad smelt naturally of rosewater. When you enter a good Muslim home therefore your host will spray you with this fragrance as a sign of welcome. In less traditional homes you will be sprayed with one of the imported scents from India or the west which every pedlar has for sale: scents with revealing names: Serpent, Mercedes, 24 Carats. Just near the house, rounded Somali women, refugees from the fighting, were gazing with ursine cupidity at the honey coloured gold in the display cases of The Happiness Exhibition.

I had met Yusuf at the British Club on Saif bin Dhi Yazzan Street. He was sitting alone at the bar chewing *qat*, and sipping a beer. He had an Islamic style beard but was wearing jeans and a Princeton T-shirt. He spoke perfect Arabic,

English and French and told me he was an American Muslim, born in Chicago of Palestinian parents. He wrote a bit, did occasional work for the US embassy, thought of doing a PhD, collected stories, slept with two beautiful Somali women. I told him about my journey, about the Judaising Lemba, about my search for the Lemba's lost city of Sena.

'There used to be thousands of Jews here in Sanaa in the Qa – the Jewish quarter. They all left for Israel in 1948. Now there's only one left. Nice guy. He comes and goes. He's not really supposed to be here.'

Yusuf's Jewish friend was a goldsmith who had a portable stall in the market. He told me about the plight of the Jews in the north near the Saudi border and the difficulties he had working in Sanaa illegally. But he knew nothing of any ancient Jewish migration to Africa. In the seventeenth century, he said, there had been a forced exile to Mawza, a desolate and insalubrious town near the Red Sea coast. The Imam of the time had decided that Muhammad's words about clearing Arabia of its Jews and Christians ought to be taken more seriously. The community died in their thousands before the remnant was allowed back to Sanaa. But apart from this he knew of no ancient Jewish migration from the Yemen to Africa or to anywhere else.

During our qat session Yusuf had told me that in his travels in the country he had heard rumours of some ancient Arab migrations to Africa from the Hadramaut. He had been planning to go there the following week in a borrowed Toyota Landcruiser and he suggested I accompany him.

I'd heard that Landcruisers were not the best vehicles for crossing the desert because of their high status among the Bedouin. Nobody would deign to steal a Land-Rover, for instance, but Toyotas were regularly hijacked.

'This one won't be,' said Yusuf smiling. 'This one's got

what I'd call a fuck-off number plate. It was once owned by a sheikh in tribal country. No Bedouin would dare mess with him. Only one thing to bother about: it's not fully insured – just third party and blood money.'

Yusuf said he would meet me in Aden in a few days' time. In the meantime I took the bus down the length of highland Yemen to the south.

From Sanaa at 7,500 feet to the coastal plain the road winds first through the hard, shiny rock of the high plateau. The slopes are adorned with yellow patches of sorghum and green squares of *qat* surrounded by high walls and protected by towers perched on top of which you sometimes glimpse a man or a dog. But on the whole you don't look at the view. You watch the driving and pray.

In the seat behind me a man was chewing *qat*. He grasped a large bunch of the precious shrub wrapped in pink cellophane. His chewing cheek was bulging, his eyes fixed on the Egyptian movie which starred a lush heroine who spent most of her time in bed. Some of the Yemenis complained about the film, others were spellbound. He offered me several tender leaves from the tip of the branch and then proceeded to exact payment. I was ordered to close the window; to accommodate his sleeping child on my lap and to push my reclining seat further forward so that his wife who was breast feeding would have more room for this activity. After a decent interval I suggested that it might be fairer if he and his wife changed places so she could have more room at his rather than my expense. He laughed but stayed where he was.

The movie soundtrack seemed overly dramatic for the bedroom scenes but provided perfect background music for the real life and death struggles of the road. Half way to Aden, impelled by a sense of self-preservation, I decided to part company with the bus and find other means of getting there, Safari Tours in Taizz provided the answer. For $100 a day they would allocate a four-wheel drive vehicle and a driver. Muhammad was a northern tribesman with a long, lugubrious face decorated with a gold tooth. He had a good provision of *qat*, an AK47 assault rifle on the passenger seat and a traditional curved *djambiyyah* in his belt. Muhammad undertook to drive me to Aden. I said I wanted to engage him for three days, at the stated rate, and to make my way to the south at a distinctly sedate pace, via the lesser known byways. The first day passed uneventfully. On the morning of the second Muhammad abandoned the country tracks, swerved out onto the main road and headed for Aden at high speed.

'Muhammad what's the hurry? We've still got two days.'

'Wallah!' he snarled, overtaking a convoy of *qat* lorries. 'We have but two hours,' and he accelerated fiercely.

'Muhammad,' I said 'I promised you three hundred dollars for three days. One hundred dollars per day.'

'Indeed,' he replied 'You are right.'

'We have therefore two days left.'

Muhammad looked over his shoulder as he sped into a bend.

'We agreed on thirty-six hours, English. Is it not true in Britannia that a day has twelve hours, and a night has twelve hours. We agreed on three days. Which is three periods of twelve hours.'

I had no wish to make a scene but I didn't feel like being cheated. Muhammad's misunderstanding, if that is what it was, was not very credible. After all I wasn't the first western traveller to call on the services of Safari Travel.

Shortly after noon, we found a police station in a small, hot town near adh-Dhala. The gendarmes, enveloped in white *galabiyas*, were seated on cushions in the commandant's office, chewing *qat*. The arbitration took most of the afternoon. The Englishman, it was finally conceded, had a sound argument. Muhammad too had a valid point: no one could deny that there were but twelve hours in a day and therefore thirty-six hours in three days. But as the Englishman was a guest in the Yemen they would be obliged to find in his favour. Muhammad was humiliated and angry. I had no desire to spend a further day and a half in his resentful company and told him to drive me straight to Aden.

We stopped in a side-street near Steamer Point and Muhammad helped himself to a handful of *qat*. He remarked softly that I had ill-used him. Faced with this quiet assessment I softened and allowing him the benefit of the doubt I shrugged and handed over the full three hundred dollars. One hundred and fifty of them were counted off and disappeared into one of the deep pockets of his *galabiya*. Lips pursed he handed back the rest and drove off without a word.

In 1839 Aden was stormed by British and Indian forces and until 1937, when it became a separate colony with its own Governor, it formed part of British India and was administered by the Government of Bombay. Aden town had been totally absorbed into the British Empire and had been the busiest port in the world after New York and Liverpool. Thirty years after the British left in 1967 disturbing traces of their presence were everywhere, from the neo-gothic church at Steamer Point to the no-nonsense austerity of the military establishments. Although little has been built in Aden since the British withdrawal, the occasional newish and dismal structure and the general air of grey dilapidation give the town the air of a simmering Belgrade or Bucharest. Muhammad had left me next to the Crescent Hotel which once, long ago, had been the place to stay. It is no longer. It has been replaced by a Bulgarian hotel on the Gold Mohur Beach and a smart Swiss place at the other end of town.

You could hardly imagine Queen Elizabeth II staying at the Crescent today as she once did. But it was not a disappointment. The red polish on the steps had faded now to an almost imperceptible blush, but the solid pre-war British furniture was still largely intact. I climbed the grand staircase to my room – the lifts had long ago stopped working. The room was in a terminal state of decay. The carpet had lost its colour and nap, and the creepers of some tropical plant had penetrated the room via a broken window. In the adjoining bathroom a rectangular hole in the floor was the only sign that a bath had once stood there. The cavernous and empty dining room was graced with a full size grand piano and magnificent chandeliers but the man at the desk did not recommend that I eat there. He suggested the old British Sailors' Club just down the road. Built for other ranks this nondescript building still boasts bakelite plaques above the rooms with the names of the donors: Clacton Branch of the BSS Guild 1961, Wareham and District another. The club's Mariners' Bar had become a haven for hard drinkers. Jordanian and Syrian engineers sat drinking vodka at one table discussing the likelihood of getting a contract in the Yemen. A few Palestinians from the PLO-owned night club next door were arguing over a belly-dancer. 'I am a poet. I am a cat,' wailed an Arab swaying past them, a bottle of Stolichnaya in his hand. 'I walk the night, I climb the trees, I look at the moon.' He paused and bawled suddenly: 'Scientists. They send scientists in rockets to see the moon and the sun. They should send poets. And cats.'

I sat watching the sun set with this drunk. He had some shellfish for sale. 'Good to make love,' he said making a mighty erection with his arm. If I didn't like shellfish he could get me some honey from the *wadi* Do'an, the best and most expensive in the world. It had the same effect. Or some special Hamdani *qat*: 'Makes you want it more and makes you go longer.' I said I had no one to go longer with. I was going to the Hadramaut, travelling with a male friend, following some kind of a lead, writing a book. 'I don't believe you,' he said. 'You're not a writer – you're a spy. But you can tell me the truth. It's almost night now. We say in Arabic "The word of the night is blotted out by the sun".'

At Steamer Point, Russian and Japanese merchant ships lay at anchor. Past them a dhow slipped through the red water. The boat moved slowly, making little impression on the smooth surface of the water, the pink triangle of its sail billowing slightly. Had it come from Zanzibar, Sofala? I felt that this same dhow would still be here when the last rusting hulk of modern shipping had finally been been transformed by the alchemy of time to its constituent chemical parts.

Yusuf arrived a day and several hours late. He had been to visit a Muslim divine in Taizz although he would not say why. He was dressed in a striped *futa*, a white shirt and wore a crocheted skullcap. 'We're going to the Muslim holy city of Terim,' he said. 'Got to be dressed right. And anyway it's hot as shit in the Hadramaut. Nothing as cool as a *futa*.'

It was afternoon before we set off. Chewing a rough lorry driver's *qat* called *sau'di*, Yusuf drove fast through the heat and dust of the desert. 'This stuff keeps you awake,' he said laughing. 'I'll not sleep for a week the amount I've taken.'

He kept the branches of *qat* hidden under a blanket, taking a small bunch when he wanted it.

'I'm travelling as a fully paid-up Muslim fundamentalist,' he said. 'Some of them don't approve of *qat*.'

On the road towards Habban, during a flash downpour, we stopped at a roadside eating place in a hamlet called Al-Ahmar. A concrete construction, open on all four sides, provided some protection from the rain. In one corner kids were being roasted, in another, men were slaughtering a goat. People squatted on the floor watching an Egyptian TV soap and displaying with outstretched hands the green oranges they had for sale. The water pouring off the roof like sheet glass reflected equally the butchering of the goat and the banalities of Cairene life. Except for the wet concrete floor there was nowhere for us to sleep. A few miles down the road we found a simple *lukanda*. This, the cheapest form of overnight accommodation in the Yemen, was on the main street of a village where there had been no rain. A rickety metal spiral staircase joined the street to the hotel veranda. In the communal sleeping room beyond this, a dozen or so men were lounging in the half-darkness on blackened mattresses, smoking, chewing *qat*, watching TV. The smell of rotting shark mixed with stale tobacco hit me like a tidal wave. I asked for mattresses to be put on the roof. As we lay down to sleep, in the cold clear air, it was just possible to pick out mountains by the light of the stars but I could not grasp either their proximity or their size.

What had been beautiful the night before was less so in the light of dawn. The street below was strewn with rubble: empty packets of Kamaran cigarettes, cans of Shelltox cockroach killer, Shams washing powder, lengths of wire, spark plugs, greasy bits of Toyotas. South Yemen until recently had been a hard-line socialist state. Signs of some transient modernity were indeed visible: there were cement block buildings although they were all painted in traditional white and green: there was not one without rusty metal rods sticking out of the roof, as if everyone had plans to add a storey when they could afford it. The only decent building was a new stone-built mosque. But the call to prayer had a bleak, socialist ring to it as if it had been pared down to its most utilitarian parts.

To my surprise Yusuf was urging the lorry-drivers to make the morning prayer. He had slept very little and seemed nervous and irritable. A group of drivers were squatting next to their vehicles on the filthy, oil-soaked ground and were listening to his harangue with embarrassment. I wished he would stop. Beyond the asphalt road a dusty golden track led towards the fields; men could be seen trudging to work as they always had, and beyond the narrow plain, table-top mountains, pink and moss-brown in the morning sun, were making obeisance to a solitary peak.

'What's all this fervour about?' I asked Yusuf.

'I'm just in fundamentalist mode. Extremist mode.' he replied giggling. This mood continued as we entered the *wadi* Habban. Yusuf stopped the Landcruiser and started shouting at a group of young unveiled women at the side of the road. With good humour they shouted out that he should go back to the north and stay there. 'It's a total disgrace being unveiled like that,' Yusuf said. 'I'm not surprised the people in the north think the south is a sink of iniquity and that the women are whores.'

In Habban you see for the first time the multi-level houses which the Arab poet Alqama described in the early years of Islam as 'climbing the height of heaven, in twenty storeys'. These have been the characteristic feature of the Hadramaut since Sabean times. Dominated by the palace of the Sultan, Habban used to be divided into hierarchically distinct quarters for Jews, *Seyyids* – descendants of the Prophet – and sheikhs. These quarters were pretty squalid. And I supposed they always had been. When a certain Major Miles of the

Aden Residency staff visited Habban in 1870, one of the first westerners ever to do so, he remarked that there was universal equality of wealth in Habban: everyone was equally impoverished. Even the Sultan, whose sway did not extend beyond the town limits, possessed but a single slave and no furniture.

The town used to have one of the most important Jewish communities in the area. Here the Jews were very different in appearance to those elsewhere in the Yemen. The men wore their hair long, wore ribbons around their head, and broad silver belts around their waist. Traditionally they had carried arms for the Sultan. Habban had been the most easterly of the Jewish communities of the Yemen and one of the most remote in the world. But in earlier times there had also been a community further east, in the *wadi* Hadramaut itself, until the Jews were expelled as a result of the activities of a Jewish pseudo-Messiah towards the end of the fifteenth century.

One reason for Habban's inaccessibility was the constant warring between different tribes and factions in the area. Until recent times if an unwary stranger made the mistake of entering the town the Habbanites would drive him out. And he would be made to carry on his back whichever beast of burden he made the mistake of arriving on: otherwise his blood would be on his head.

I asked the men sitting in the market place about the Jewish community. A *Seyyid* looked at me suspiciously and muttered that they had all gone to Israel. Yusuf stood aloof frowning. The town square stank terribly of fish. A shark, the staple diet of this inhospitable coast, was being cut up in the dust. Everything for sale in the market seemed to have something to do with fish. Even the plastic thonged sandals of the suspicious *Seyyid* were adorned with fish. 'I've often thought how ghastly it must have been for Jews living in Germany and central Europe to live in a culinary culture devoted to the pig,' I remarked. 'In fish eating cultures like this there must have been fewer problems.'

'Why are you so interested in the Jews?' he grumbled. I explained that I taught Jewish studies in an English university and had a particular interest in the Jews in Islamic countries. This seemed to more or less satisfy him and we went to get a drink in the little café on the square.

'I'll have tea,' I said, sweet mint flavoured tea being the national beverage.

'Libtun?' asked the waiter.

'What?' I asked.

'He means Lipton's,' said Yusuf. 'It's the local way of saying tea-bag. You have the choice between a tea bag or a traditional brew'.

The waiter told us there was a *wadi* outside the town which had once been used as a place for ritual bathing by the Jewish community and we headed off to look at it. In a part of the *wadi* still called 'pool of the Jews' generations of Jews had carved their names – Moses son of Solomon, Isaac son of David, Joseph son of Abraham. However one of the fresher Hebrew inscriptions carried a defiant message: 'Cursed be the Ruler'. No doubt these words were scratched in the soft rock in 1948 before the departure of the Jews from Habban and refer to the anti-Jewish persecution of the Sultan of Habban of the time. Another inscription, in Arabic, carved high up on the same cliff face in a particularly inaccessible place, contained a more enigmatic message, simply: 'the tears of Zekhariah'. I stared at this trying to imagine the circumstances that led to a young man carving this and I noticed Yusuf looking at me with a wry smile.

'It's a weird thing being interested in Jews,' he said. I shrugged and said nothing.

After Habban the road swings south-east towards the squalid coastal town of Bir Ali. Not far away the pre-Islamic town of Qana once stood: Qana of the frankincense country, Qana 'which yields frankincense from the trees'. Sheltered from the open sea by a hill called the Fortress of the Crows, this city would have completely dominated the bay. Qana was the principal southern port of the incense route and one of the great entrepots of the ancient world. It was from here, from the port of Araby the Blest, that 'north-east winds blow Sabaean odours from the spicy shore' where the smells of cinnamon, pepper and spikenard from India mingled with Persian dates and wine and the fragrant gum from Qana's rocky hinterland. And where men grew rich on the trade in pearls and muslin from Ceylon, Indian diamonds and sapphires, tortoiseshell from the Malaccan Straits and perhaps gold and ivory from Sofala. But more than anything it was the trade in frankincense and myrrh, indispensable for the great religious systems of the Near East and India, which made the pre-Islamic state of Himyar, in which Qana stood, one of the wealthiest countries in the world.

Himyar was greatly influenced by Judaism. According to Arab sources, Himyar converted to Judaism during the reign of King Abu Karib As'ad (c 385–420 AD). According to others the conversion occurred during the reign of the last king of Himyar, Yusuf Ashar Dhu Nuwas (d.525) otherwise known as Masruk, who drove his horse into the Red Sea and accepted death by drowning rather than fall into the hands of his African enemies from Ethiopia.

As we sat by the sea in Bir Ali, Africa seemed not far away. There was a crowd of boys playing drums, they were all black, African looking. No doubt their ancestors had come to this grim coast as slaves perhaps from Zanzibar or Kilwa. Not far from here in 1834 Captain Haines saw 700 Nubian slave girls being offered for sale. We asked the boys where we could eat. They explained that Bir Ali had no real restaurant but they found us fish and chillis and rice flavoured with cinnamon and cloves which we ate with our hands on the sand. There was no hotel so we went off to sleep on the beach next to the ruins of Qana.

We lay in our sleeping bags in the shelter of a sand dune. But Yusuf could not sleep. He wandered around the beach, smoked cigarette after cigarette, and finally crouched next to me and said in a whisper:

'I've got a confession to make.'

'What's that?'

'I think I'd better introduce myself.'

'I thought you already had.'

'Yeah. But there's a bit more to it. The truth is I'm a Jew. I'm not a Muslim. And my name's not Yusuf. My mother is a Palestinian Arab, that's how I know Arabic. My father is a Hungarian Jew brought up in Paris. They met in Israel in the 1950s. My mother converted when they married. They moved to the States just after.'

'What in God's name are you doing dressed up as a Muslim, going round the Yemen preaching hellfire and brimstone to the Arabs?'

'It's a long story. I had this idea. I'd like to bring peace to the Middle East. You know? What people don't understand is that Islam will never give up Palestine. My mother made me understand that. It cannot. Palestine is part of Islamic territory – what they call the House of Peace – Dar as-Salaam. Arab politicians can do what they like, say what they like. Muslims will never surrender Palestine, never surrender

Jerusalem. Unless,' he paused, looking back at the imposing silhouette of the Fortress of the Crows rising from the desert, 'unless they can be made to believe that the return of the Jews to the Land of Israel is somehow part of the divine plan, part of the design of Allah, part of the Prophet's message.'

'But Islam makes no such point,' I protested.

'Yeah. I know. I've been looking for support in the texts. No luck yet. If I don't find it I'll have to invent it. Forge it. Create a sort of holy lie that people will believe in. That Muslims can buy.'

'So what's your real reason for being in the Hadramaut?'

'Well, I kinda like your story about a lost tribe of Israel disappearing into Darkest Africa. But I'm mostly interested in looking out for old Arabic manuscripts dealing with the return of the Jews. I guess you'd call it my mission. And there is an amazing collection of old books and manuscripts in Terim. There's a great Islamic library there. I know it sounds a bit crazy but anyhow that's my story'.

And sticking his hand out he said, 'Hi – my name's Harvey Gold.'

The Hadramaut runs parallel to the south coast of Arabia and eventually turns south and joins the sea by the *wadi* Masila. Explained in the Bible as signifying the place of death its true etymology may come, credibly enough it seemed to me, from an Arabic root meaning searing heat. Terim is set on the left side of the *wadi* between precipitous walls rising from the valley floor to the high plateau – the *djol*. To the north the plateau merges with the sand-desert of the Empty Quarter. According to tradition this valley was the home of the prehistoric people of Ad, destroyed by God for failing to worship Him as recommended by the Quranic Prophet Hud. As if to compensate for the sins of their forbears the people of Terim are intensely religious. Terim is a city which traditionally claimed to have three hundred and sixty four mosques. When Freya Stark visited Terim in the 1930s there were still sixty mosques functioning and there are still mosques everywhere with sand lapping at their doors. The central mosque, cream and green, extravagant and tiered, bedecked with neon lights, is transformed by the changing light of twilight from robust vulgarity to something exquisite. It rose and grew before my eyes reacting against and then merging gracefully with the peach sky and its restrained handful of stars.

Surrounded by fields, gardens and palm groves which invade the town along with the sand, Terim is also a city of palaces built by Hadramis who have made their fortunes overseas in Java or Singapore. Terim is called the town of death and sleep. Real work was always done elsewhere: people came back from the East to spend sleepy holidays in their Terim gardens and to die. These retirement mansions are all larger than life: their pediments, arches and doorways are inappropriate in the narrow valley of the Hadramaut with the desert sands whipping over the top. They are grander than any need could justify, more rhetorical in their purpose, ridiculous but not afraid of being so. Set against the glowing rock of the side of the *wadi* these pastel coloured edifices look like a Hollywood film set – not to be used – simply there to impress.

Outside the palaces and mosques Terim is a town of more human scale, a place of tiny alleys, of mud-brick houses, intense heat, palm trees in mosque gardens shuddering slightly in the breeze, sturdy studded wooden doors. Across the square in front of the great mosque sides of fly-covered shark are manhandled onto wooden wheelbarrows and carted away through the sand. The stench of fish-heads the size of footballs, abandoned in every alley, stays with you for days.

I wandered through the streets where crisscrossing wires cast shadows on carved blue shutters and neon tubes stick out of the houses at weird angles. Townsmen hurried home, taking short rapid steps as demanded by the ubiquitous Indonesian *futa*. The Bedouin, long hair shiny with ghee, moved less surely. And so did I. As I walked aross town to the Qasr al-Qubbah hotel, with its gardens, pools and technicolour cupola, I wondered if this strange town could possibly harbour the key to the puzzle which had exercised me for so long.

The following morning Yusuf took me to the Islamic library where he hoped to find the elusive documentation which would change the course of Middle Eastern history. We both spent the morning reading. Shortly before noon we were joined by the head of the library, Sheikh Ali Salem Bukair, who was also the Mufti of Terim like his father before him. The Mufti had an unusually hoarse voice caused no doubt by decades of haranguing the faithful. He was a slight, ascetic man with a habit of cracking his knuckles and twisting his arms behind his back like a contortionist. He was polite but austere. After a few minutes' conversation, during which I managed to explain the purpose of my journey, to my surprise he invited us back to his home for lunch. Running ahead up the stairs with the agility of a much younger man he shut all the doors leading onto the stairwell to prevent us glimpsing the womenfolk of his household. With energetic arm movements he showed us into his *mafraj* where small carved shutters filtered the blinding white light of Terim at midday. We sat on the floor propped against the cushions lining the room while his younger sons brought us flag-shaped raffia fans, cold water and tea, and, soon after, a splendid meal of rice, goat curry, chillis, a salad of tomatoes, onions and bananas. The conversation was urbane and general. But as we finished lunch we were joined by another elderly man summoned by Shaykh Ali to meet us.

Sheikh Abdul Rahman Abdul Karim al-Mallahi was a poet and playwright who was now enjoying his retirement from the old socialist ministry of culture. But his real passion was the history of Arab navigation. Sheikh Ali asked me to repeat to Sheikh Abdul Rahman the legends of the Lemba and their claims to have come from the north, from Sena, to have crossed Pusela and to have arrived finally in Africa. I suggested to him that the celebrated Hadrami town of Seiyun with its similarity to the Sayuna of the Arab geographers might be a candidate for the Lemba's Sena.

'Impossible,' he snapped. 'To this day people from the western and central parts of the *wadi* have links with the east, with Indonesia, with Singapore, not with Africa. Except perhaps in the *wadi* Do'an where they used to go to Egypt, Somalia and Ethiopia. You've seen these palaces in Terim built by families who made their fortune in Java – it's the same in Seiyun. It's the people at the eastern end of the *wadi* who have links with Africa. They travelled to Mombasa, to Tanzania to Zanzibar – in the old days to Kilwa, to Sofala. The men used to leave to make a living. It's always been poor here. There was poverty and appalling misrule. There were different Sultans ruling over every hamlet in the Hadramaut. And most of the time they were at war with each other. We have an expression here: "We have Sultans – but it is better to go to the coast and eat fish." The traditional rulers did nothing for people here, so they went abroad and left their women and children behind. Sometimes they would return. Sometimes they perished, sometimes they could not get back.

But you know,' he said after a pause, his voice softening, 'there is in fact a town called Sena at the end of the *wadi* Hadramaut, just before the valley turns off towards the sea. You won't find it on your map,' he said smiling, 'it's too remote. But once, before the Sena dam burst many hundreds of years ago it was an important town with a rich agriculture. It lay on the trade route – the old incense route – from the sea to Terim. May I suggest that the Pusela of your Lemba refers to the Masila – the valley which leads from Sena to Sayhut – the old port of Africa. What was it you said? "They left Sena, they crossed Pusela." Well – they left Sena and in order to get to the sea they would have to cross the Masila and once they had crossed the Masila they would have found themselves in the great mediaeval port for sailors bound for the African coast!'

I could hardly believe what he was telling me. I had scoured every Middle Eastern map for place names that would help identify the origins of the Lemba. I had never found anything half as convincing as this. I was momentarily thrown off balance and had difficulty in taking in what he was saying. He carried on talking airily about the tides and currents of the Indian Ocean: how there are two kinds of currents – the deep and the shallow. The deep starts in the southern end of the Red Sea and continues from March to the end of August; whereas from September to March an easterly deep current flows from India to the Arabian and African coasts. Then there are the winds: the *dubur* wind which comes from the south-west, from the African coast and blows around to Arabia from April to the end of July, and then the *ayzab* which goes from the north-east to the south-west. Thus with a perfect conjunction of current and wind it would sometimes be possible to get from Sayhut to Zanzibar in about twelve days. The traditional time, then, for leaving for Africa was in

December – the time of the strongest south-west winds and currents. You could not embark even from al-Mukalla to Africa – you would get pushed into the gulf of Aden. You have to go from Sayhut.

Shaykh Abdul Rahman was clearly fascinated by the story of the Lemba. He found Hadrami names for many of the Lemba clans and sub-clans: Ba-hamisi for Hamisi, Ba-sadiki for Sadiki, Ba-Kandishi for Hamandishi, equivalents for Duma and Bakari and Seremane and Hajji. Again he spoke of the depopulation of the eastern end of the *wadi* after the destruction of the Sena dam. As I listened, bemused and befuddled, Sheikh Abdul Rahman offered to take us and the Mufti the following day to the far end of the *wadi* – to Sena.

An air of festivity attended our procession. The Mufti was wearing a green *futa* and a long, not very white shirt covered with a white cotton shawl and a white crocheted skull-cap. Sheikh Abdul Rahman, the navigator, was royally attired in a purple plaid cloak. Yusuf was wearing a maniacally pious scowl and a remarkable assortment of supposedly Islamic garments crowned by a red fez. To better look the part of a Muslim scholar he had bought a second-hand pair of gold-rimmed glasses in the bazaar of Terim. These prevented him from seeing anything and gave him a headache. For the rest of the day he said almost nothing. Before we set off we looked at the *Lonely Planet Guide* to Yemen. The Mufti was pleased to see a photograph of his spendid mosque and I was pleased to see that there was nothing on the map east of Terim. The Mufti blew his nose in a satisfied way and twisted his arms behind his back as a sign that we could go.

Along the route children greeted us with respectful enthusiasm. At intervals along the track you see small white *siqaya* domes and feudal mud-built castles mostly in ruins on jagged pinnacles. The road to Sena follows the water course of

337

the Hadramaut – the *sailah*. The river, jewelled with white boulders, repeatedly bursts out of the *wadi* floor only to go underground again. As the river reappeared around a bend, the Toyota splashed through the moving water disturbing men submerged up to their necks like water buffaloes. Along the banks acacias, *samr* and *ilb* trees and palms gave the kind of deep shade where you could imagine going to sleep for ever.

The road passed the tomb of the Prophet of God Hud where a ghost town of hundreds of houses, some of them palatial, are built against the cliff face of the *wadi*'s side and are maintained in readiness for the four days a year when Muslims come to venerate the Prophet. The Bedouin particularly love this place and one of them, long haired and green eyed, his Kalashnikov wrapped in a pretty piece of purple cloth, was lounging by the ford through the *sailah*, gazing at the small metropolis with what seemed like awe. And awe was an appropriate response to this place, for here there is a true sense of sanctity. I thought of the magnificent Bahai temple at Haifa where this sense is absent. Sanctity it seems to me is something that cannot be counterfeited. It is perhaps an organism that grows very slowly, nurtured by centuries of prayers and tears. Hud was the first of the five Arab prophets. It has been suggested that since the word Hud is used in the Quran as a collective noun denoting the Jews, and that the root there means 'to practise Judaism', Hud may be equated with the ancestor of the Jews.

We were about to continue when Yusuf came to life. He was playing his part a bit too well, I thought, treating the Mufti with a haughty but more or less benevolent condescension as if he were representing stricter and more authentic Islamic values. He now insisted on praying at the shrine. In fact he insisted that everyone pray at the shrine. I felt embarrassed and kept my distance but when he marched back to the Toyota I whispered to him that he could treat Sheikh Ali with a little more respect.

'But I let him lead in prayer!' he said.

'OK, but he is the bloody Mufti,' I snapped.

Sena is a small town, but no more insignificant than many other towns in the Yemen which figure on maps. It is built on high ground which rises sharply up from the *sailah*. We stopped the Toyota in the square near the mosque. A group of people soon joined us. They were surprised, even excited to see us. No one ever comes here. I started to tell them about my quest. They all had some connection with Africa, mostly with Kenya and Tanzania. As we chatted a terrible voice boomed something in Swahili.

'I know Afrikiya. Don't tell me about Zimbaboy. And come in out of the sun!' Shooing wives and daughters out of the way, the village *mukhtar* ushered us up the stairs into his *mafraj*. The burly old man was dressed in a red shawl and white *futa*. His beard and hair were dyed red with henna and he had a *djambiyyah* stuck in his belt. A *Seyyid*, a descendant of the Prophet, he had an easy manner and natural authority. As soon as we had seated ourselves he clapped his hands and called for his slave. His *mafraj* was decorated with ostrich eggs, photographs of his ruined castle, swords and *djambiyyas*. As we drank ginger tea and ate dates and grapes from his orchards he pulled a sword off the wall and brandished it playfully. I told him about the Lemba. He showed no surprise. 'We have always gone to Africa from here,' he said. 'My own sons are mostly in Africa. I always treated them hard. And they've done well – most of them are cabinet ministers – but they hate me.' He grinned as if this was of little consequence. As for the Lemba, he said – they would be welcome to return to Sena whenever they wished. The old man talked about his village and his travels. He told me about the tribes of the *wadi* Sena, about the customs and traditions of the eastern Hadramaut. He told me about their method of seeing the new moon at the beginning of Ramadan. They captured the moon in a bowl of water, he said. The bowl was set a little in the shadow and reflected the moon even during the day. Using this technique they would never transgress the laws of the fast. This was the moon of the Lemba, I thought. He confirmed that most of the Lemba clan names were to be found in the Hadramaut.

Sheikh Ali had, at Yusuf's insistence, provided us with a driver. He was a surly little Bedouin with kohl-smeared eyes one of which harboured a sty. He had not spoken all day. Now he was engaged in an intense conversation with the *mukhtar*'s slave. It seemed that in the village there was a remarkable woman known as *Um al-ayun* – the mother of eyes. Before leaving Sena the driver insisted on going to see her. We walked past mud brick houses the same colour as the cliffs and surrounding hills their cornices decorated with ibex horns. At noon the light reflected from the white sand and beige walls was blinding and one could well imagine that an eye healer would not go hungry here.

On the edge of the town there were gardens full of mango trees and limes, green finches and golden clusters of dates resting in the heart of young palms. In a nearby house *Um al-ayun* was waiting for us. She was sitting with her back to a window, unveiled, a red scarf around her head and crescent shaped scars on her cheeks. She peered at the driver's eyes and muttered to herself. Her method of treatment consisted of inserting a piece of cloth between the eylid and the eyeball of her patients. She ordered the driver to rub his eyes as hard as he could. While he did this she prepared her piece of cloth, trimming it carefully with a pair of not very sharp scissors, wetting the trimmed edge with her tongue. She started to pronounce on the eye in front of her: she could feel that there was something wrong, that some kind of an object was attached to the skin behind the eye-lid. The driver by now had rubbed all the kohl off his eye. It had become red and swollen. She held his head, pulled down the skin of his cheek and pushed her grubby piece of bandage into the eye until only a small piece was visible. The healer's mother had also done this she told us. She used to be able to thrust her tongue right up behind the eyeball and deal with any infections that way.

I felt a kind of anti-climax. This was the end of my journey and that imposed a sort of solemnity upon me. I was not sure that I wanted to share this moment with this somewhat unappealing woman of Sena. I wanted to reflect on my journey, decide if I had been faithful to the task set me by Mathiva, by Ephraim the Detective, by the irascible Phophi, by Sevias, by the dying chiefs Mposi and Ndouvhade. Ndouvhade had said he would see me perhaps in Sena. Was he in Sena? But this conclusion was perhaps appropriate. Whatever I had discovered here was a function of my own eyes. I had seen what I took to be a solution to the origin of the Lemba. But were my eyes good enough? Was I blinkered? Would other people see it in the same way? Did my journey and experiences constitute proof?

Um al-ayun of Sena patted the pouched, bruised eye of the Bedouin and kneaded the surrounding flesh with her thumb. With a swift movement of her wrist, like a prestidigitator, she pulled out her soiled little rag and with it the source of her patient's malaise: a small, smooth, white stone.

AFTERWORD

The publication of the first editions of this book followed by various radio and television treatments of the story have brought the previously unknown Lemba tribe of southern Africa to the attention of a wide international audience. Even within South Africa, the Lemba were practically unknown, almost like a secret society. But on 31 October 1999 three of the Lemba elders were invited to the Pretoria residence of President Thabo Mbeki. Mbeki had seen the documentary based on this book while he was abroad: he was fascinated and wanted to hear more about the Lemba. In their own land the Lemba have been recognised as the unique tribe they are. Terribly excited by this official recognition, Professor Mathivha wrote to me and said 'The crown of the Lemba is yours!' At the same time the Lembas' links with the Jewish people have become stronger, and their own sense of 'Jewishness' infinitely more robust. On 1 December 1999 Yaacov Levi, a Jewish educator with degrees in animal science and fisheries science, left the United States for South Africa. His mission was to bring normative Judaism to the Lemba. Thousands of books and other aid have been sent by Jewish communities in the United States. In the future the Lemba will be totally transformed by these events, but they are already no longer the same people I knew ten years ago.

The Lembas' remarkable story has struck a chord across

various disciplines and particularly with geneticists. Unknown to me, in the latter stages of my work, a fellow Welshman, Professor Trefor Jenkins of the South African Institute for Medical Research and the University of the Witwatersrand in Johannesburg, had the idea of trying to solve the mystery of the origin of the Lemba by collecting genetic material from the tribe. The reason is that one tradition has it that the original Lemba immigrants from the north, from Sena, were males who subsequently took local African wives. Jenkins argued that if the Y chromosome of the Lemba, which is passed down through only the male line, could be shown to originate in some specific part of the world, we might be able to determine where the Lemba were from. On the basis of samples of DNA taken from 49 Lemba men, Jenkins wrote a scientific article that was published in the *American Journal of Human Genetics* (59:1996). He was able to show that '50% of the Lemba Y chromosomes are Semitic in origin—40% are Negroid, and the ancestry of the rest cannot be resolved. These Y-specific genetic findings are consistent with Lemba oral tradition.'

Jenkins's pioneering efforts reached a popular audience with the transmission of the BBC Television series *Origins* and the book based on the series, *In the Blood: God, Genes and Destiny* (1996) by Professor Steve Jones, a geneticist at University College, London. Relying on Jenkins's data, Jones noted:

> In the pedigree of the Lemba there is a surprise. Most of their genes—blood groups, enzymes and the like—unite them with the African peoples around them. However, those on the Lemba Y chromosome . . . have a different origin. On a family tree of the world's male lineages the Lemba are linked, not with Africans, but with the Middle East. The Lemba legend of their origin contains a hidden truth.

Long before the television series was shown, one of my Lemba friends had sent me a copy of Jenkins's article. It was incredibly exciting to see some apparent corroboration of the conclusions that I had reached on the basis of my journey. From reports I received from the Lemba in the mid 1990s it was clear that they, too, were excited: one of them wrote to me, 'You have given us our history back, Jenkins has given back our blood.' Jenkins's work immediately started having an impact on the Lembas' sense of their own identity.

A short while later Neil Bradman, the brother of an acquaintance of mine, invited me for lunch. This was the first of many meals we were to share, although most of them would be in less luxurious settings than the Charlotte Street restaurant where we met. Bradman, a wealthy Jewish businessman with interests in the study of genetics, had just established the Centre for Genetic Anthropology at University College, London, under the directorship of Professor Vivian Moses (who in time kindly consented to explain some of the rudiments of genetics to me). Bradman wanted me to get involved in a project to create a genetic map of the populations—most of them Jewish—in which I had a particular interest.

My first field trip with Bradman was to Ethiopia where we had the idea of collecting DNA samples from two unusual groups that claimed to be Jews—the Falasha, or Ethiopian Jews, and the Qemant from the region of Lake Tana. Later we collected samples in Kenya and Uganda. Soon after, I persuaded Bradman that we should return to the Lemba. It was clear to me that the tantalising results produced by Jenkins's research left a number of questions unanswered. To say that the Lemba had 'Semitic' genes did not solve the riddle of their religious origin, nor was the term 'Semitic' particularly precise. As applied to language, the term 'Semitic' could refer to languages from many parts of the Middle East and North

Africa and to much of North-East Africa as well. As applied to people, the term seemed less useful: clearly it could not be used to label speakers of Semitic languages who include a vast variety of peoples. We discussed whether genetics could help us to determine what religion the Lemba had traditionally practised. It seemed unlikely. In the past Judaism had been a proselytising religion that had attracted hundreds of thousands of converts from around the Mediterranean and the Middle East. A striking example of this was to be found in the very area from which I believed the Lemba had once come—namely the conversion of the South Arabian kingdom of Himyar to Judaism. In addition, the pillage and pogroms to which Jewish communities in Christian Europe had regularly been subjected were frequently accompanied by rape: this must have led to all sorts of genetic admixture. Given this history, why should Jews have a strikingly homogeneous genetic makeup? I was convinced that a larger Lemba sample and more detailed anthropological information about each donor might reveal something of value.

By now I was persuaded that the Lemba had probably come from South Arabia. It seemed, then, a good idea to compare South Arabian and Lemba DNA. Given the clan structure of the Lemba and the similarity of clan and family names in the Yemen, I thought that genetic affiliations between Lemba clans and Arabian subtribes might even show up. In the absence of any documentary or archaeological evidence, DNA might conceivably provide some sort of proof that my theory on the origin of the Lemba was correct.

In January 1997 in the Vendaland area, and in October 1997 mainly in Sekhukuneland, I collected DNA from 136 male Lemba. Samples were collected from paternally unrelated but otherwise random males identified as Lemba by the donors themselves and by the elders who were present. The clan affiliations of 108 subjects were recorded: some Lemba, to my surprise, were ignorant of their clan affiliation.

The first thing you have to do when collecting samples is put on thin rubber gloves. It was hot during the testing, and the gloves filled up with sweat. Using them is unpleasant on another count: in a country where whites do everything they can to create a cordon sanitaire around themselves, interacting with black friends while wearing sterile gloves was embarrassing. The technique I had been taught to employ was to vigorously rub a cotton swab over the inside of both cheeks of the donor. This procedure, I was assured, produces sufficient DNA for the purpose of analysis. The DNA is then stored in test tubes along with a preservative agent.

My first port of call was a black township near Louis Trichardt. I entered its ramshackle streets with a sense of unease. First there was the question of 'informed ethical consent,' which any researcher doing this sort of work has to secure. That is, both individually and collectively, the Lemba would have to authorise my collection and use of their DNA. The Lemba leadership had been happy to give their consent and to give me letters of introduction to facilitate the work. Most of them knew of Jenkins's research and had an idea what genetics was all about. But explaining what I wanted to simple, unlettered villagers would present practical as well as moral difficulties. In addition, the process was much more invasive, it seemed to me, than anything I had done before. By now I had some idea of the kind of impact my book and other work was likely to have on the future of the Lemba. The genetic work I was now undertaking was likely to be even more explosive.

In the township there were plenty of people who knew me from previous visits. From their standpoint this research might confirm beyond any possible doubt what they thought about themselves—and what they wanted to think about themselves—that they were of Jewish origin. For each donor I filled out a sheet listing the donor's name and age, his father's and paternal grandfather's name, their first and second languages, their place of birth and their clan. The samples were then sent back to London for analysis.

What I now wanted was to collect DNA in South Arabia so a comparison could be made. In May 1997 Neil Bradman and I retraced my original journey to the eastern end of the Hadramaut and collected 120 male DNA samples, some from Seiyun a few miles down the *Wadi* from Terim, some from Sena itself. Collecting DNA samples in a pious Muslim country has its difficulties. The first collection point was a teachers' training college in Terim. The principal kindly permitted us to address the student body—some 70 students—and to explain our mission. Although common prudence dictated that I keep off the question of Jews—after all, this was a devout Muslim country—I explained that it might be possible through genetic means to show that in the remote past Hadramis had played a part in the construction of Great Zimbabwe—one of the great African civilisations. They seemed less than charmed by this idea. One of them stood up and explained firmly that the Quran forbade the collection of DNA. He did not vouchsafe how he knew this. Nonetheless there was a growl of assent. The spokesman stood up and walked out, and all but two students followed him. The two who stayed behind were manifestly more secular than the majority: this was clear from the cut of their beards and from their clothes. They were happy enough to give their DNA. One of them muttered under his breath that he did not think the Prophet would have any objection. Neil had the inspired idea of rewarding the men's independence of spirit by taking their photo using the expedition Polaroid. As the gleaming photographs were spooled out of the machine I handed them over. Brandishing their spoil, they marched out into the blistering heat of the yard. These were probably the first colour photographs of themselves they had ever possessed. Within a minute the rest of the students were queuing up to give their DNA and to receive their gift.

Overall a total of 399 samples—Lemba, Bantu, Yemeni, Ashkenazi, and Sephardi—were collected. The results were analysed by Dr. Mark Thomas at University College, London, Dr. David Goldstein at the University of Oxford, and Neil Bradman, who by now was doing a doctorate at Oxford under Goldstein's supervision. The first results clearly showed a significant similarity of markers among many of the Hadramaut Y chromosomes and those of the Lemba, although there was no specific overlap with the population of Sena—which, in fact, as we discovered, is thought to have arrived in the area in relatively recent times. These findings seemed to confirm that the Lemba may well have come from the general area of South Arabia. But these results left the question of the religious origins of the Lemba unanswered. It was possible now to attest with some certainty that the Lemba had come from Arabia, but there was nothing here to confirm the Lembas' claim that they were of Jewish extraction. A parallel study, however, was producing data that would, indeed, have something to say about the religious origins of the Lemba. To understand the implications of this research one must first understand a little more about Y chromosomes and DNA mutation as well as something of the inherited Jewish priesthood—the Cohanim.

DNA is a long molecule consisting of a string of bases (known as T, C, G, and A). About 98 per cent of the DNA in human beings appears not to have any relevance to our structures or our well-being; indeed, it may not be relevant to anything at all and may be utterly redundant. This great mass of our DNA is normally referred to as junk DNA. The remaining 2 per cent of our genetic material codes for all the proteins that make up what we do and what we are, everything from the colour of our eyes to the shape of our toenails. These proteins have very precise structures tightly governed by the DNA coding. Proteins are (often) hundreds of amino acids long, each amino acid being determined by three consecutive bases on the DNA; those sections of DNA specifying particular proteins are called 'genes.' If for any reason a DNA base is replaced by another, or if it is deleted, or if, by chance, another is added, or sections of DNA are duplicated (all hazards that do indeed occur), the structure of the DNA at that point will be different from the original and, hence, variant.

Sites on the DNA that have been found by experiment to exhibit such variety are called 'polymorphisms.' They can occur in both the coding and the junk regions of the DNA. If polymorphisms occur in the former, they may confer some disadvantage because of the consequent modification of a protein structure, and they are likely to be weeded out of the population by natural selection (although if the disadvantage is not great, they may survive). Changes in junk DNA have no consequences as far as we know: they simply sit there, generation after generation.

Those junk variants (polymorphisms) get passed down from one generation to the next. The argument is that they occur by chance. Since human DNA contains so many bases, and since the frequency of polymorphic change for most sites is not very great, the chance that through history any one of them will have been struck more than once is low (but not zero—some sites are known to have been hit more than once) and for that reason are called 'UEPs' or 'unique evolutionary polymorphisms.' They are the stuff of these studies. Although UEPs are not easy to find because they have no consequences for the carrier, a number have been identified. Such mutations, in turn, permit people to be grouped in various ways. Importantly, the Y chromosome does not recombine and remains practically unchanged from generation to generation. Thus using the Y chromosome we can hope to trace the ancestry of certain groups back through history, ultimately to points of common ancestry, which is precisely the kind of genetic mapping the Centre of Genetic Anthropology was engaged in. Its findings would yield data that would shed light on the Lemba. But first to some early Jewish history.

Somewhere between thirteen and fifteen centuries BCE the Israelites left Egypt and spent years languishing in the desert areas of the Sinai, Negev, and Transjordan. The Bible tells us that during this period the tribe of Levi was selected for certain religious duties that included carrying the Ark of the Covenant. Both Moses and his brother Aaron were members of this tribe, and descendants of Aaron in the male line were designated Cohanim or priests.

In 587 BC the temple of the Israelites in Jerusalem was destroyed by Nebuchadnezzar, and many of its inhabitants were taken into captivity 'by the waters of Babylon.' Until this cataclysmic national event, the sources paint a confused picture of the relationship between Levites and Cohanim. In some sources the term 'son of Levi' is synonymous with 'priest,' and the impression is given that any Levite may officiate as priest; in other sources a sharp distinction is drawn between Levites and 'sons of Aaron.' There are also indications that foreigners such as Gibeonites were given some of the Levites' Temple functions and perhaps even became Levites. Other non-Levitic temple servants—'the sons of Solomon's servants' may also have assimilated to Levites. After the return of the captives from Babylon, a very much clearer distinction was made between priestly Cohanim and nonpriestly Levites, and every effort was made to keep non-Levites out of Temple service.

Levitical status, like priestly status, has been passed from father to son to this very day. It is true that a Jew is defined as being someone born of a Jewish mother, but priestly status and Levitical status pass down through the male line. Thus priestly status is transmitted exactly like the Y chromosome. What our study showed was that although Levite Y chromosomes are diverse, the Cohen Y chromosomes are remarkably homogeneous. Specifically, among the Cohanim it was found that over 50 per cent of the sample had one specific haplotype (the specific set of markers in each cell that are passed on from the sperm), which became known as the Cohen modal haplotype. The Cohen modal haplotype is, then, that combination of genetic markers on the Y chromosome in the sperm of Cohanim that distinguishes them, more or less, from other sperm producers.

It was the Cohen modal haplotype that was to open a new window on the Lembas' past. We discovered that one of the South African subclans—the Buba—carries this haplotype at a very high frequency—over 50 per cent of the Buba I tested had this haplotype. Among Levites 3 per cent have the haplotype; among the general Jewish population about 10 per cent (but the general Jewish population also includes Cohens and Levites).*

The date of entry of this haplotype into the Lemba is unknown. It could be that a carrier of the haplotype—probably a Cohen—was responsible for introducing this genetic ele-

*M. G. Thomas, K. Skorecki, T. Parfitt, H. Ben-Ami, N. Bradman, and D. Goldstein, 'Origins of Old Testament Priests,' *Nature* 394 (9 July 1998) pp. 138–40.

ment in relatively recent times. Yet the haplotype was found in Buba communities that were geographically quite distinct from each other. It is more likely, then, that the gene flow occurred over a hundred years ago—and therefore predates regular contact between the Lemba and Jews—which started on a small scale from the time of the colonisation of the northern Transvaal around the turn of the century. Prior to that we know of no Jews, and precious few Gentiles, who penetrated the inland areas inhabited by the Lemba. It is altogether more likely that when the ancestors of the Lemba arrived in Africa they were carrying this haplotype with them.

These results could therefore with caution be interpreted as indicating that at some time in the past Jews inhabited South Arabia. We know that at the time of the death of Muhammad there were Jewish tribes in the *Wadi* Hadramaut who may well have subsequently converted to Islam. Some of the present Muslim population of the Hadramaut may be descended from them. The fact that the Lemba share some of the markers found in other Jewish populations could indicate that in the past Jews—or descendants of Jews—emigrated to the shores of Africa. Whether this was for religious, political, or economic reasons it is not yet possible to say.

December 1999

NOTES

CHAPTER 1

14 5 N. J. Van Warmelo, *The Copper Miners of Musina and the Early History of the Zoutpansberg* (Pretoria, 1940), p. 67. According to a Lemba informant: 'The Whalemba insisted that their daughters be not married by any others than their own people lest they be only partly shaven according to Venda custom and lose their wits. On the other hand, if the daughter of a stranger should be married by a Mulemba, she would become cleverer by having her head shaven.'

14 19 *Ibid.*, p. 66.

15 32 *Rand Daily Mail*, 15 September 1982.

16 22 Van Warmelo, *op. cit.*, p. 6.

CHAPTER 2

18 14 R. Oliver, 'Discernible Developments in the Interior *c.* 1500–1840', in R. O. and G. Mathew (eds), *The History of East Africa* (Oxford, 1963), p. 169.

22 3 Quoted in D. Kessler, *The Falashas: The Forgotten Jews of Ethiopia* (New York, 1985), p. 111. It is worth noting that the Agau people, of whom the Falashas are part, share the tradition that they originally came from Sennar. See J. Halévy, *'Excursion chez les Falacha, en Abyssinie'*, in *Bulletin de la Societé de Géographie* (Paris, March 1869), p. 9.

355

36 32   On ritual purity among the Lemba, see M. N. Mphelo, 'The BaLemba of the Northern Transvaal', *Native Teachers' Journal* (October, 1936), p. 39; and H. A. Stayt, 'Notes on the Balemba', in H. A. Stayt (ed.), *The Bavenda* (Oxford, 1931), p. 235.

40 12   There has been no demographic work done on the Lemba. On the basis of what I observed, Mathiva's estimate is on the high side. Cf. I. Schapera, *The Bantu Speaking Tribes of South Africa* (Cape Town, 1946), p. 65: 'Some hundreds of adult males in the Union ... in Southern Rhodesia ... 1,500 males'; J. Blacking, *Venda Children's Songs* (Johannesburg, 1967), p. 41: 'There are probably no more than about 2,000 Lemba living scattered or in little pockets among the Venda ... a few others may be found in different parts of the Transvaal.' *Rand Daily Mail*, 15 September 1982: 'South Africa's 250,000 "black Jews" the Lemba'. At a recent meeting of Lemba in the northern Transvaal more than eight thousand people were counted; this can serve as a minimum figure, but clearly suggests a total population many times greater. In Zimbabwe there are many sizable concentrations of Lemba. In the area round Mposi I estimate there may be around twenty thousand Lemba at the very least.

40 23   On the Lemba and Sabbath see H. von Sicard, *The Ngoma Lungundu: Eine Afrikanische Bundeslade* (Upsala, 1952), pp. 166–8. Cf. G. Beyer, '*Die Malepa Nordtransvaals*', in *Kolon. Rundschau*, 17, 8, 1924, p. 272. On circumcision see index; on burial practice see index; on the secrecy of the Lemba see e.g. D. C. Chilgiga, 'A Preliminary Study of the Lemba in Rhodesia' (unpublished seminar paper, 1972), p. 2; on sacrifice see von Sicard, *op. cit.*, p. 166; on moon rituals see index.

41 3 It is not clear whether there is any connection between *zanj* and the Greek *Azania* mentioned in *Periplus of the Erythrean Sea*, the *Zingis* of Ptolemy or the *Zingion* of Cosmas Indicopleustes. The etymology of the word is uncertain: it has been connected with the Persian word *zangi* meaning 'fool', although etymologies based on African words have also been suggested. It could just be that *zanj* comes from *wasenzhi* and not the other way round. In this case it might be that the term was originally used by non-Muslim peoples inhabiting the east coast of Africa to describe the peoples of the interior and was taken over in the same sense by the Arabs. See M. Tolmacheva, 'Towards a definition of the term *Zanj*', in *Azania: Journal of the British Institute in Eastern Africa*, vol. xxi, 1986, p. 105ff. In modern times the term *wasenzhi* is used on the east coast as the opposite of *waung-wana* – free and civilised peoples. See E. A. Alpers, *Ivory and Slaves in East Central Africa* (London, 1975), p. 8. See also A. A. Jacques, 'Notes on the Lemba Tribe of the Northern Transvaal', in *Anthropos*, 26, 1931, p. 247.

Page Line CHAPTER 5

45 16 For further information see E. J. Krige and J. D. Krige, *The Realm of a Rain-Queen* (London, 1943).

46 32 H. A. Junod, 'The Balemba of the Zoutpansberg', in *Folklore*, 19, 1908, p. 277.

Page Line CHAPTER 6

60 14 M. L. Daneel, *The God of the Matopo Hills* (Mouton, 1970). See below p. 95.

61 4 Schlömann, in *Zeitschrift für Ethnologie*, 26, 1894, p. 64.

61 8 Stayt, *op. cit.*, p. 234.

61 11 Jacques, *op. cit.*, p. 247; see also Junod, *op. cit.*, p. 284;

C. Bullock, *The Mashona and the Matabele* (London, 1950; first edn, 1927), p. 21; Van Warmelo, *op. cit.*, p. 66.

61   18   H. A. Junod, *Bantu Heritage* (Johannesburg, n.d.), p. 44; see also Van Warmelo, *ibid.*

62   4   Junod, *ibid.*; see also J. E. G. Sutton, 'The settlement of East Africa', in B. A. Ogot (ed.), *Zamani* (Nairobi, 1974), p. 80.

62   26   T. Huffman, 'Expressive space in the Zimbabwe culture', in *Man* (NS), 19, pp. 593–612.

67   24   Cf. Jacques, *op. cit.*, p. 246; Stayt, *op. cit.*, p. 235; L. C. Thompson, 'The Ba-Lemba of Southern Rhodesia', in *NADA*, 19, 1942, p. 77; Van Warmelo, *op. cit.*, p. 66.

67   31   Cf. Junod *op. cit.*, in *Folklore*, p. 281.

68   1   A. A. Jacques calls it *sindja* or *sindza*, but cf. Mphelo, *op. cit.*, p. 41.

68   20   *Ibid.*

68   24   Thompson, *op. cit.*, p. 77.

68   30   *The Matabele Journals of Robert Moffat 1829–1860* (Salisbury, 1976), p. 369.

69   12   Van Warmelo, *op. cit.*, p. 66.

69   28   Stayt, *op. cit.*, p. 235; G. M. Theal (ed.), *Records of South Eastern Africa*, 9 vols (Cape Town, 1898–1903), vii, pp. 189, 268, 306; Junod, *op. cit.*, in *Folklore*, p. 283; Van Warmelo, *op. cit.*, p. 64; N. Sutherland-Harris, 'Trade and the Rozwi Mambos', in R. Gray and D. Birmingham (eds), *Pre-Colonial African Trade* (London, 1970), p. 252.

73   17   Cf. Schlömann, *op. cit.*, p. 67.

73   29   Cf. Jacques, *op. cit.*, p. 249: 'Other words used in these prayers were: *A sasa sa e se a bona, Mose a a vuye popa, munhu umbi mutša mbona kwava ku fa, waenda.*' An approximate and partial translation of this is 'Let Mose [Moses?] come back here, man is bad, you will not see him again, to die is to go on a journey.'

Page Line **CHAPTER 7**

84 9 Thompson, *op. cit.*, p. 79; see also Bullock, *op. cit.*, p. 21; M. E. R. Mathiva, *The BaLemba* (unpublished paper, 1972), pp. 7–8. It is of interest to note that some Lemba-like graves were discovered by Hall at Great Zimbabwe: R. N. Hall, *Great Zimbabwe* (London, 1905), p. 94.

84 12 Jacques, *op. cit.*

84 18 Stayt, *op. cit.*, p. 234.

84 26 Von Sicard, *op. cit.*, p. 160.

84 27 Thompson, *op. cit.*, p. 79; Professor Mathiva told me in a private communication that 'souls return to Sena'.

85 4 Mathiva, *op. cit.*, p. 7; Jacques, *op. cit.*, p. 249.

85 15 M. E. R. Mathiva, 'Lemba Characteristics' (unpublished paper, 1987).

85 20 Ritual suicide was encouraged particularly in cases where the king had some pronounced defect, e.g. his teeth had been knocked out; see Theal, *op. cit.*, p. 194.

87 15 Some Lemba-like groups are thought to exist in Mozambique; private communication from Margaret Nabarro, Johannesburg, and cf. von Sicard, *ibid.*

Page Line **CHAPTER 8**

92 28 Van Warmelo, *op. cit.*, p. 66.

93 15 João Albasini, iv, *João Albasini 1813–1888* (Pretoria). See also J. B. de Vaal, 'João Albasini 1813–1888', Camoes Annual Lecture, no. 3, University of the Witwatersrand, Johannesburg, 1982; D. Fernandes Das Neves, *A Hunting Expedition to the Transvaal* (London, 1879).

Page Line **CHAPTER 9**

100 24 Van Warmelo, *op. cit.*, pp. 63, 65.

101 3 F. N. Ravele, Secretary, Mphephu Tribal Authority, in *Bantoe*, July 1958, pp. 76–8.

101   9   Cf. Blacking, *op. cit.*, p. 41.

101   22   W. Grundler, *Geschichte der Bawenda – Mission in Nord Transvaal* (Berlin, 1897), pp. 13–14; see also Stayt, *The Bavenda*, p. 6. D. N. Beach, *The Shona and Zimbabwe* (Gweru, Zimbabwe, 1984), p. 212.

101   29   N. J. Van Warmelo, 'The classification of cultural groups', in W. D. Hammond-Tooke, *The Bantu-speaking Peoples of Southern Africa* (Johannesburg, 1937), pp. 80–2.

101   31   Jacques, *op. cit.*, p. 248.

102   1   Cf. N. M. N. Ralushai and J. R. Gray, 'Ruins and Traditions of the Ngona and Mbedzi among the Venda of the Northern Transvaal', in *Rhodesian History*, 8, 1977, p. 8.

102   8   A. Anderson, *Twenty-Five Years in a Wagon in the Gold Regions of Africa.* (London, 1887), ii, p. 144.

102   28   g. Caton-Thompson, *The Zimbabwe Culture: Ruins and Reactions* (Oxford, 1931), and especially Appendix iv by H. Sayt, 'Notes on the Bavenda and their connexion with Zimbabwe', p. 244 ff; and more recently: T. Huffman, 'Iron Age Settlement Patterns and the Origins of Class Distinction in Southern Africa', *Advances in World Archaeology*, 5, 1986, p. 304.

Page Line   CHAPTER 10

108   13   Cf. H. von Sicard, 'Lemba Clans', in *NADA*, 39, 1962, p. 72; Thompson, *op. cit.*, p. 81.

109   6   Cf. G. Lindblom, 'Copper Rod "Currency" from Palabora, N. Transvaal', in *Man*, 89–90, August 1926, p. 144.

109   24   E. Axelson, *Portuguese in South-East Africa 1488–1600* (London, 1973), p. 143: an unlikely alternative is that the hoe represents the sort of ceremonial hoe which was given to Rozwi troops who were occupying new territory

for the *Mambo*, see N. Sutherland-Harris, *op. cit.*, p. 244.

110 1 Junod, *op. cit.*, in *Folklore*, p. 279ff; Thompson *op. cit.*, p. 82ff.

110 20 Von Sicard, *Ngoma Lungundu*, p. 157ff.

110 21 See P. S. Garlake, *Great Zimbabwe* (London, 1973), p. 114. Garlake writes, 'Similar sets of tools [i.e. similar to those found at Great Zimbabwe] were used in recent times by the Venda, a tribe closely related to the Shona . . . renowned for their . . . metal-working skills.' But as we have seen, it was the Venda who learned these skills from the Lemba. In an appendix to G. Caton-Thompson's book, *The Zimbabwe Culture*, H. Stayt, demonstrating the connection of the Venda with Great Zimbabwe, wrote: 'Metallurgy was practised among the BaVenda until recent times. . . . I know definitely that copper mining and smelting was done in this area until about 45 years ago, as an old MuVenda, Netshsaula, a petty chief of Chief Masekwa, gave me a complete description of the methods employed. He had himself been a copper worker, having learnt his trade from a MuLemba . . . . The chief metallurgists among the BaVenda belong to the alien BaLemba group, who worked at Messina under the protection and patronage of Venda chiefs.' Stayt, while arguing that metallurgy was one of the things linking the Venda with the Zimbabwe civilisation, in fact shows that such a link must have been via the Venda's close relationship with the Lemba. The tools found at Great Zimbabwe were found in a hut which adjoined the conical tower in the Elliptical Building and in the Eastern Enclosure on the Hill, both areas, as Garlake points out, 'that seem from other evidence, to have been centres of ritual' (p. 116). See also: H. J. Taylor, 'The Amandabela and other tribes of Matabeleland', in *Proceeds of the Rhodesian Scientific*

Association, 6:1, 1906, p. 22ff; C. Beuster, 'Ruinen von
Zimbabye im Mashona Lande' in Zeitschrift für Ethnologie, 25, 1893, p. 289; cf. Sutherland-Harris, op. cit.,
p. 263.

111	8	H. von Sicard, 'Shaka and the North', in *African Studies*, xiv, 1955, p. 147.
111	14	Jacques, *op. cit.*, p. 248.
111	18	Stayt, *op. cit.*, p. 231.
111	23	Von Sicard, 'Lemba Clans', p. 78.

Page Line CHAPTER 11

121	5	See e.g. J. Blake-Thompson, 'Mlimo and Mwari: Notes on a Native Religion', in *NADA*, 1956.
121	14	Von Sicard, *Ngoma Lungundu*, p. 152.
121	17	R. Summers, *Zimbabwe: A Rhodesian Mystery* (Cape Town, 1963), p. 100.

Page Line CHAPTER 13

| 134 | 18 | Van Warmelo, *Copper Miners*, pp. 63–5. Von Sicard, *Ngoma Lungundu*, p. 145. |
| 134 | 25 | The white powder was known by a name which Van Warmelo's informants could not translate: *zhwangala vhutshena zhwa madzi-kande*. |

Page Line CHAPTER 14

| 141 | 18 | The suggestion that the Lemba came from Egypt was made by a number of informants. Cf. e.g. Chigiga, *op. cit.*, pp. 5, 8. See index. |

Page Line CHAPTER 15

| 150 | 16 | On the Lemba dialect see N. J. Van Warmelo, 'Zur Sprache und Herkunft der Lemba', in *Hamburger Beitrage zur Afrika Kunde*, 5, 1966, pp. 273–83; see also P. J. Wentzel, *The Relationship between Venda and* |

Western Shona (D.Litt. and Phil unpublished thesis, UMOA, 1981), pp. 32–9.

152 25 See J. T. Bent, *The Ruined Cities of Mashonaland* (London, 1893), p. 242; see also C. R. Boxer, 'A Dominican account of Zambezia in 1744', in *Boletin de la Sociedade de Eustudos de Mocambique*, 1960, p. 10.

153 3 *Cape Argus*, 22 September 1953, referred to by W. G. L. Randles, *L'empire du Monomotapu du XVe au XIXe siècle* (Paris, 1975), p. 69.

156 29 *The Matabele Journals of Robert Moffat 1829–1860*, pp. 250, 369; see also Junod, *op. cit.*, in *Folklore*, p. 280: 'The Balemba used to do a good business also in special medicines which they sold at high prices to the Ba-Suto'; *ibid.*, p. 284, among the Ba-Suto: 'They used to be the surgeons trusted with the physical operation [circumcision]. They provided the special charms by which the circular fence of the lodge was doctored to protect it against malign influences from outside. They also used to perform the last operation, viz. burning the lodge on the day of the liberation of the boys [from the initiation period] as nobody else dared to do it. The newly initiated as is well known must leave the lodge and run to a pool to bathe there, it is strongly prohibited to them to look backwards when the houses of the initiation are burned, as the sight of that might pierce their eyes and make them blind. The Balemba, masters of the *ngoma*, do not fear that.' Thompson, *op. cit.*, p. 77: 'Amongst the Ba-Lemba is a class of hereditary high priests. Owing to the superior intelligence of the Ba-Lemba, some of the chiefs of other tribes had a Mu-Lemba priest attached to them and today this practice is still continued. He is a very important person, whose kraal is next to that of the chief, to whom he is adviser, doctor, priest, rain-maker and diviner; he is president of the circumcision lodge of the tribe. The Ba-Lemba priests were responsible for the

introduction of circumcision and other Semitic rites into the ritual of the tribe with whom they dwelt.' See also T. Trevor, 'Some observations on the relics of pre-European culture in Rhodesia and South Africa', in *Journal of Royal Anthropological Institute*, LX, 1930, p. 392: 'Most of the smiths and the doctors were Balemba'; Jacques, *op. cit.*, p. 247: 'They play a prominent part as surgeons and medicine men in the circumcision ceremonies practised by the Venda, Thonga and Sotho; *ibid.*, p. 248: 'The Lemba were keen traders who travelled far and wide to buy and sell their merchandise. This . . . would often consist of medicines'; Chigiga, *op. cit.*, p. 10: 'Besides, the Lembas were renowned for their use of magic in fighting. They were "doctors"'; von Sicard, 'Lemba Clans', *op. cit.*, p. 70: 'Sadiki . . . This was the clan of the medicine-men of war, as they knew all medicines'; 'Hamisi . . . They were known as medicine-men who treated people in order to get children.'

159	23	Cf. Stayt, *op. cit.*, p. 234; Jacques, *op. cit.*, p. 246; Thompson, *op. cit.*, p. 79; Bullock, *op. cit.*, p. 22.

Page	Line	CHAPTER 16
165	12	Jacques, *op. cit.*, p. 246.
165	16	Mphelo, *op. cit.*, p. 36.
165	22	*The Matabele Journals of Robert Moffat 1829–1860*, p. 250.
166	1	Schlömann, *op. cit.*, p. 67.
166	13	Van Warmelo, in Hammond-Tooke, *op. cit.*, p. 81.
166	14	Stayt, *op. cit.*, p. 235.
166	16	Alpers, *op. cit.*, p. 22.
166	21	Garlake, *op. cit.*, p. 176.
167	18	Beach, *op. cit.*, p. 32.
167	20	Theal, *op. cit.*, I, p. 93.
168	7	Translated by Guy Butler.
168	18	Thompson, *op. cit.*, p. 81.

168 32 Jacques, *op. cit.*, p. 249.

169 8 I have already mentioned in the text that Solomon Sadiki in Soweto and Phophi in Vendaland explained the term 'Lemba' as 'those who refuse', i.e. refuse banned foods, inter-dining, etc. Indeed, this explanation was proffered by all of my Lemba informants and has been accepted by some scholars. There are, however, other explanations. It has been suggested that 'Lemba' should be connected with word *Lembi*, which occurs in a number of northern Bantu languages and which means non-African, European, respected foreigner, etc. V. H. Velez Grilo preferred to connect the name with the word *Ma-Rembane*, which refers 'directly to the act of procreation displaying the abhorrence shown by aborigenous peoples towards the endogamous and polygamous customs of the Lemba'. Velez Grilo in the same article also put forward the somewhat more plausible suggestion that the term may be connected with a Zulu word meaning 'hoe'. It is also noted by a number of observers that the Lemba do not particularly like the name and that it is more often used of them than by them. I have chosen to connect the name with the Swahili simply because it seems an altogether likely etymology and because the Lemba are more likely to have come from the coast than from the north or the south. See Van Warmelo, in Hammond-Tooke, *op. cit.*, p. 82, and *Copper Miners*, p. 63; von Sicard, *Ngoma Lungundu*, p. 140; V. H. Velez Grilo, 'The dispersion of the "Wa-Remba" (or "Vha-Lemba") and tribes related south of the Zambesi', in *South African Journal of Science*, 54, 5, 1958, pp. 111–17.

Page Line CHAPTER 17

173 27 Cf. von Sicard, *Ngoma Lungundu*, p. 167.

173 33 Jacques, *op. cit.*, p. 247; Stayt, *op. cit.*, p. 232; Mphelo,

op. cit., p. 41. It seems that the Lemba are not the only South African tribe to practise this custom of moon watching. It was found also among the Suto – although it may well be that they acquired the technique from the Lemba. See D. E. Ellenger and J. C. MacGregor, *History of the Basuto* (London, 1912), pp. 49 and 50.

174   3   Jacques, *ibid*.

175   2   P. Kirby, *Musical Instruments of the Native Races of South Africa* (Oxford, 1934), p. 65.

175 12   Stayt, *op. cit.*, p. 236.

175 14   Theal, *op. cit.*, p. 202–3.

175 23   *Ibid*.

177 19   *Ibid*.: 'The Lemba usually marry among themselves only. Marriage was considered a serious affair. The girl had to subject to inspection by some old women and if she was found to have lost her virginity she was sent back to her parents. She had to remain in the village of her parents-in-law for a year before the consummation of marriage. If they were satisfied with her character and capability for work she was led to her husband at the end of this period. A "doctor" was then called in to make incisions on their bodies and to mix their blood . . . Most of these customs are not peculiar to the Lemba, but are met with among the Venda also, except that the probationary period is there reduced to a few months.' On marriage among the Lemba see also Bullock, *op. cit.*, p. 20; Stayt, *op. cit.*, p. 234; Jacques, *op. cit.*, p. 246; Thompson, *op. cit.*, p. 79.

Page Line   CHAPTER 19

185   4   See above, pp. 78–9.

185 13   Van Warmelo, in Hammond-Tooke, *op. cit.*, p. 80.

187   4   See Abu Salih the Armenian, *The Churches and Monasteries of Egypt and some Neighbouring Countries*, tr. B. T. A. Evetts (Oxford, 1895), p. 286, f. 105b.

188　9　Von Sicard, *Ngoma Lungundu*, p. 159.

188　23　Al-Idrisi (Abu Abd Allah Muhammad b. Muhammad b. Abd Allah b. Idris al-Hammundi al-Hasani) was born in Ceuta *c*.1100, studied in Cordova and became the court geographer of the Norman king, Roger II of Sicily, whose great silver-plate map of the world provided the basis for Alfidrisi's *Kitab Rujar* or *Book of Roger*.

186　30　It is perhaps worth noting that in southern Arabia proclamations by town criers and the like were always preceded by beating on a drum. See R. B. Serjeant, *The Portuguese off the South Arabian Coast* (Oxford, 1963), p. 35.

190　6　Private communication from Dr Margaret Nabarro, Johannesburg.

190　8　Thompson, *op. cit.*, p. 85.

Page Line　CHAPTER 20

195　11　H. von Sicard, 'The Lemba Ancestor Baramina' in *African Studies*, 12, 1953, pp. 57–61.

196　22　H. A. Junod, *The Life of a South African Tribe*, ii, p. 424.

196　2　D. Livingstione, *Missionary Travels and Researches in Southern Africa* (London, 1857), p. 660.

197　2　Bullock, *op. cit.*, p. 22.

197　24　Van Warmelo, in Hammond-Tooke, *op. cit.*, p. 83.

198　33　N. Chittick, 'The coast before the arrival of the Portuguese', in B. A. Ogot (ed.), *Zamani: A Survey of East African History* (Nairobi, 1974), p. 103; G. Mathew, 'The East African Coast until the Coming of the Portuguese', in R. O. and G. Mathew (eds), *The History of East Africa*, pp. 103–4; Theal, *op. cit.*, VI, p. 233.

Page Line　CHAPTER 21

201　11　See 'Dyke Neuk', 'Dumbghe', in *NADA*, pp. 51–4; H. von Sicard, 'The origin of some of the tribes in the Belingwe Reserve', in *NADA*, 1948, p. 98.

209 25 Seremane, which has been identified as a Bantuised form of Suleiman, the Arabic form of Solomon, is in addition to a clan name a designation for the whole Lemba tribe. See von Sicard, 'Lemba Clans', *op. cit.*, p. 76.

Page Line CHAPTER 22

212 22 Cf. Scott T. Carroll, 'Solomonic Legend: The Muslims and Great Zimbabwe', in *The International Journal of African Historical Studies*, 21, 2, 1988, p. 233ff.

215 15 H. T. Norris, 'Did Antarah ibn Shaddad conquer Zimbabwe?' in A. K. Irvine, R. B. Serjeant and G. Rex Smith (eds), *A Miscellany of Middle Eastern Articles: In Memoriam Thomas Muir Johnstone 1924–83* (London, 1988), p. 85.

215 29 *Ibid.*; see also H. T. Norris, *The Adventures of Antar* (London, 1980).

Page Line CHAPTER 23

218 9 M. Van Wyck Smith, 'Waters flowing from darkness: The two Ethiopias in the early European image of Africa', in *Theoria*, 68, 1986, pp. 67–77.

220 28 T. Baines, *Gold Regions of South Eastern Africa* (London, 1877), preface, p. v; Bent, *op. cit.*, p. 209.

220 33 Baines, *op. cit.*, p. 83.

221 23 *Ibid.*, p. v.

224 14 E. P. Mathers, *Zambesia* (London, 1891), p. 35.

Page Line CHAPTER 25

244 10 E. C. Mandivenga, *Islam in Zimbabwe* (Gweru, Zimbabwe, 1983)

Page Line CHAPTER 26

251 3 S. Mendelssohn, 'Jewish Pioneers of South Africa', paper read before the Jewish Historical Society of England, 3 June 1912.

253 7 C. Mauch, *Reisen im Inneren von Sud-Afrika 1865–1872* (Gotha, 1874).

258 19 Garlake, *op. cit.*, p. 65.

258 30 A. Wilmot, *Monomotapa* (London, 1896), pp. 49, 58.

259 30 Quoted by Garlake, *op. cit.*, p. 66.

260 26 G. Page, *The Rhodesians* (London, 1912), p. 1.

264 3 Anderson, *op. cit.*, pp. 197, 200.

264 7 Beuster, *op. cit.*, p. 292.

264 11 C. Peters, *The Eldorado of the Ancients* (New York, 1902), p. 127.

264 33 Hall, *op. cit.*, p. 101.

268 1 G. Caton-Thompson, *op. cit.*, p. 199.

Page Line CHAPTER 27

271 23 T. N. Huffman, 'The Rise and Fall of Great Zimbabwe', in *Journal of African History*, 1972, pp. 353–66; see also T. N. Huffman, 'Iron Age Settlement Patterns and the Origins of Class Distinction in South Africa', in *Advances in World Archaeology*, 5, 1986, pp. 291–338.

274 14 Trevor Tudor, 'Some observations on the relics of pre-European culture in Rhodesia and South Africa', in *Journal of Royal Anthropological Institute*, LX, 1930, p. 390: 'On three separate occasions I have seen in M. Pathlele's location, Pietersburg, conical altars connected with the circumcision rites, which much reminded me of the conical towers of Zimbabwe ... in each case there were two conical altars ... all built of dry stones and in all cases the batter was curved, not in a straight line.'

277 2 K. Mufuka, *Dzimbahwe: Life and Politics in the Golden Age* (Harare, 1983), p. 22.

277 33 Summers, *op. cit.*, pp. 75, 94.

278 18 Lemba claims to have participated in the building of Great Zimbabwe are sometimes cited: e.g. Chigiga, *op. cit.*, p. 15: 'With regard to the Dzimbabwe, Marhondo said, on their way from Malawi, they met a certain Arab

called Aribaniguzani who joined their company . . . This Arab and the four Lemba found the buildings of Zimbabwe already started, and they too joined in the building process . . .'

Page Line CHAPTER 28

290 4 Cf. T. Price: 'The Arabs of the Zambezi', in *The Muslim World*, XLIV, no. 1, 1954, p. 31ff. Price concludes his article: 'Socially they offer a remarkable parallel with the Jews in Europe, and it is not impossible that there is a Jewish strain, cultural if not physical, in their mixed ancestry.'

290 24 J. M. Schoffeleers, *Mbona: The Guardian Spirit of the Mang'anja* (unpublished B.Litt., 1966), p. 26.

Page Line CHAPTER 30

312 13 See: R. E. Gregson, 'Trade and Politics in South-East Africa: The Moors, the Portuguese and the Kingdom of Mwenemutapa', in *African Social Research*, 116, 1973, p. 417; P. Kahle and M. Mustafa, *Die Chronik des Ibn Ijas* (Istanbul-Leipzig, 1931), V, p. 109; G. S. P. Freeman-Grenville, *The East African Coast* (London, 1975), p. 14; *The Encycopaedia of Islam*, IV p. 469ff.

312 20 Al-Idrisi's work *Nuzhat al-Mushtak* was compiled in 1154 and was exploited by a number of later Arab geographers including Ibn Abd al-Munim al-Himyari. Al-Himyari's work *The Fragrant Garden* was written in the fifteenth century but was in fact a re-cast of a thirteenth-century work written by an ancestor of his with an identical name. See T. Lewicki, *Arabic External Sources for the History of Africa to the South of Sahara* (London, n.d.), p. 93; A. Malecka, *'La côte orientale de l'Afrique au moyen age de al Himyari (xve s.)'*, in *Folia Orientalia*, IV 1962, p. 331ff.; Abu al-Fidah wrote Seruna, which is certainly an error for Sayuna which looks similar in Arabic script.

312 26 *Encyclopaedia of Islam, iv, p. 409ff.*

313 16 See Serjeant, *op. cit.*, p. 157; Freeman-Grenville, *op. cit.*, p. 18; Axelson, *op. cit.*, p. 27; H. von Sicard, 'The Ancient Sabi-Zimbabwe Trade Route', in *NADA*, 40, 1963, p. 7; T. Shumovsky, *Tre Neizestnye lotsii Achmada ibn Madjida* (Leningrad, 1957). G. Mathew, *op. cit.*, pp. 111, 118, 121, 123; G. Ferrand, *Textes relatifs à l'extrème orient* (Paris, 1913), II, p. 321ff; R. Summers, *Ancient Mining in Rhodesia and Adjacent Areas* (Salisbury, 1969), pp. 115–19, 151; Huffman, 'The Rise and Fall of Zimbabwe'; *op. cit.*, pp. 353–66; Serjeant, *op. cit.*, p. 32.

Junod, *op. cit.*, in *Folklore*, p. 277: 'Some old Balemba of both the Spelonken and the Modjadji country told my informant the following legend: "We have come from a very remote place, on the other side of the sea. We were on a big boat. A terrible storm nearly destroyed us all. The boat was broken into two pieces. One half of us reached the shores of this country; the others were taken away with the second half of the boat, and we do not know where they are now. We climbed the mountains and arrived among the Banyai. There we settled, and after a time we moved southwards to the Transvaal . . ."'

Cf. Serjeant, *op. cit.*, p. 32: 'The Indians resident in the larger ports (of South Arabia) . . . were mostly Hindus. They are always known as Baniyan . . .'

313 27 See M. Tolmachera, 'Towards a definition of the term Zanj', in *Azania: Journal of the British Institute in Eastern Africa*, XXI, 1986, p. 106; Freeman-Grenville, *op. cit.*, p. 15.

314 5 Theal, *op. cit.*, VIIpp. 188, 199, 253, 530. D. P. Abraham, 'Maramuca: an exercise in the combined uses of Portuguese records and oral traditions', in *Journal of African History*, II, p. 212.

314 32 See Axelson, *op. cit.*, p. 27; von Sicard, 'The Ancient Sabi-Zimbabwe Trade Route', pp. 6–7. Gregson, *op. cit.*, p. 419; but see also D. N. Beach, *The Shona and Zimbabwe 900–1850* (Gweru, Zimbabwe, 1984), p. 108. D. P. Abraham, 'Ethno-History of the Empire of Mutapa, Problems and Methods', in J. Vansina, R. Mauny and L. V. Thomas (eds), *The Historian in Tropical Africa* (Oxford, 1964), p. 107.

315 12 See G. Liesenbang, 'New light on Venda traditions: Mahumane's account of 1730', in *History in Africa*, 4, 1977; N. Sutherland-Harris, 'Trade and the Rozwi Mambo', p. 261, and A. Smith, 'Delagoa Bay and the trade of South-Eastern Africa', pp. 275–6, in R. Gray and D. Birmingham (eds), *Pre-Colonial African Trade* (London, 1970).

Page Line CHAPTER 31

336 16 The Hadramaut was unvisited until relatively recent times. Leo Hirsch visited part of the *wadi* in 1893 and Theodore Bent and his wife followed later the same year. The first western traveller to mention Sena was Harold Ingrams who is still remembered in the eastern end of the Hadramaut. See Theodore and Mrs Theodore Bent, *Southern Arabia*, London, 1900; H. Ingrams, *Arabia and the Isles*, London, 1952, p. 203. The area to the east of the *masila* was unsettled during my visits and I was unable to see the site. In the 1930s the dam was described as having been made of mud and having 'existed in pre-Islamic times between Qabr Hud and the sea'. According to 'a local expert' of the time the dam had been destroyed some 600 years before. See D van Meulen and H von Wissmann, *Hadramaut: Some of its mysteries unveiled*, Leyden, 1932, pp. 182–3. Ingrams refers to the destruction of the dam and found some traces 'strongly built of masonry and cement'. (p. 204)

340　8　See above pp. 173ff. Apart from the Hadramaut I have
not come across this custom elsewhere in the Islamic
world. The importance of the new moon however is well
attested and gives rise to a variety of practices. See e.g.
B. A. Donaldson, *The Wild Rue*, Luzac, 1938, pp. 102ff.
I am indebted to Dr Nancy Lindisfarne for this reference.

NOTE ON THE JOURNEY

The journey described in this book took place more or less as narrated. I repeated the journey as far as Zanzibar for the radio series 'King Solomon's Tribe' and some of the incidents have been incorporated into this book. The journey to the Hadramaut took place the following year although I revisited the area in May 1997 to collect DNA samples. Again some of the incidents from the second journey have been incorporated into the text.

INDEX